W9-BJE-833

BLUE SKY,
NIGHT THUNDER

The Utes of Colorado

A Novel
by
JESS McCREEDE

Affiliated Writers of America/Publishers
Encampment, Wyoming
Printed in the United States of America

Published by

Affiliated Writers of America, Inc.
P.O. Box 343
Encampment, Wyoming 82325
1-800-292-5292

ISBN: 1-879915-08-1

Library of Congress Catalog Card Number: 93-73778

Dedicated to the *Nüntz,*
Spirit of the People
Maiquas!

RESERVATION

The Grasslands of Paradise,
Indian hearts as cold as ice.
Scouts and Braves,
Lost in an uncharted maze.
Wilderness and forests,
Squaws gathering the harvest.
Gathering in the rain,
Gathering with shame.
Shame of what they are,
Having to travel far,
To get to where they must call home,
The Reservation!

—Halle E. O'Neal
Age, 12 years

AUTHOR'S NOTE

I have tried to walk carefully across the quicksands of time in telling the history of the events leading up to the battle at Milk River and the subsequent massacre of Nathan Meeker, Indian Agent for the White River Utes, and his employees that fateful autumn day, September 29, 1879.

What is described here; the places, the people, and how they each were forced into making life and death choices under desperate situations, are real.

It is the story of a long forgotten group of gentle and shy Utes known as the *Nüpartka,* who once resided in a most beautiful place in northwest Colorado, along a river they called Smoking Earth.

GLOSSARY OF TERMS

Aveinkwep - the "cave of sticks" where Bear Dance is held.
Bear River - known today as the Yampa River.
Carniva - Ute lodges.
Grand River - the Colorado.
Iniputz - "ghosts of the dead".
Little River - known today as Milk River.
Maiquas - Ute greeting.
Mericatz - Ute word for white man.
M'sut t'quigat - Ute word for shaman or medicine man.
Nüntz - the People.
Nüpartka - that band of Utes living along Smoking Earth River.
Pana - Ute fried bread.
Piwán - Ute wife.
Pöorat - shaman's medicine tobacco.
Quap - smoking tobacco.
Quatz - what the People called the Spanish, "Iron Shirts".
Quigat - the sacred bear power every Ute shaman possessed.
Smoking Earth River - known today as White River.
Swerch - Ute word for white soldier.
Tav-mois - Ute word for tomorrow.
Tawacz viem - Ute word for chief.
To-Mericatz - Ute word for black soldiers.
Yampatika - the "root eaters", what the Shoshoni one time called
  the Nüpartka.

CHAPTER 1

Swaths of lemon aspen lay like thick threads of miner's gold between borders of dark emerald that covered the flanks of the rising expanse of gray-tipped mountains, granite cold and bare of snow. These vast high mountains interlaced with deep forests, alpine meadows of tall grasses, sparkling lakes and rushing rivers were home to the *Nüntz*, the People. It had been that way far longer than any of the old ones could remember. Fiercely proud and possessive of this sky blue land of tumbling, climbing mountains, the *Nüntz* were well known to their Plains neighbors to the east of this great fortress of rising, mysterious country. The Kiowa called them *K'opk-i'ago*, or mountain people. To the Sioux they were *Sapa Wichasa*, black people. But to most of the tribes of the Northern Plains, the

1

Nüntz were simply the Blue Sky people, so named for their lofty control of this vast land they called the Shining Mountains.

It was from this rugged fortress, the People had watched the coming of the *Mericatz*, the white man. At first their numbers were few and remained scattered across this broad expanse of folding mountain valleys and parks. But as their numbers continued to grow like spring grass in sheltered meadows, the People became alarmed. Many councils were held to discuss these strange white people but no one knew what to do about them. For they saw how the *Mericatz* fought the Comanche and the Kiowa who had lived on the Plains for as long as the *Nüntz* had the mountains, forcing them on to small pieces of hot, dusty land where they suffered sickness and death. And, unlike the Plains people who sometimes came to their mountains to raid and steal horses, the *Mericatz* showed no fear and pushed deep into their country where they dug into the earth for strange stones. And they did not leave. The more they dug for these stones, the more their frenzied excitement attracted others. Soon the mountains were thick with *Mericatz* scurrying about with their digging tools, scaring away the game and spoiling the rivers. The People retreated higher into the mountains, yet the *Mericatz* came with paper and double words and took away most of their lands. Even the *Mericatz* soldiers could not keep those who dug for the stones off the very lands agreed to by treaty. The People became angry, yet in the end it did no good.

One day, *Mericatz* came from a place far to the east, beyond the land of the Comanche and Cheyenne. A place called Washington. They claimed to represent the most powerful of all *Mericatz* who lived in that place. They came with more papers, telling the People they must now learn to live like other Indians, on small pieces of lands not of their choosing. On lands not able to support hunting. The *Mericatz* from this Washington promised to give the People many goods things to eat and warm blankets to keep away the cold . . . but now two winters had passed and the People had received nothing.

Hunger. There was always hunger and the waiting . . . it pinched the land together like rocks around a narrow passage and sapped the strength of its People. It was the middle of the Last Fall Moon, yet the prairies stood empty and white as snow flew down from the tall standing mountains far to the west of the buffalo plains. Soon the snow moons would follow, bringing with them the intense cold. And trees along the rivers would once again resemble brown sticks, upright and lifeless . . . like the old people.

Like lean wolves following a fruitless hunt, hunger stalked the country of Smoking Earth River. It pressed against the people of the Nüpartka Utes like hard ice in winter, stripping away the children's laughing smiles and dancing eyes of summer. And with the hunger came sickness . . . and death.

Quinkent pulled the blanket about his shoulders against the dropping temperature and watched as the golds and reds of quaking aspen and cottonwood leaves reflected the fading sunlight across Smoking Earth River. He marveled at the way summer's robust green was so easily drained from the leaves by the Fall Moon. At night, the haunting song of the spirit birds, the loons, were pleasant music to ears grown tired of hearing empty promises. Quinkent was a man of over sixty snows, somewhat short and wispy with a massive head and dark eyes that were as hard as serviceberries in winter. Two points of a gray mustache extended downward over his broad mouth. His hair, now streaked with gray, was cut close to his head and a single hawk feather slanted downward in Ute fashion, pointing to one shoulder. When he met with the *Mericatz*, he often dressed like them, for it seemed to please them. And Quinkent was ever ready to please Washington, even in the face of hunger and death.

But today, in spite of the sharp winds blowing across the undulating Danforth Hills rising two thousand feet above the valley floor,

Quinkent wore only a breechcloth and a colorful blanket draped about his shoulders.

Quinkent looked around at the twenty or so *carniva* that gathered like so many trees along the river, reassured by its presence and life giving waters. Cook fires were being lit and those with food prepared their evening meal. His searching eyes found his *piwán,* Singing Grass, bent over a cook fire making, what he knew to be, the last of their coffee. For Quinkent, thoughts of dwindling food supplies rested heavily on his heart. He had expected the fall hunt to make the difference, to carry them through another hard winter. They couldn't depend on promised supplies from the *Mericatz.* For two years now they had waited patiently for the much needed supplies of blankets, flour, sugar and rice from Washington. Quinkent had spoken with the agent many times, but his words, like so many falling leaves, were dry and brittle. Nothing ever came of their talk.

The heat of summer had been long and without much rain. The prairie grasses quickly turned brown and shriveled away, their brittle stalks rattling in the dry wind. Even in the sheltered mountain valleys, the normally lush grass remained thin and provided little nourishment for their ponies.

And in the First Fall Moon, hunting parties had gone north from this place to where the Shining Mountains sank beneath the brush-covered sage of the buffalo country to search for meat. The hunters had found the plains dry and dusty and worst of all, nearly empty. A summer of searing heat and no rain had pushed the herd even deeper into the hunting grounds of the Arapaho and Cheyenne. The hunters found only a few buffalos, stragglers mostly. Animals too weak or sick to migrate east with the herd. Not enough to see them through a hard winter. But what else could they do? Most of the lodges under Quinkent contained only old men. Men too old to fight their ancient enemies, the Arapaho.

Like himself, his small band of *Nüpartka* Utes, wished only to be friends with Washington—to do what was asked of them—to keep peace for the good of all the People. And after two years, they still clung to the hope the *Mericatz* would deliver their supplies before the First Snow Moon.

Quinkent left the Smoking Earth River and entered his *carniv* where he sat on a bed of furs before the small center fire and waited for Singing Grass to bring coffee. Even as the sun left the sky, Quinkent felt the cold stealing into his *carniv*, reminding him that as hunger gnawed at his belly, winter would force him to make a decision he did not wish to make. It made his heart feel bad like when the *Mericatz* first came into their mountains. At first, they were few, then, suddenly, many. And they brought presents for the People. Clothes not made of skins and strange-tasting food that could not be gathered from the mountains, only from a *Mericatz* store. They also brought guns and saddles for their horses and brightly colored things that flashed back the sun.

And then things turned bad. It happened so slowly, none of the *Nüpartka* knew when it started, but suddenly their country grew smaller and some of the People began wearing the *Mericatz* clothes and eating his bread. And in order to get the things that tasted good, the People sold their hides from the hunts at the *Mericatz* stores. Everyone was happy. Presents came from Washington every year and very soon all the People, not only the *Nüpartka*, but the other six bands of the People grew accustomed to these gifts. But these gifts had suddenly stopped and no one could tell him why, except that they could do nothing. The People had grown dependent on these gifts and without them, some of the old ones and small children would become sick and die during the long winter moons.

These were the things that occupied Quinkent's thoughts as Singing Grass pushed aside the entrance flap of elk skin and handed him the steaming coffee without speaking. As *tawacz viem*, chief of the *Nüpartka*, it was Quinkent's responsibility to look after his People, to see to their needs. If he did not, the People would no longer follow him. And Quinkent liked being *tawacz viem* and sending his *Mericatz* name—"Douglas"—to Washington.

A horse came up, blowing loudly and stamping his feet against the hard ground as its rider dismounted heavily and entered Quinkent's *carniv* without asking. Quinkent knew without looking up it could only be the big bellied Colorow. Like a huge bull buffalo in prime, Colorow pushed through the door of Quinkent's *carniv* and took a seat opposite Quinkent, warming his hands at the center fire. Colorow usually kept a fierce scowl on his face to frighten the *Mericatz* women, but tonight his expression was one of worry and sadness. Like Quinkent, he too had seen over sixty snows.

Colorow was not even a Ute, but the product of a Comanche father and a Jicarilla Apache mother. Adopted by the Muache Utes, Colorow, the red-shirted Chief Blanco and Kaneache finally joined the *Nüpartka* band after their anti-Ouray sentiments grew to a fevered pitch following their attack on old Fort Pueblo in which they murdered a dozen drunken Mexicans. Chief Ouray scolded them by saying their actions cast a dark shadow on all Utes, not just the Muache, since most *Mericatz* did not know one band from another.

The three-hundred-pound colorful Colorow was known for telling exploits of himself upon entering a *Mericatz* house unannounced, demanding biscuits, sugar cubes and soup in a rather loud voice, a fierce scowl on his face. There were few times frightened *Mericatz* women did not feed him as demanded.

Colorow took the coffee from Singing Grass and slurped loudly, his dark eyes darting around the *carniv* for signs of food. Quinkent passed a leather pouch containing the last of his *quap* to Colorow. Quinkent knew, as did everybody, that Colorow carried two pipes, a small one and a huge clay pipe he used when smoking another man's tobacco. Colorow emptied the contents of the leather pouch into the big bowl, looking even sadder now that the tobacco only half filled his pipe. He lit the pipe with a small stick from the center fire and blew huge lungfulls of smoke upward towards the slit of an opening at the top of the lodge. His dark eyes glittered in the light of the small fire, missing nothing when Quinkent's *piwán* moved to the far side of the lodge and began taking her cook pots from a large hide bundle.

Quinkent knew Colorow would stay as long as there was food to eat and *quap* to smoke. Quinkent thought the huge Indian may decide to tell a story about how brave and fierce he was but Colorow remained silent for a while, staring into a fire that gave off little heat and smoking his pipe. Quinkent wished now he had rolled a cigarette before passing his pouch to Colorow. With nothing more to do, Quinkent sat before the fire and thought of the presents locked up in a warehouse in the *Mericatz* village called Rawlings. Tobacco was one of the many gifts locked up there as well. It made his heart heavy to think of such things again.

Colorow broke the silence in his deep rumbling voice. It was a statement rather than a question. He spoke the Old Language, a language of many words that flowed through a man's mind like a soft wind through trembling aspen.

"Washington sends *Mericatz* who steal the presents meant for us. That is how it is now: they have something and we have nothing to feed the crying children."

Quinkent let Colorow's words wash over him like water boiling over a rock in the Late Spring Moon. His words stirred deep feelings in Quinkent and he thought again of what the *Nüpartka* must do before the long snows filled Smoking Earth River.

"Perhaps I will visit Danforth tomorrow and ask again for what is ours," Quinkent finally answers. E.H. Danforth was a Unitarian

Reverend and the Indian Agent for White River Agency, located a dozen miles upstream of Quinkent's winter valley encampment.

"This agent believes and lives all the best teachings of his God. He wants to do the right things for our People," Quinkent added.

Colorow remained silent, puffing on his long-stemmed pipe and staring into the yellow flames of the fire as if the answer somehow lay within the glowing red coals.

"This agent has sent words on paper to the *Mericatz* holding our presents and still nothing is done," Colorow finally said, thinking of his empty belly that lay against his spine like sheet ice in winter. He sucked loudly at the coffee from the tin cup. The dark liquid intensified his own hunger.

"Perhaps this agent will go with us to the Mericatz village and get our presents." They both fell silent as Singing Grass busied herself with the evening meal. Soon the smells of cooking meat drifted through the lodge and Colorow's big belly rumbled like distant thunder.

Later, after Colorow had eaten all there was, he mounted his horse and rode down to his own *carniv* as a quarter moon eased above the hoary head of Sleep Cat Peak, spilling its weak light across Smoking Earth River. Long after Singing Grass had gone to sleep beside him, Quinkent lay awake in his blankets thinking of the course he must take if Agent Danforth refused to go with him to the *Mericatz* village one hundred eighty-five mountainous miles away. He only knew his People could not survive a bad winter with no more meat than they had managed to jerk. Quinkent lay there listening to the night sounds, waiting for the spirit birds to sing to him, to ease this feeling of heaviness in his heart. The pale moon was shifting to the western sky before Quinkent found troubled sleep and still the birds had not called to him from the river.

The next morning, Quinkent ordered his *piwán* to saddle his horse as he lifted the bridle from a lodgepole and went out into the early light. The morning air was brittle cold and still. Threads of white mists lifted from the surface of Smoking Earth River while a line of dense clouds formed to the west above the yellow plateau region, a barren, rolling benchland of gray sage and greasewood. Quinkent's encampment of twenty lodges were in the heart of what was called winter valley by the Utes and Powell Park by the *Mericatz*.

Quinkent had chosen well. Separated from the White River agency by a two-mile-long narrowing of Smoking Earth River that cut its way between the Danforth Hills to the north and the Grand Hogback that bunched up to the river from the south, winter valley was warmer in winter, less windy and usually snow-free. Over ten thousand grassy acres supplied forage for the two thousand horses that grazed here during the summer months when other Ute bands came together.

Quinkent thought of his friend, Major Powell, his *piwán* and his brother Walter who had spent the winter here in '68. Quinkent liked the Powells and had learned a little English from them that winter while Powell's men surveyed some of the valley and learned Ute customs and language. John Wesley Powell was a government geologist and ethnologist who had lost an arm at Shiloh. He had also accomplished one of the most rugged feats of American exploration by descending through the terrible canyons of the Colorado and Green Rivers the year following his stay with Quinkent.

Thinking of these things now caused Quinkent's heart to be happy, yet when he turned his rugged little pinto down river, the pressing problems of being a chief flooded his mind and sickened his heart once again. Should he move his People to the *Mericatz* village in hopes the supplies would be released or should he continue to wait here in winter valley where the sharp winds did not come? Maybe this agent would know what to do. He would ask him. But when he got to Agency Park, Quinkent found himself facing a crisis altogether different from his own.

Quinkent rode up to the familiar two acre stockade, taking in the rundown condition of the dirt-roofed buildings and sagging porches. The Agency seemed deserted as Quinkent stepped down. Only two horses stared back at him from the corral. Quinkent tied his pony to the hitch post, climbed the worn steps, and pushed open the Agency door. A rather tall, angular-faced man was busy packing papers and books into boxes. His gray hair was disheveled and his face drawn into a frown as if deep anger rode his shoulders.

Rev. Danforth looked up at the silent-eyed Quinkent as he shoved a thick ledger into the box, closed the lid and expertly tied a thin string around it.

"Hello, Douglas, what brings you up here?"

"Where your men?" Quinkent asked in passable English.

Danforth waved his hand absently, "Hunting, up at Trappers Lake."

Quinkent looked slowly around the Agency office at other boxes stacked neatly against one wall. His heart felt even heavier than before.

"Where presents?" Danforth picked up the box and carried it over to the stack and sat it down. He looked at Quinkent with a pained expression.

"It's like I said last month, Douglas. I don't see how I can make you understand but . . ." Danforth went over to the scarred desk and sat down heavily. He looked up at the nut-brown face of Quinkent and shook his head. How could he make an Indian see when he didn't fully understand it himself.

"I don't have the authority to release the supplies to you and Captain Jack. There is the matter of payment for shipment of goods on the train. Do you understand?"

Quinkent stared at the Agent for a full minute. The *Mericatz* words were like the last time—useless and dead. His words made no sense. Didn't the presents from Washington belong to the Nüpartka? How was it a *Mericatz* could lay claim to them?

"Did you send my words to Washington? Tell them how the People suffer . . . children grow sick?"

Danforth passed his hand before his eyes and sighed deeply. "I'm sorry, Douglas, but I'm afraid anything I do at this point will be useless."

"What you mean?"

"As of this moment I'm no longer the White River Indian Agent."

"You no like Ute?" Quinkent was thinking of the brawl the agent had had with Canávish, the one the *Mericatz* called Johnson. Canávish was a Yampa Ute medicine man who now belonged to the *Nüpartka* band of Utes. At one time, Canávish was a splendid specimen of a man, tall and powerfully built, but he was thin and wasted now that he possessed the great powers of bear medicine.

"It's not that. It's . . . everything." Danforth got up from his chair and wandered over to the stacked boxes, his hand trailing over their tops as he walked by. He turned back to the watching Indian.

"I came here three years ago full of great hope and with a genuine desire to help your people become self-sufficient, to build homes and to take up farming." Danforth shook his head sadly. "I can't point to one thing I've accomplished in the years since. Another reason, which I don't expect you to understand, is political. There is a new Secretary of the Interior, Carl Schurz, who found my common brawling with your medicine man, Johnson, a little too much," Danforth said, referring to a two hour fight with Canávish after the Utes threw their farming tools into the White River. "I sent him my resignation yesterday."

"What of our presents Washington promised? Will new agent come quick?"

Again, Danforth shook his head slowly and took his seat behind the agency desk. He lifted tired eyes to Quinkent.

"I honestly don't know, Douglas. It could be many months before a new agent is appointed. Impossible to say. As for the annuities in Rawlings, it's anybody's guess when they will be released. I'm sorry, I know how important they have become now that winter is upon us."

"The snow moons soon come," Quinkent said, choosing his words carefully so that the *Mericatz* would understand them. That was the trouble with the *Mericatz* language, making the ancient words of his People clear enough for the *Mericatz* to grasp. Quinkent thought of Colorow's words of last night. With his elbows propped on his battered desk, Danforth waited glumly for the Ute to continue.

"Maybe we go to this Rawlings, send words to Washington?"

Danforth shook his head and stood up. There was nothing to be gained by speaking further with Douglas and he wanted to get on with his packing so he could be as far as Peck's store on the Yampa by nightfall.

"Under the circumstances, I think it would be better if you remained here in view that your agent is leaving. That way, trouble could be prevented in Rawlings."

Quinkent stared at Danforth. Again the words of the *Mericatz* made no sense. He was *tawacz viem* and as such, he had a certain amount of responsibility to his people. Why did this agent not speak out against Nicaagat leaving Smoking Earth River? With over one hundred lodges, Nicaagat was now encamped near the place the *Mericatz* called Whiskey Gap, north of Rawlings. And what was this trouble this agent spoke of? The *Nüpartka* had caused no trouble since coming to this place. In the end, Quinkent decided not to ask this agent these things for he was tired of dead words that meant nothing when spoken. It was hard to hold what a *Mericatz* said for very long anyway. He turned to leave.

"I'm sorry, Douglas, I wish there was something more I could do," Danforth called helplessly to the departing Indian.

Quinkent left the agency in a light snowfall. The words of the *Mericatz*, Danforth, reached deep inside him and caused his middle to be twisted around, like a man sick from eating too much. Perhaps he would wait awhile and try to understand the strange words of the *Mericatz*. Sometimes they were not so bad if they were studied carefully. Quinkent brushed the light covering of snow from his horse and mounted the little hard-muscled animal. The falling snow brought out a sense of deep urgency in Quinkent and he knew that there was no more time to study the words of the *Mericatz*. Winter had finally settled in across the broken mountains at his back. He pointed his horse west, giving the animal a small kick in the ribs.

Reverend Danforth watched from the window of the agency office as the squat Indian disappeared into the gathering whiteness. He knew Douglas had barely gotten a fraction of what he had just said. He turned away feeling utterly helpless. For all his effort, and his wife's, to bring together the best of both worlds, white and Indian, the troubles had come from Washington and not the Utes. Danforth suspected Schurz had someone else in mind as White River Agent and the brawl with Johnson had been the excuse to pressure him to resign. It was too late to take back angry words now, he figured. The fat was in the fire.

As Quinkent rode west, the snow gradually thinned and stopped altogether when he reached his *carniv* by Smoking Earth River. Singing Grass rushed from his lodge, a stricken look on her face. Quinkent dismounted as she hurried to his side, her face tear-stained and trembling.

"What is the matter?"

"Walks with Sky is dead," Singing Grass wailed loudly. Walks with Sky was her sister's only boy child of ten winters. Quinkent could hear Canávish chanting loudly down by the river's edge.

13

"How did this thing happen?" Quinkent asked, looking to the river again where people had gathered around Canávish who continued to use his *pöorat*, the power given to him by *Sunáwiv*, the God who resided in the Sun.

"Walks with Sky fell into Smoking Earth River while snaring a fish," Singing Grass said, tearing at her clothes. Quinkent handed her the bridle to his horse and walked down to the river where the crowd had gathered.

Several people parted as Quinkent walked up and allowed him to pass by. Quinkent came over to the kneeling Canávish and looked down at the boy who lay with his arms by his side and his eyes open, staring upward at nothing. His half-naked body was dusty gray and Quinkent knew the boy was beyond even Canávish's help.

As if sensing Quinkent's presence, Canávish stopped his wailing chant and stood up, holding to his medicinal pouch of *pöorat* in one hand and prayer stick in the other.

"*Pa ah a pache*, held him under too long," Quinkent said with proper sympathy and to ease the responsibility from Canávish's shoulders. The waterbaby, *Pa ah a pache*, was one of two evil spirits, the other, *Se ach*, the witch. Both were dangerous to human beings. The *Pa ah a pache* resembled a fish and had a mustache and long black hair and resided in deep water. When children got to close, the waterbaby would grab them and take them under until they died. And Walks with sky was very dead, Quinkent concluded. Quinkent knew that the greatest *m'sut t'quigat* could not breathe life into a body once the heart had grown cold. And there was no doubt in his mind that Canávish was the most powerful *m'sut t'quigat* of the *Nüpartka*.

"What you say is true, yet the pain comes regardless, for Walks in Sky held promise of being a great leader," Canávish said. It was true, Quinkent admitted to himself. His father, Quinkent's brother-in-law, Blue Light, was a sub-chief of moderate notoriety who had distinguished himself in many battles with the Arapaho whenever they invaded their hunting grounds and in raids against the Najavo to the south.

But that was the time that went before. The *Mericatz* had not yet come into their shining mountains and the People were strong and controlled all the mountains and even part of the frowning Plains where the earth was smashed flat and without trees. These Plains people, the Arapaho, Sioux, Kiowa and Cheyenne were constantly having wars and their ways were almost as hard to understand as the *Mericatz*. The People of the mountains took from their enemies, but would go home and the plains people would become angry because the People would not stay and fight. Yet there were many stories of fighting and of brave deeds by strong warriors.

But that was before the *Mericatz* came and made war with the plains people and pushed them onto tiny bits of hot, burning lands where they grew sick. The People had watched from their mountains and when the *Mericatz* came to them offering peace, the People agreed, giving these *Mericatz* permission to dig stones from the ground in exchange for *Mericatz* presents. The *Mericatz* spoiled the water and stripped the trees from the land, causing the game to disappear. These *Mericatz* were never satisfied and they asked for more land to dig for stones. At first, the People thought these crazy men would grow tired of digging stones, and go away, but they never did.

And now, the People had been herded onto small bits of land just like the *Mericatz* had done to the plains people. Their way of life was rapidly drawing to a close. These were the things Quinkent thought of as he continued to look down at the dead boy. There was no room left in their world for great leaders, much less warriors. The *Mericatz* had changed all that forever.

Blue Light lifted the lifeless body of his child while his *piwán* cried loudly by his side. Her bare arms and legs were covered in bright blood where she had cut herself with a small knife. In careless Ute fashion, the boy would be hidden quickly in some rock crevice and items of clothing and toys that were once his would be left outside Blue Light's *carniv* for other children in the village.

Colorow came up on his little pony who strained under the Indian's heavy weight. He came, not because of the excitement over the boy's death, but in hopes of freeloading at some sympathetic *carniv* because of it. He slid off the back of the bony horse and lumbered over to where Quinkent and Canávish stood in silent thought.

"*Maiquas.*" Quinkent exchanged greetings with the big-bellied Indian for the two of them. Canávish said nothing nor did he acknowledge Colorow's presence. The three men stood there for a long time not speaking and it was Quinkent who finally broke the silence, knowing Colorow was anxious to learn of his meeting with Agent Danforth.

"This agent says he is leaving. He has had trouble with one of the leaders in Washington. Soon we will get a new agent." Colorow's face clouded over and he hung his big head against his massive chest as if indicating his displeasure at the news. Canávish seemed to have scarcely heard what Quinkent was saying.

Quinkent continued, "Danforth will not go to this Rawlings and get our presents for us." Colorow seemed to scowl even more.

Canávish turned his eyes on the two men. "Perhaps if we had these presents, Walks in Sky would not have fallen into the river." The medicine man was looking for some way to ease the burden he felt for not having saved the child.

Quinkent looked around at his small village of aging men. They could ill-afford to lose someone as young as Walks in Sky. It brought him face to face with reality. The lodges in his camp would continue to grow smaller with the passing of the snow moons. He must act decisively or one day very soon he would no longer be *tawacz viem* . . . just another old man who pitched his *carniv* in the shadow of

Nicaagat's many lodges. Even though he had not seen Nicaagat for six moons, Quinkent could feel his steadily mounting presence. Nicaagat wanted to be *tawacz viem* of all *Nüpartka.*

"We will leave winter valley at *tavi-mois,* sunrise, and go to this *Mericatz* village of Rawlings."

"Unh," Colorow said without hesitation, thinking of the smoking tobacco and flour locked up in the warehouse. Canávish said nothing, his eyes fixed on the river as if he could somehow draw back from its dark waters the breath of Walks in Sky.

"The *Mericatz* will listen to me. They will see how our children suffer. They will send my words to Washington who will tell them to give us our presents."

"Unh," Colorow said forcibly and he lumbered slowly away to tell his *piwán* to prepare for the trip.

Later, Quinkent told Singing Grass of his decision and she immediately began making preparations to dismantle their *carniv* for the two-sleep trip to the *Mericatz* village. That night the haunting song of a spirit bird floated up from Smoking Earth River and filled Quinkent's head and heart with music. He slept soundly in spite of the mournful wailing from Blue Light's *carniv* that did not stop until the sun's first warming rays touched Sleepy Cat Peak.

CHAPTER 2

Following the completion of the Union Pacific Railroad across southern Wyoming Territory in late spring of '69, Union Pacific officials began a heavy advertising campaign to promote the fertile lands that lay along its right of way. The campaign paid off and hundreds of eager farmers and ranchers poured into the area and fanned out to take homesteads to either side of their tracks and as far away as the Little Snake which coiled its way along the border separating Wyoming and Colorado Territories.

Still others rushed in to swell the shanty town population of Rawlings to twice its previous size of four hundred over the next few years. With the rush came the miners who ranged south beyond the Continental Divide to set up hasty diggings at Bug Town and Poverty Bar below Hahn's Peak in Colorado and only fifty miles from the White River Ute Agency. Those that came to the new mining district, came by way of Rawlings or ventured across Middle Park from Denver or Central City by way of rugged Gore Pass and along beautiful Bear River.

For whatever reason that drew them to this area of the West, Rawlings continued to be the closest point of civilization for restocking supplies and receiving equipment from back east by way of the Union Pacific. Rawlings grew up like a blister in a hot land of red rocks, sage brush benchlands and little water. This great arid basin stretched west, beyond the Green River, north to old Fort Bonneville and east to the Medicine Bows.

For these newly arriving hopefuls, Rawlings appeared less than the paradise presented to them by eastern agents of the Union Pacific. The little town was nothing more than a huddle of ugly board shacks, warehouses, gambling houses and saloons where buxom hussies confronted newcomer and old alike with plunging necklines and frank invitations. Businesses in town were helped greatly by the influx of bored soldiers from Fort Steele only a dozen miles to the east.

Rawlings was already four years old by the time the Rankin brothers rode into the wild and reckless town. Other less desirables, bunco artists, pimps and prostitutes quickly found their niche along Lower Row in such places as Foote's Saloon, the Bucket of Blood or the Alhambra Billiard Hall where most of the local cowboys hung out when not trading secrets with Chippies in one-room crib cages.

Of the three Rankin Brothers, two came to build a solid future in this desert community, to uphold the law and to leave behind a proud mark. The third brother, Joe Rankin, although solid and dependable when sober, preferred the seedier lifestyle, charming women whether single or married, and the reckless adventure as a some-time army scout. All things considered, Rawlings suited Joe Rankin just fine.

"Joe!"

The lanky frame sprawled across the small cot stirred beneath the gray blanket, burrowing deeper into the straw-filled tick mattress searching for warmth.

"Joe!" came the cry, louder, more insistent this time.

The man on the cot muttered in his sleep and turned over on his side, his jaw dropping open. A loud snore escaped the gaping mouth and slack lips. In the warm pooling of his dreams, Joe Rankin incorporated the insistent call of his name with that of his younger friend, Matt, as Joe led Smokey down to the river's edge for a well deserved drink. The sun of middle summer beat down on the boys with a golden glow of late afternoon. Freckled and hard-muscled by the weeks of grueling plowing, Joe was dust-caked by the sweat of his labors, while Matt skipped along happily with enough energy for them both. The younger boy, more bother than real help, was supposed to pick up stones turned up by the biting plow, yet when Joe finished a row and turned back, likely as not, Matt was off across the plowed field chasing whatever imaginations filled his head.

"Can we go swimming, Joe, can we?" Matt's wide eyes brimmed with excitement and expectation. "Remember, you promised, Joe." The smell of plowed earth was strong in their nostrils and the cooling fragrance of the river beckoned them. While he watered the mule, Matt shucked his clothes, his fish-white body in sharp contrast to the dark waters as he splashed into the cool river, shaded by thick willows edging the bank. Dragonflies danced across the water's surface while cicadas called to them on the gentle breeze that stirred the leaves of the overhanging willows.

And then . . . Matt was screaming. Not the screams of a youth lost in the pure pleasures of the moment, but screams of fright, of the unknown.

The man on the cot began to breathe heavy and his eyelids fluttered as his body jerked uncontrollably beneath the thin blanket. His slack face tightened, the lips drawing into a tight line.

"Hold on, Matt, I'm coming!" In the sun drenched waters, a dark coiling object surfaced beside the thrashing body of his terrified friend. There was no mistaking the dirty brown, thick body of the moccasin and the cotton-white mouth now clamped firmly to the boy's leg.

"Dammit, Joe!"

The voice loomed closer. A cup raked the iron bars of the cell, sounding like a Gatling being fired at point blank range.

The man on the cot stiffened and sat up suddenly, his blood-red eyes blinking back the light of early morning. His chest rose and fell heavily, the image of the boy and snake still strong in his mind.

"Thunderation, but you sleep sound or was it the whiskey holding you down?" a grinning face asked from the other side of the iron bars.

Joe Rankin squinted up at his younger brother as he ran his fingers through rumpled hair that was slowly receding from his face in spite of his best efforts to prevent it. He had even spent fifty dollars for some oily-smelling concoction from Doc Trumbull who swore the mixture could reverse the process of thinning hair. Everyday, he had smeared the evil-smelling mixture into his scalp for three weeks, enduring his two brothers' laughing comments with quiet assurance and belief in the product. For a week or two it did seem that his hair was becoming a little fuller, a little thicker. But then he ran out of tonic and another fifty dollars at the same time. Joe guessed he would never know if the treatment would have worked. In the end, Joe figured he could best spend fifty dollars in a more productive way down on Lower Row or over a bottle of good whiskey. He burped and the taste of last night left his stomach feeling queasy from the smell.

He pushed aside such thoughts and looked around the cell as if realizing for the first time where he was. Rankin stared up at his cheerful-faced brother and gave him a sour look.

"Why in hell did you wake me?" Joe asked, yet glad that he had. This wasn't the first time he had dreamed of the boy and the snake . . . except this time he almost touched the boy's hair.

He was getting closer with each dream. Rankin shook his head to clear such foolish notions from his head. No matter how many times, no matter how many ways he dreamt of the episode, it wouldn't change facts. Matthew J. Bedford was dead and that was that. No stupid dream was ever going to bring back his friend of long ago, no matter how badly he wanted it to happen.

"Want some breakfast? Coffee maybe?" Bobby Rankin asked his brother, seeing his pain.

Joe Rankin got unsteadily to his feet, his tall lanky frame seemed to fill the small cell. "Coffee will do just fine," he replied, feeling his stomach lurch at the idea of food. He flexed his jaw muscles, feeling the tenderness along the ridge line. His fingers explored the raised area. "When you gonna learn, Joe? Port Weems's a big man. His fist'll make two of yours."

Rankin managed a tight grin. "Hadn't expected on needin' my mitts," he said ruefully.

"Expect you'd need them a lot less if you left the married ones alone and took your needs down to Lower Row."

"Can I help it if all the pretty ones are married and find me irresistible? And you know full well not to mix business with pleasure," Rankin replied, referring to his little known business interest in the prostitutes who worked the lower side of Rawlings. He belched again, the sour smell of whiskey flooding his nostrils. Rankin grimaced.

"Thought you was gonna fetch me some coffee?" he said to his jailer brother. "Or will you make your older brother get his own?"

Bobby Rankin, jailer for their third brother, Sheriff James

Rankin, smiled broadly at his distressed sibling. Unlike Joe, Bobby was a good four inches shorter and carried more meat on his frame.

"Ain't got no choice," Bobby Rankin said, moving down the hall. "Port Weems filed charges against you for trifling with his wife's affections," he called over his shoulder.

Joe Rankin stood there for a minute not fully comprehending what his brother was saying until he moved to the cell door and found it locked.

"What the hell—" Joe shook the door. "Dammit, Bobby! unlock this door," Rankin screamed down the hallway. Bobby reappeared carrying a tin cup of coffee for his brother.

"What in hell's the meaning of this, locking the door against your own flesh and blood?"

Bobby Rankin passed the cup through the bars. "Told you, Port Weems is pressing charges against you, not to mention the three hundred dollars it's gonna take to soothe Blacky's feelings. Damn, but you and Port musta had an expensive fight."

Joe stared at his younger brother, his aching jaw hanging open. *Trifling affections? Three hundred dollars!* Had everybody gone crazy since last night? Blacky Stillwell didn't have three hundred dollars worth of nothing in his so-called saloon.

"This is some kinda joke you and Jim cooked up, ain't it, Bobby? To put a heel on my womanizing."

"Nope. Port Weems and Blacky is behind it and that's the truth."

Joe Rankin looked stunned. "Hell, Bob, it was Port come looking for me. He done most of the damage to Blacky's place. I was too near drunk to defend myself much less bust up furniture."

"Joe, you was lucky Port didn't come gunning for you instead."

"Listen, Bobby, you gotta let me outa here now. I got a livery to run. For Christsakes, I ain't leaving town." Joe's voice had taken on a pleading tone. He had spent many a night in his brother's jail, but never locked up. When morning came, he had simply paid up what damages he owed and waltzed on back to his livery until he was ready to buck the tiger again. This was something completely new to him.

"Can't open it, Joe, you know that."

"Then go get Jim, he's, by God Sheriff, ain't he? He can damn sure let me out." His brother shook his head, "Jim's rode over to Fort Steele." The jail grew quiet after that as Joe absorbed this bit of distressing news, the forgotten coffee still clutched in a white-knuckled fist.

Joe's face finally grew a deep crimson. "First thing I'm gonna do is shoot that stinkin'-eyed Weems for having me locked up. And ain't noway I'm gonna fork over three hundred dollars to Blacky Stillwell either," Joe fumed. "Might even be forced to shoot him too. Whole place ain't worth Chinaman spit. And to think. I fixed him up with that little bug-eyed whore, Sally, just to help him out. Yes sir, just might have to cripple him as well," he said grimly.

"Joe, wish there was something I could do," Bob Rankin said, a feeling of helplessness sweeping over him at the sight of his distressed brother. Joe stopped his fuming and looked at Rawling's jailer. A thought struck him and he put it to words.

"Don't I get a chance to bail myself out like other bad men you've locked up?"

Bobby Rankin's face flooded with blood, "Judge Walker hasn't been around to his office to set bail yet, Joe."

"Then you best get over to his place and roust the old scalawag outa bed and tell him to hop to it. And tell him if he don't keep it low, the next time he rents a buggy and horse from me it will cost him six months wages." Bobby stood there looking at his brother though the bars. He had never seen Joe so cold-eyed sober and angry.

"Well, you just gonna stand there all day? Get to moving, boy!" Joe Rankin commanded. Bobby sprang away from the cell and retreated down the hallway.

Joe listened as the door closed and then he finally forced himself to relax. Wasn't much else he could do under the circumstances. He took a sip of the forgotten coffee and found it cold. His anger flared like a match stuck to pitch pine and he flung the cup against the far wall, where the spilled coffee sprinkled the cot and his soft deerskin jacket. Joe eyed the wet marks. Port Weems and Blacky Stillwell were gonna pay for that, he promised himself. And then he thought of Linda Weems, so soft and yielding and his anger quickly turned to desire. He could smell the richness of her skin even now. What he couldn't figure was how that ugly-faced Port had managed to marry such a sweet and beautiful creature, two dozen years his junior. He shook his head at such mysteries and picked up his leather coat and tried shaking off the residual coffee before it took hold and the drops left a permanent stain. He sat down glumly on the cot and stared into space for a long time. Sometime later, the outer office door banged open and Joe moved to the cell door and craned his neck, trying to see down the empty hall.

"Who's out there? That you Bobby?"

There was movement and the bulk of a large man filled the hallway, his angry eyes searching for the man in the cell. He stepped deeper into the hall, bringing with him a Winchester which he gripped tightly in both massive hands.

Rankin recognized Port Weems and stepped deeper into the tiny cell. Desperately, he looked around for something he could use as a weapon or a shield.

"Ain't gonna waste words on low down scum like you, Rankin!" Port Weems shouted down the quiet hall. "Just gonna blow your worthless hide full of holes. That way, the womenfolk of Rawlings will be safe to walk the streets once again, free from your kind."

"Hold on, Port. You don't want to do that," Rankin said, edging deeper into the cell. He began to sweat profusely, the coffee-stained coat clutched in his hand, now forgotten. *Where the hell was Bobby? Of all the times...*

"You kill me, my brothers will see you hang, Weems," Joe called, as he felt the thin mattress of corn shucks. No way it could be used for padding to ward off a shot from Port's rifle. He was trapped like a rabbit in a cage. There wasn't any way Port could miss.

"Decent, law-abiding citizens ain't hung fer shooting low lifers that mess around with married women," Port said, as he edged deeper into the dim hall.

"You'll hang all right," Joe continued, wiping away the sweat now stinging his eyes. "Better think of Linda . . . Mrs. Weems and them two boys of yours. They gonna need a father around to raise them proper."

"It's a cinch you don't know what's proper," Port Weems said as he stepped up to the cell holding Rankin. His cruel face was blood engorged and red from an early morning infusion of alcohol. An evil grin spread across his features. "Well, well, lover boy, looks like your tomcat days are about over."

Rankin had his back against the wall with his hands out in front of him. "Now Port, think about what you're doing."

"Spent most of the night doing just that," Weems said, jacking a shell into the .44-40. To Rankin, the sound was like the very gates of hell being opened to receive his soul.

"Dammit, Port, it ain't all my fault. Linda was more than willin'," Joe said out of desperation as the burly man brought the Winchester to hip level and pointed it at him through the bars. He hated to bring the woman into it, but with death staring him in the face, he figured he had to do something to keep Weems at bay for a little longer.

The words stung the big man and his face turned grim. "Done knocked some sense into her as well. Won't be tomorrow when she throws a petticoat over some jasper like you, not the way I fixed her face." A gleam came into his eyes just from the telling.

"Why you dumb muleskinner. Don't you know that ain't noway to treat someone as kind and gentle as Linda."

"Don't you try and, by God, tell me how to treat my wife!" Port Weems roared, his face a dusty purple.

"Hold it, Port!" Bobby Rankin ordered from the hall doorway. "Now drop the Winchester." Port Weems turned his head slightly to see Bobby standing there holding a Colt on him.

"This ain't none of your affair, jailer, just 'cause he's your brother. What he done is wrong. Made me the laughing stock of Rawlings."

"Drop the rifle, Port," Bobby Rankin said evenly. "Won't ask again." Weems seemed to sag just a little and the barrel of the Winchester dropped slightly. His burning eyes pinned Joe Rankin.

"This ain't settled. Remember that, Rankin." Weems allowed the rifle barrel to tip further towards the floor. Bobby Rankin moved forward cautiously and took the rifle from the big man. Both he and Joe heaved a collective sigh of relief. Joe moved to the front of the cell. Port Weems continued to stare hard at him.

"Thought you'd never get back," Joe said, looking at his younger brother. "Next time I'm hemmed up like this, make damn sure you lock the front door before you leave."

Bobby grinned at his brother who was white as alkali. "Me and Jim been trying to tell you about fooling around with married women. Nothing can come of it but grief."

"Spare me," Joe said. "What you gonna do with this crazy man?"

"Why lock him up, of course." With that, Bobby stepped back an opened the cell door next to Joe's.

"You locking *me* up?" Weems said, incredulous.

"That's generally what happens when a person tries to commit murder," Bobby said matter-of-fact. He swung the door open as far as it would go. "Get in, Port."

"You can't put him in here next to me," Joe said, as shocked as Port Weems was by Bobby's actions.

"Why not," Bobby grinned, "might do both of you some good. This way you two can talk out your troubles. Besides, you know we ain't got but one jail and two jail cells."

"Dammit, Bobby, you can't do this to me," Joe pleaded. "Least let *me* go."

Bobby Rankin shook his head. "Can't do that either."

"Didn't you talk with that sot of a judge Walker about me?"

"I don't want to be stuck here next to *him*," Port Weems bawled. Bobby locked the door and smiled at both men in their misery.

"Shouda let the law handle this, Port. This ain't going to look good when it comes up in front of Judge Walker."

"I don't care a damn how it looks to Dan Walker!" Weems almost screamed. "I ain't the one been messing around with another man's wife."

"That's right, Weems, you just visit the girls down on Lower Row when you feel the need," Joe Rankin interjected sarcastically. "Can't understand a man with a wife as pretty—"

"Damn you, Rankin!" Weems roared, "What would you know about my needs?"

"Guess I'll leave you two to talk it out," Bobby said, smiling at his brother.

"Bobby, you can't do this to me," Joe said, but Bobby was gone. A long silence fell over the jail as the two prisoners eyed one another with obvious hatred. Joe turned his back to the other man and sat down on his cot, staring at the floor. Port Weems looked ready to break something in his agitated state as he clenched and unclenched his big fists. He looked through the bars at the source of all his troubles.

"You can't hide behind your brothers forever, Rankin," he warned. Joe Rankin looked up at the fuming man with cold eyes. He got up from the cot and came over to stand just inches from the bars.

29

"Never hid behind no man, Weems, especially my brothers. As soon as we clear of these cells, you can find me down at the livery anytime you think you got the stomach for it, which we both know you don't." Port Weems stepped back involuntarily. He was familiar with Rankin's prowess with a short gun and his dead-shot accuracy with a rifle. Confronting Joe Rankin when he was locked up and defenseless was one thing, but facing him with a gun in his hand was another. Some of the heat drained out of Port Weems.

"And while it's just the two of us, you mistreat Linda again, you'll have to deal with me and you best have your gun handy." Joe Rankin stared the big man down and it was Weems who turned quietly away and sat down on his cot, who buried his face in his big calloused hands. Silence filled the void for the next few minutes and Joe returned to his cot and picked up his coat once more. The coffee stains were barely visible now that they had dried.

"Know I don't deserve her," Weems started in. "Hell, look at me. I'm twenty-two years older and ugly as a piebald pinto." He looked through the bars at Rankin. "You don't know what I've been going through. I see the way other men look at her. All I've ever done is wrangle mules and wagons. Can't give her the proper things in life I know she wants, the pretty clothes and such," he said, "but I do love her and that's the honest to God truth."

Rankin looked at the miserable man for a moment before speaking. A lot of what a man is, the way he views himself and how he interacts with others are tied up in what he believes the world expects of him. Most men would go to any length to protect this image. God knows, he had over the years. And when he came along and found Linda Weems so willing . . . well, not that he intended to tell Port Weems, but he could see how the man might grab up a Winchester and come gunning. Maybe his brothers were right. Maybe he should just stick to whores. At least a man didn't have to worry about keeping his pants handy in case a husband came home unexpectedly.

"Listen, Weems, I ain't saying what's right or wrong, but I can tell you, your wife . . . well, she's not to be blamed for what happened, no matter what I said a few minutes ago. You got to understand, women are like a sickness with me. And with that Winchester pointed at my gut, it seemed the right thing to say at the time."

Port Weems visibly shuddered, "Ain't never come that close to killing a man before," he confessed. He raised his head and looked at Joe Rankin with tired eyes. "Don't think I could have gone through with it anyway, no matter the hurting inside."

Joe Rankin got up off the cot and came over to the bars separating the two men.

"Well, I'm willing to forget it happened, if you can overlook the one indiscretion your wife ever had. She loves you man," Rankin said. "It ain't those pretty things she's needin'. All you got to do is show her a little attention."

Port Weems sat there for a long moment in silence. Finally, his big shoulders slumped and Weems nodded his head slowly as the fire inside slowly dissipated. No further words were needed between the two men.

Bobby Rankin came in later with the news that Judge Walker was willing to accept a bail of nothing less than the three hundred dollars owed to Blacky Stillwell to which Joe expressed outrage.

"I'm dropping the charges I lodged against Joe," Port Weems said quietly to the jailer. Bobby Rankin looked as though he hadn't heard the man correctly.

"Planning on gunning my brother down later?" Bobby inquired, looking from one man to the other.

"No, nothing like that," Weems replied quietly. "We've reached an understanding, that's all." Bobby looked perplexed. Joe merely shrugged his shoulders when his younger brother glanced his way.

"Well, no matter," Bobby responded, "there's still the charges Blacky brought against you, Joe."

"For Christsakes, Bobby, whose side you on?" Joe snapped.

"We can split the damages," Port Weems broke in, "since I broke most of Blacky's furnishings anyway." Both Rankin brothers were surprised by Weems generosity even if what he said was true.

Bobby tested the waters once again. "But now you aren't mad at Joe anymore?"

"I'm plenty sore at him, I just don't want any further trouble is all." Weems looked at Bobby with pain in his eyes. "I just want to go home now . . . to my family."

"What about it, Joe, any reason why I can't turn Port loose?"

"Go ahead, and you can open my door while you're about it."

"Got the hundred and fifty you gonna owe Blacky?" Bobby asked, grinning at his brother while he let Port from his cell.

"Dang it, Bobby, when I do get outta here, you best find a hole."

"What I thought you would say. I'll be back directly with your lunch. Come on Port." They started down the hall with Bobby leading the way.

"Bobby! . . . Bobby!" Joe called, but his brother ignored his cries and closed the hall door behind him. Joe banged the bars with a clenched fist.

"Damn!"

CHAPTER 3

The trail to Rawlings from the White River Ute Agency was at best, rigorous in the summer, but in the First Snow Moon, a thick carpet of white lay across the steep slopes, plunging wild rivers and deep canyons, making the trip treacherous for man and horse. As the People moved slowly away from the protective mountains, the old men and young children suffered the most from the stinging cold winds that cut across the treeless prairie, freezing toes and fingers solid. At night the cries of frostbitten children could not be quieted by the screaming winds as feeling returned to extremities with unrelenting agony. The old ones suffered in silence. To them, this was simply another injustice by the *Mericatz* they were made to endure.

Now a full moon had passed while they waited patiently by fires that warmed their bodies but not their stomachs while Quinkent rode into the *Mericatz* village of Rawlings to ask for the presents Washington was holding in the building next to the tracks of the *panakarpo*, the railroad. Each day, Quinkent returned to the *carniva* by the Sweetwater with nothing more than empty *Mericatz* words to feed his village.

Quinkent held faint hope that the *Mericatz* would give them the presents before spring thunder, but he said nothing to Singing Grass when she brought him a cup of weak coffee after the cold ride to Rawlings. It was late afternoon and pewter clouds, thick with snow, hung heavy over the frozen river, casting a bleakness across the frigid landscape that drove Quinkent's spirit deeper into him.

Even though he knew his *piwán* was anxious to learn if the *Mericatz* in Washington had sent word to release their presents, Quinkent sat before the center fire in stony silence. He had watched his words being shot to Washington like bullets, yet even before the *Mericatz* who sat before the little machine spoke, Quinkent knew the words that rattled back at them were not good. His pleading with Washington for food and blankets for the People was again ignored. And when the answer came back, Quinkent had simply stood up, gathered the reins of his horse and rode back towards the river. All *Mericatz* words were the same. Even when they talked to men, they sounded as though they were speaking to children. They laughed at the wrong time and at the wrong things. What was richly funny to an Indian, a *Mericatz* would simply frown at and turn away. There was no understanding *Mericatz* Quinkent concluded although he felt compelled to try because the *Nüpartka* must survive above all costs. Singing Grass broke the cold silence as she rummaged in her food bundle for items to cook.

"Nicaagat is camped on the Shoshoni." Quinkent never acknowledged her words, but continued to stare into the small fire, his soul suddenly made cold by what she said. The Shoshoni was known as the Little Snake River by the *Mericatz* since this river was on the edge of their country. Quinkent did not like to hold in his head the thought that Nicaagat camped there with over a hundred lodges of *Nüpartka* around him. It meant that hunting had been poor for Nicaagat's band as well. Nicaagat normally wintered in the Green Mountains north of the place the *Mericatz* called Whiskey Gap, named for a wagon train of whiskey that was destroyed by Company "A" 11th Ohio Cavalry under the command of Major O'Ferrell in 1862. A noteworthy act since it was the first official prohibition raid on record for the Territory of Wyoming. It was a place Quinkent never ventured, preferring the sheltered valley along Smoking Earth River or Roan Plateau along Grand Mesa for his winter encampment.

But now the *Nüpartka* were far from their home, cold and hungry in a land of sage brush and angry winds that blew incessantly. Quinkent did not like this open, flat land other than to hunt buffalo, but even they were gone from this prairie and the People were starving because the *Mericatz* would not give them the presents from Washington.

The shadow of a man played across his *carniv* and without preamble, a stout Indian, the color of fall acorns entered Quinkent's lodge and stood tall before the center fire. The backward slope of his proud head was adorned with a silver ornament signifying *one who leads others*. Nicaagat stood silently for a moment while awaiting Quinkent's greeting to his lodge and fire.

"*Maiquas!*" Quinkent said forcefully and Nicaagat answered in kind and took his seat across from Quinkent, his two tightly woven braids of black hair lay like thick twisted ropes against the beautiful buckskin coat his *piwán* had made for him. Nicaagat was fifteen winters younger than Quinkent.

Quinkent and Nicaagat were rivals and neither man made no pretext of liking the other. Quinkent had never visited the *carniv* of

Nicaagat, yet Nicaagat would sometimes visit Quinkent when there were important things to discuss. At such times, Quinkent was more than willing to receive his rival for it helped to strengthen his position with his own band of *Nüpartka*. It was only through the intervention of Ouray and his sister Tsashin's husband, Canávish, that Quinkent became *tawacz viem* of the *Nüpartka*, and not Nicaagat following the death of Chief Nevava.

While Singing Grass went outside the *carniv* to start the cook fire to prepare the evening meal, Quinkent drew forth the leather pouch that held tobacco he had gotten from the *Mericatz* store in Rawlings. Next, he produced corn husks for rolling cigarettes which he passed over to Nicaagat after he shook out some of the rough-cut tobacco into a cupped husk.

They rolled their cigarettes and lit them with pieces of glowing coals from the small fire. In the ancient ways of the People, both smokers drew in lungfulls of smoke and held it, releasing it slowly through their mouths. Just as quickly the smoke was sucked deep once more into their lungs where it was held for a long time against the heart. This time when the smoke was released, both Quinkent and Nicaagat rotated their heads with a swishing motion and the expelled smoke was blown around them in big circles towards the ground. Again they repeated the ritual except this time the smoke was blown upward over the center fire where it mixed with the woodsmoke and escaped through the ears of the *carniv* toward the darkening sky. Only good could come from their talk now, for they had given the truth of their hearts to the earth and sky. Such was the way of those who were not friends and wished to speak about grave matters that concerned all the People.

Quinkent thought of the People and their hunger. Without asking, he knew Nicaagat was here to find out if Washington was going to release the presents. Both bands of the *Nüpartka* had suffered much from the poor fall hunts. The drying summer winds had been hard on man and animal, preparing neither for the cold snows that now covered the ground. Quinkent also knew through Colorow, that Nicaagat had been to see the soldiers at Fort Steele and he was anxious to know what Nicaagat had learned.

Of all the People, Nicaagat possessed more of the *Mericatz* words and knowledge of their ways than anybody except possibly, Ouray, *tawacz viem* of all seven Ute bands. Nicaagat was friends with the soldiers and had served as a special scout for General Crook during their wars with the Sioux. Placed with a Mormon family in Utah, Nicaagat spend his youth going to a white man's school and later worked for six months driving a salt wagon until he decided all *Mericatz* were crazy and rode east to join the People on Smoking Earth River. He was a powerful leader, even his name, Nicaagat, "leaves turning green," bespoke of his power held in the Spring Moon. Gradually, the *Mericatz* language became hidden deep within his head and only when he was alone with *Mericatz* would he speak their language.

Quinkent was the first to break the silence. "Washington is good to us and we need to be their friends."

Nicaagat looked at the aging man with the wispy mustache and knew that for all his knowledge, Quinkent did not yet understand the *Mericatz* and how they thought.

"The *Mericatz* will not release our food and blankets until those that carried these things west are paid. That is how it is. That is how it has been now for two winters," Nicaagat reminded Quinkent. His voice was deep and rumbled out of him like thunder on a spring day.

"Washington is my friend . . . and to all the People," Quinkent insisted. "They will see how we grow weak and sick and soon they will grow tired of holding our presents and give them to us."

Nicaagat seemed not to hear Quinkent. "The soldiers will not help. My people suffer too." It was the first time Nicaagat admitted his band were in need of the food and other items now locked away in the warehouse.

Quinkent's heart was heavy at the news concerning the soldiers. He had hoped they would share with them, enough at least, until the *Mericatz* in Washington freed their presents. Everyday they waited, another child died and Quinkent was weary of the anguish of his people.

Nicaagat continued in the ancient musical language that flowed like slow water over smooth rocks. "We should take some of these things and go back to our mountains. Soon the snows will fill the passes. The *Mericatz* will not follow."

Quinkent could not believe his ears. "To take without asking would only bring trouble to all Utes. The *Mericatz* will come next spring," Quinkent warned.

Nicaagat rolled another cigarette and this one he smoked like a *Mericatz*, taking short, steady pulls and releasing the smoke immediately. He was suddenly nervous as he spoke of breaking into the warehouse that very night.

"If you did this thing tonight, we would be forced to break camp and run south." Quinkent shook his head, "My brothers are old, we cannot move fast in this terrible weather. Many of us would die."

Nicaagat sat for a while smoking and thinking of Quinkent's words that now filled his head. He was caught by the urgent need to provide for his own band, yet knowing that he must learn to be sensitive to the concerns of all *Nüpartka* if he was to be *tawacz viem* someday.

Singing Grass stepped through the entrance and placed before them a steaming pot of dried elk meat, boiled to tender richness. A few wild herbs floated on top of the thick mixture, adding the distinctive Ute flavor to the food that was preferred by the *Nüpartka*. Next, she placed wooden bowls before them and brought cups of coffee and fat-fried *pana*, bread, to serve with the meat. Small cakes of dried meat and ground serviceberries from the fall hunts rounded out the meal.

Quinkent knew the meal before them represented the last of their provisions, yet he was pleased Singing Grass had prepared such a feast. Serious talks between such men as Nicaagat and himself called for special preparations.

After they had finished with the meal, Quinkent once again produced his *quap* and they rolled cigarettes and smoked in silence for a time. On full stomachs, the world presented itself in a different light and angle. The sharpness no longer pushed its way into the center of a man, blinding him to the obvious. Men could come to reasonable decisions that were wise and honorable. Perhaps now, Nicaagat could see the danger in taking some of the presents without the *Mericatz* permission.

When Nicaagat finally spoke, his words stirred things around in Quinkent and left him feeling sad again.

"We will take what is ours. But we will wait one sleep while you break camp." Singing Grass slipped around and cleared away the food pots and replenished the center fire with small pieces of wood. Outside, the winds of the day gave way to the night and its moaning sounds through the trees lining Smoking Earth River died to a faint whisper with the fading light.

Quinkent smoked in silence, his thoughts busy with the implications of what Nicaagat was planning. True, the presents were theirs, but in the *Mericatz* strange ways, until the words on all the papers were signed, the *Nüpartka* could not have the presents. It was the way of the *Mericatz* and try as he might, there was just no understanding them. Even as these thoughts filled his head until it hurt to hold them there any longer, in the end, Quinkent did what was expected of a *tawacz viem*.

"I will go see the *Mericatz* tomorrow. Maybe Washington will hear my words and listen with their hearts."

"They will not listen," Nicaagat said with conviction. "Only after the freight costs are paid will the *Mericatz* release what is ours. We have been waiting two winters. We will wait no longer." Nicaagat stood up and looked back at Quinkent as he drew aside the door. "Remember, We will wait only one sleep." And then he was gone into the evening dusk.

Later, the pressing cold found Quinkent seeking his bed earlier than usual. He beckoned Singing Grass to join him. Tonight, he needed the comfort of her softness, her gentle caresses that never failed to work their magic on him. Maybe then all the troubled thoughts that filled his head would go away.

Singing Grass released her pinned up hair and the dying fire reflected a thousand tiny lights from its silky blackness as she dropped her garments and slipped beneath the thick robe that Quinkent held open for her. Thirty winters younger than her husband, Singing Grass was still slim of form, smooth-skinned and eager for their infrequent love making. She pressed herself to Quinkent, seeking his warmth, stroking his back and sides lightly with subtle fingers, her breath steady and even, filled the hollow beneath his jaw.

Quinkent sighed and closed his eyes to her caresses, feeling the pain in his head floating away by her gentle ministrations. He had sought only to hold her, to be comforted by her familiar softness but he was soon aware of her taut body, her heavy breasts against his chest and her encircling thighs entwined with his own, beckoning and drawing him closer. His heartbeat throbbed at his temples as his hands explored her supple body. As he ran a calloused hand down the small of her silky back and over the rounded curve of her bottom, she trembled and moved her hips eagerly against him like a mare waiting to be mounted. And he was surprised at his readiness. He whispered her name and Singing Grass took him in one hand, guiding him gently to her and they were soon lost in their mating.

Even though Ute custom allowed for a man to have more than one *piwán*, Quinkent had taken no other woman since Singing Grass came to his *carniv*. That was not to say there had not been others before her. As with all men of the Blue Sky People, Quinkent had bedded his share of young girls on the way to manhood. It was an accepted practice and many times he had entered the lodge of sleeping parents to make love with a willing girl. The parents found nothing wrong with this and only disapproved if they were awakened by their love making, for it was considered rude to make much noise over such matters.

Singing Grass lay cradled in his arms afterward, the smell of her, like sweet grass in summer, was strong in his nostrils. It had been a long time since they had enjoyed each other. In the dying light of the center fire, Quinkent could see his breath in the frigid air as he pulled the robe close about them once more, their bodies damp from the exertion.

"Do you think Nicaagat does the right thing?" he suddenly asked, wanting her opinion. As *tawacz viem*, he felt his great responsibility returning in the afterglow of their love making.

"The *Mericatz* keeps what is not theirs," Singing Grass murmured, half-asleep on his shoulder. It was not the answer he was seeking and he lay there for a few minutes turning this over in his mind.

"Even if we do not ride with Nicaagat, the *Mericatz* will blame us as well. *Mericatz* are like that. They do not see differences from one Indian to the other."

Singing Grass lifted her head from his shoulder and looked into his eyes. "The children starve and the *Mericatz* do not care. Either way, death will claim some of us," Singing Grass said matter-of-fact before settling her head on his shoulders once more.

"I will try one more time to get them to hear our pleas," he said doggedly. "While I am gone, the camp will join those lodges along the Shoshoni where Nicaagat now camps. If they do not listen, we will come as swiftly as we can once we take the presents. So tell the others to be ready. We must ride deep into the mountains and hope the *Mericatz* will be stopped by the Snow Moons."

"You can do nothing less," she whispered, falling into a satisfied sleep. For a long time, Quinkent lay there, holding her to him and listening to her gentle breathing, her last words echoing deep within his brain. *He really could do nothing less.*

Early morning found Quinkent fighting a driving snow pushed along by a cold wind that tore at his clothes like wild brambles, forcing its icy fingers inside to freeze the flesh.

The half foot of new snow hid the ugliness of Rawlings, not that anyone at this early hour would have noticed in the swirling madness of white. Hunched over the neck of his horse, Quinkent had the street to himself as he walked the animal over to the familiar building that bordered the Union Pacific tracks. A yellowed light barely cut a path through the flying snow to mark the presence of life inside the drab building. A little ways off stood the warehouse, dark and silent and covered with snow. It was here the presents from Washington were being held. Quinkent did not look at the building as he rode up.

Quinkent dismounted stiffly and led his pony to the side of the building and out of the direct wind. He tied the animal to the bare limb of a bush that grew out from beneath the raised building and returned to the front door and stepped inside. Cold wind brought with him a small snowstorm.

"Christ! Hurry and close the door," a red-faced man said from behind a wire cage that housed the ticket office. The young man never lifted his head from the documents that were spread before him.

"There's coffee on the stove, help yourself." A few rough hewn benches and a large pot-bellied stove occupied the rest of the cramped quarters that was the depot. Across one wall was a large colored map showing a major portion of the United States and highlighting the complete railroad system of the Union Pacific.

Quinkent had spent time looking up at this great map, at the indecipherable marks and wondered at its meaning, but the *Mericatz* who worked here had shown no inclination to explain it to him. Perhaps, today the *Mericatz* could tell him about this map. That was another thing Quinkent could not understand about *Mericatz*. They were always busy with what they called "work" and never took time to relax, smoke and laugh with others of their kind until the sun touched the distant horizon. This "work," so peculiar to *Mericatz*, was part of the reason they were losing Danforth as agent. Quinkent hoped the next agent would not expect the same of the People, but deep down near his heart, he knew all *Mericatz* were the same.

Quinkent moved next to the stove and warmed himself before reaching for the coffee pot. The man came out of the cage holding a sheaf of papers in his hands. He was in his early twenties, clean-shaven and dressed in a dark brown suit and stiff white shirt. Grayson Toliver took his job as Union Pacific agent and expressman seriously and he insisted on dressing the part. He ran a tight office and had received praise and recognition from his superiors back in Omaha on several occasions plus a small increase in salary for his dedication to duty. And he had been doing his duty for five years now.

"Oh, it's you, Douglas. What on earth are you doing out in such awful weather?" Quinkent looked at the *Mericatz* and slurped the strong coffee, liking its rich taste.

"Talk to Washington. Need presents, now," Quinkent said, wondering why the *Mericatz* could not see why he had come.

Toliver laid the papers on a small desk and turned to look at the old Indian. He smiled for the first time and most likely his last for the day at Quinkent.

"Sorry you rode all the way in here for nothing. Can't talk to Washington today. Snowstorm's brought down the lines somewhere between here and Cheyenne. Most likely in the Medicine Bows. Bet there's ten feet of new snow up there."

Quinkent stared for a long moment at the *Mericatz* before he spoke again. His broken English held the defeat he felt inside for his People and for his failure to have the presents released peacefully.

"You cannot give presents?"

Toliver shook his head and turned back to the small desk and sat down. "I've told you before, Douglas, I don't have the authority to do that."

"Who give this authority then? These things are ours."

"I know how you feel, but this decision must come from the Department of Interior. Until then, I can do nothing." Toliver picked up the papers before him and pretended to read them, slightly annoyed at the old chief's presence.

Quinkent stood there for a long time, watching the *Mericatz* read the marks on the papers before moving to the door. He no longer wished to know more about the map on the wall. His heart was heavy and full of sorrow. He had promised to be Washington's friend, but now Washington was acting like little children while the People starved. There was no more food in his camp and now Nicaagat would have his way, breaking away a piece of Quinkent's power from his own band in the process. The *Mericatz* spoke behind him.

"I'm sorry, Douglas. As soon as the lines are repaired, I'll send another message. Come back in a few days after the storm passes." Quinkent gave no indication he had heard the agent and continued out. Toliver shook his head and dropped his eyes to the papers once more.

Quinkent returned to the blinding snow and leaden sky and found his pony nibbling at the frozen branches of the bush. Even the animals suffered because of Washington, for the warehouse held oats and hay as well as flour and sugar. He brushed the snow from the gaunt animal and turned back towards the river where he knew Nicaagat waited.

CHAPTER 4

Quinkent's angry eyes were like two hard berries in winter as he sought out the dark face of Nicaagat across the burning fire. Six others shared the makeshift council fire while the figures of still more watched from the flickering shadows. Colorow sat next to Quinkent, his face expressing the unhappy state of his spirit. The rumblings from his huge belly emphasized the reason for this council.

Rawlings lay a few miles to the south of the thinly sheltered ravine where they now camped without benefit of a lodge to break the icy wind that rattled the bare limbs of the alders and cottonwoods like clinking bones of the dead.

Quinkent had spoken first, trying to convince Nicaagat and the others not to carry through with their plans but the silence that greeted him when he had finished left no doubt his words had fallen on closed ears and hearts. Even Colorow seemed to grow sadder by his words. In the gloom of the small fire and pressing cold, everyone waited for Nicaagat to speak.

Nicaagat finished smoking the last of his cigarette and let the smoke escape slowly through his nostrils the way a *Mericatz* does as he looked up at the glittering heavens. In the cold of a black night, the stars were like broken glass reflecting to earth the light from an invisible sun. Bringing his eyes back to the fire, Nicaagat said slowly, "We have listened to your words, with our ears and our hearts. There is wisdom in what you say and it is good to think of such things, yet we must now learn to listen with our heads as well. The *Mericatz* treat us like little children. For two winters they have denied supplies that rightfully belong to the People. Do you see any *Mericatz* going hungry? Do they lack warm blankets for their beds and good tobacco to smoke before a comfortable fire? Do their children grow thin and cry out at night for something to eat like the wolf when there is too much snow on the ground for hunting?"

"Unh!" Colorow grumbled and several others mumbled their feelings as well.

"Even the *Swerch* at Fort Steele can offer us nothing," Nicaagat said, using the Ute word for soldier. *Swerch* was not a word the *Nüpartka* liked to hear, even during high council, and those around the fire reacted sharply to the harsh-sounding utterance.

"Swerch!" came a whispered exclamation from Canávish who sat next to the big-bellied Colorow. "They are like all other *Mericatz,* except worse." A rumble of voices gathered strength from Canavish's words. As shaman, no other in the village was held in higher esteem. The interruption was excusable, even for the oldest and wisest of men. The *Mericatz* soldiers frightened the People even now for they still remembered the massacre of Black Kettle's village at Sand Creek vividly and his subsequent death and that of his wife, Mayiuna, at

the Washita River at the hands of George Armstrong Custer's Seventh Cavalry. The dawn attack in a heavy snowstorm left over one hundred Cheyennes dead, ninety-two of whom were women and children. Custer ordered his troopers to slaughter the village herd of eight hundred ponies, burn every lodge and all their food supplies. More than fifty women and children were taken prisoners.

Even though ten winters had now passed, there had been whispered talk that unless the Utes fell into line, a repeat of Sand Creek or Washita was possible. And it was the *Mericatz* soldiers who always came with the treaty makers as if to provide an added threat in case the People did not sign the paper.

Nicaagat reached out and removed a burning twig from the fire and held it up for those around him to see. Gray smoke curled away from the glowing end of the half-consumed stick.

"We are like this piece of wood. Like the fire that slowly consumes it as it is pushed deeper into the flames, so are we being consumed by the *Mericatz*. Very soon we will become lifeless and used up like this twig when it gives us its heat and dies." Nicaagat's dark eyes searched out each man at the fire. His voice trembled with the feelings that were stirring around his heart, taking over his thoughts.

"The only way to deal with *Mericatz* is to be like Red Cloud. Listen, I know these things for I rode against the Sioux with the *Swerch*. Like us, the Sioux signed treaties and their lands grew smaller. It became hard to hunt on such lands and the people began to suffer. And like us, the *Mericatz* came again asking for more lands, except this time, Red Cloud said no. That he would fight for his homeland. With his men, Red Cloud forced the *Swerch* to leave their lands and the Sioux burned their forts as they left." The men around the fire stared silently at Nicaagat. Was he asking them to go to war with the *Mericatz*? Quinkent's expression did not change while Colorow seemed to grow sullen by Nicaagat's words.

Quinkent felt compelled to speak, even though proper time had not lapsed for a man to study Nicaagat's words. To speak too quickly was considered rash, expected only of a boy not yet fully grown into a man's body. Quinkent did not care for he could not wait for Nicaagat to continue without speaking.

"It is true what you say about Red Cloud," Quinkent said softly, staring into the flames. "But it is not the same as with the People." Quinkent looked up at Nicaagat and thought he detected hate in the man's ebony eyes. "We are too few . . . even with our lodges combined. Red Cloud had the Sioux nation behind him as well as the Northern Cheyenne. That is why the *Mericatz* left their country. We are *Nüpartka*, only one band of seven. Do you think Ouray will allow his Tabeguaches to ride with us against the *Mericatz*? Or the Capotes? How about our northern brothers, the Parianucs?" A heavy silence filled the numbing cold as eyes shifted around the circle and back again to the fire. Their eyes said it all. There was no need for words, both Quinkent and Nicaagat knew their thinking. There would be no war against the *Mericatz* because Ouray controlled the other six bands and had strong ties with the *Mericatz* in Washington.

The lines around Nicaagat's mouth flattened and he angrily threw the half burned stick back into the fire, causing the sparks to fly.

Slowly, Nicaagat rose from his place by the fire, his chest heaving with hot anger. He looked around at the most powerful men of the *Nüpartka* band and from beneath his blanket, he drew his knife. While the others watched, Nicaagat held it out from his body by the handle. Suddenly he slashed at an exposed arm, leaving a red streak that gathered a pool of blood that dripped from the tips of his fingers.

"That is how the *Mericatz* drains away the life of our People . . . one drop at a time. When there is nothing left and we are too weak to fight, they will take the land of Smoking Earth River from us as easily as a pony swats a fly." Nicaagat continued to stand there with bright blood running down his arm. His act had an immediate effect on the others, just as he knew it would. Nicaagat was not above using strong symbolism to win a point. And there was nothing stronger than the sight of blood to focus men's hearts and minds.

Colorow was the first to speak in his rumbling deep voice. "Here we sit in council with not even a *carniv* to protect us from the wind and snow. We have no tobacco with which to smoke and offer our prayers to mother earth and sky. Our bellies are empty and our families suffer. Nicaagat speaks the truth. We grow weaker with each passing moon. The *Mericatz* do not care how we suffer. My heart sickens of this cold place. I long for the mountains."

There was a murmur of agreement around the circle and a nodding of heads. This flat land that covered the mountains was not a good place to spend the winter. The ancient mountains beckoned, tugging at their souls.

Canávish removed a small sprig of sage from his pouch and touched the tips to the fire. A twisted trail of white smoke sprang away from the sage and when it was burning sufficiently, Canávish pointed the smoldering branch at the four corners of the earth and then to the sky. This was their blessing to *Sunáwiv*, the Great Spirit that lived in the sun, asking his help in making the right decision. The pungent smell of sage filled each man's nostrils and the smoke was taken deep into their lungs where it was held for a long time. Everyone waited for Canávish to speak for his words carried as much weight as any *tawacz viem*. And only Canávish had the power of *Quigat*, the bear, and there was nothing stronger than this power. Canávish had always helped the People, his heart guiding them straight and true in all matters.

"We should leave this place before we grow weaker," Canávish said carefully, keeping his eyes glued to the smoldering sage he held in his hand. "But we can not go without those things that are rightfully ours."

"Unh!" Colorow rumbled, for he was cold and his huge belly ached from being hollow.

Quinkent sat immobile, staring at the flames while Nicaagat smiled broadly and took his seat. In the cold wind, the streak of crimson along the knife wound had already clotted and turned dark. They sat for a long while in silence, each man holding the words spoken here close to his heart so only good could come from such thinking.

Quinkent finally stirred, knowing that he must speak now for the final words belonged only to the *tawacz viem*. He was saddened by the outcome of this council, yet he knew there was little he could say to change their minds. They needed food and blankets and the warehouse in Rawlings could mean the difference between surviving the winter for some of his people. His only hope was that Washington would not be too angry. This hope was thin at best.

"We will go to this warehouse and take only what is necessary; flour, salt, coffee and blankets to feed and warm our people. Leave everything else." Quinkent had not mentioned tobacco yet the men before the fire knew that it was not part of the items to be overlooked. A man needed tobacco.

In the cold light of a quarter moon, the men of the *Nüpartka* gathered beside the dark silent building in Rawlings. The streets were empty, the blowing snow and cold having forced the *Mericatz* inside their warm shelters.

One of the men dismounted and tried the door of the building and found it padlocked. He turned back to the others. Nicaagat gestured towards the opposite side of the structure were a lone window was located. The dismounted man hurried over to the black window and with the butt of his knife, broke the pane of glass. The shattering glass was loud in the white stillness and every pair of eyes were glued to the other buildings to see if the *Mericatz* had been alarmed by the noise. But no *Mericatz* came to their doors.

Swiftly and silently, the men climbed into the warehouse and immediately stumbled into things in the pitch blackness. Something crashed to the floor and a man cursed loudly as the object struck his foot.

"We must find a lamp," Quinkent whispered in the darkness. Why hadn't they thought of bringing a small torch? The plan called for swift entry, fill a sack with food and be gone. If the *Mericatz* found them here now . . . Quinkent did not want to hold such thoughts in his head. Suddenly a match flared in the darkness and a weak yellow flame outlined Nicaagat's dark face as he bent over a lamp. The match touched the wick and a wide band of flame grew along its edges. Nicaagat adjusted the flame so that its light was weak, yet enough to provide a dim view of their surroundings. They were standing in an office filled with file cabinets, several chairs and a battered desk.

Nicaagat picked up the lamp and motioned the others through the opened doorway while he held the lamp high behind them. At the outer reaches of the light, wet eyes caught the glow of the flame and scurried away into the darkness. The warehouse was overrun with rats. The place smelled of rat urine, rotting grain and old clothes. Two winters was a long time for supplies to be left to the fate of insects and rats.

Nicaagat pushed his way to the front and the light fell across stacks and stacks of boxes, some now broken open from the weight of other boxes, while others were riddled with holes where the rats had gnawed through, spilling their contents across the floor. And through this mountain of supplies, the rats ran freely. Clearly, many of the boxes were spoiled which made Nicaagat and the others angry.

Colorow lumbered up with a stack of gunny sacks in his arms and he passed them out to the others who quickly sorted through the boxes, filling them with needed items. A large box fell from the pile and trade tobacco scattered across the floor. Several men scooped pieces of the dark squares into their sacks. A box containing tins of molasses were found and the carton was soon emptied. Within minutes their sacks were full and Nicaagat led the way back to the office and waited until each man had passed through the broken window before blowing out the light.

The others were already mounted and held their sacks across the front of their ponies as Nicaagat emerged from the building. As if sensing each man's excitement, their ponies pranced back and forth in the frigid night, filling the air with their powdery breaths.

Even Quinkent was excited by their boldness and the food they now carried for their families. Washed away was the concern for what the *Mericatz* might do when they discovered the break in. His heart filled again with anger as he recalled the spoiling food infested with rats. The *Mericatz* had no right to keep food from the People while they were starving only to see it spoil. He was glad they had broken into the warehouse but he did not tell the others this.

Nicaagat was in the process of swinging his leg across his horse when a low growl came out of the shadows from the nearest building, a dozen yards away. Awakened by the noise, a huge rough-coated dog charged from beneath the building, circling to their right and barking loudly.

All Quinkent saw was a large dark object against a background of white as the animal raced back and forth. Immediately, he heard the zip of an arrow and the high-pitched yelp of the dog followed by a sudden return to silence. Quinkent looked around and found Nicaagat's sub-chief, Sowówic, grinning at him with his bow raised over his head.

A faint glow behind a curtained window grew to a yellow-white light from the building where the dog had come. The animal had awakened a *Mericatz* and Quinkent gestured to the others to follow.

They trotted away from Rawlings and headed south, the hoofbeats of their ponies covered by the soft snow covering the frozen ground. Dawn was two hours away as the quarter moon slipped towards the frigid horizon to the west.

They had already disappeared into the pale whiteness of sagebrush country before the man stuck his head from the doorway and called softly to his dog. Greeted by silence, the man figured the dog had gone back under the building once more for shelter against the icy winds and quickly closed the door against the penetrating cold.

CHAPTER 5

Other than to take a quick check of the weather and the condition of the tracks now completely covered by last night's snow, Grayson Toliver didn't stick his head outside the office door again until ten minutes to eight. Even then he didn't stray beyond the icy platform while he scanned the eastern horizon for sign of the billowing black smoke that would signal the arrival of the eight-ten train. He knew it was a useless gesture, but it was hard to break old habits. Toliver knew the train would be at least an hour late, probably later, by the telegraph he had received that morning from Laramie. And the train still had to cope with the Medicine Bows.

A cold wind whipped the pants legs of his suit around his ankles and he took one last look across the bleak landscape before deciding to head back to the warmth of his office. His eyes strayed to the large black and white lump near the warehouse. He shivered in the cold, his eyes tearing in the wind as he focused on the object. There was something vaguely familiar . . . Before Toliver realized what was happening, he found himself running across the snowy field, his dress shoes and suit forgotten for the moment. He drew up ten yards from the object, breathing hard. There was no mistaking his dog now. He started forward again slowly, not wanting to believe the horror his eyes were showing him.

"Railhead!" Toliver shouted as he knelt down beside the stiffened creature. The snow was dark with the dog's blood. It was then he noticed the arrow protruding from the big dog's chest. Eight inches of shaft had gone clean through the animal. It was a minute before Grayson Toliver realized his animal had been killed by an Indian and not some miner or cowboy after an all night drinking spree.

Toliver stroked the stiffened fur now matted with the frozen blood of the animal that had been his constant companion for the past five years. Everybody in the valley knew and liked the big lovable dog who greeted arriving train passengers with a friendly wag of his tail and an exuberant bark. It became standard practice for the engineer to save a tidbit of food for Railhead whenever the dog jumped into the cabin of the locomotive after checking out the passengers.

Suddenly Toliver had a mental picture of the old Ute who had visited him yesterday. Was Douglas the one who had killed his dog? The Indian had certainly seemed upset after he found out the telegraph wires were down and that their annuities could not be released. Another thought struck him and Toliver stood up and looked around at the warehouse for the first time.

The ground near the building appeared to be torn up by a number of horses and he looked quickly at the gaping window.

Sudden realization flooded his brain and instantly Toliver knew what had taken place. He barely remembered stumbling to the door late last night to stop his dog from barking, warning of the intruders' presence. Had he gone home to his small cabin, Railhead would still be alive. But he had stayed over at the office, as he did sometimes when trains were running late, to catch up on paperwork. He kept a cot there for that purpose.

He left the dog and hurried over to the broken window and peered in. Broken glass littered the interior of the office. Toliver looked around him at the moccasin tracks in the snow and knew his hunch was correct. The Utes had broken into the warehouse and carted off as much of the supplies as they could carry. Toliver looked toward town and the near-empty street. He could see bundled figures of men hurrying between buildings and realized how badly he was shaking from the cold. He had to get out of this weather but more importantly, he had to notify his superiors in Omaha. It was the Union Pacific who was responsible for withholding the Ute annuities because the freight had yet to be paid.

Grayson Toliver ran back to the depot, his grief for his slain dog momentarily forgotten. He stood for a few minutes before the stove until his teeth were no longer chattering and his hands were sufficiently thawed to handle the key.

As soon as the pain in his fingertips had subsided, Toliver stroked the telegraph key to alert the expressman in Laramie and Cheyenne to clear the line for a priority message through to Omaha headquarters. He hated having to send such a message to his superiors for he partially blamed himself for the break-in. Had he heeded his dog's warning, perhaps he could have stopped them. Then just as quickly, he realized the folly of such thoughts. He had grown up in eastern Iowa, the son of an attorney. When it came to handling guns, he was sorely lacking and had completely missed out on the Civil War because he was barely eleven when Lee met Grant at Appomattox.

Grayson Toliver hunched over the key and tapped out the message to Omaha. When completed, he sat back in his chair and waited for the telegraph operator on the other end to acknowledge his wire. He stared at the silent key for a few minutes, wondering if his message had even gotten through, considering the weather. While he waited, Toliver poured himself a cup of tea and strolled over to the door and looked out. It was snowing again, feathery flakes the size of half-eagles. He closed the door against the cold and took his seat before the telegraph key. Once he was through here, he had to get over to the sheriff's office and tell him about the Utes. Suddenly the key came alive with a burst of metallic activity at gatlin gun speed.

Toliver translated the code and looked down at what he had written once the key fell silent.

> ACKNOWLEDGE RECEIPT OF WIRE. HAVE YOU DETERMINED EXTENT OF SUPPLIES MISSING? NOTIFY ARMY AT FORT STEELE AND LOCAL AUTHORITIES TO TAKE PROPER ACTION. KEEP THIS OFFICE POSTED.
> F.W. BOUTWELL, SUPERINTENDENT

Grayson Toliver stared hard at the message. Damn! why hadn't he at least checked to see how much had been stolen. He shoved the paper into a vest pocket and flashed an acknowledgement to Omaha. Next, he tried calling the operator at Fort Steele, but got no response. It was still early and there were times the telegraph was not manned for an hour or two at a stretch. He decided to try later. Toliver put on his heavy coat, locked the office door behind him and hurried over to the warehouse. A knot developed in his throat as he passed by the lifeless form in the snow and wondered how he was going to bury his dog with the ground frozen hard as a skillet. He sighed heavily as he unlocked the door to the warehouse. It was going to be a long day and there was still the eight-ten to worry about.

Later, Grayson Toliver found the sheriff's office empty. He looked down the opened hallway that led to the jail cells and thought he detected movement.

"You back there, Sheriff?" Toliver called, taking a timid step toward the open doorway.

"Sheriff ain't here now. Who's out there?" a voice called.

Grayson Toliver stepped further into the hallway, trying to make out the figure in the cell.

"You know where the sheriff is?" Toliver asked, ignoring the prisoner's question.

"Probably out having a hot breakfast while I sit here freezing my ass off," the man said sarcastically. Toliver peered hard down the darkened hall at the man.

"That you Joe?" Toliver edged further into the hallway.

"Cold sober and hard-assed mean," Joe Rankin growled. Grayson Toliver relaxed, his breathing growing steady once more as he came up to the cell and peered inside.

"What you doing in here, Joe?" Toliver asked, forgetting for the moment his own urgent business. On occasions when he found the time, Toliver had rented horses from Joe Rankin for exploring the nearby countryside. So far, he had fished the North Platte were it makes a cut between the Haystack Mountains and Cedar Ridge. He had even visited Major Henry Thomas at Fort Steele and was thankful he was not in the military. The place was drab and life there seemed awfully dull to him.

Joe Rankin stared back at the young, well-dressed man, whose eyes seemed larger than usual. Rankin was wearing a thin blanket over his leather coat and he stood there in the middle of the jail cell looking much like a starving wolf in winter.

"It's a long story, boy," Rankin said, waving a blanketed arm in the air as he paced back and forth in front of the bars. Rankin stopped suddenly and looked down on the Union Pacific agent.

"You're still young enough and maybe you'll heed another man's advice. Stay away from spirits, boy, no matter the flavor or color. And confine your activities to Lower Row. Fooling with married females and such will only bring you grief once the pleasure's a distant memory." Toliver looked up at the tall lanky Rankin, his jaw dropping open. He was so taken back by the advice, Toliver could only nod his head in the affirmative, not that he intended to ever pay a visit to the painted women in that part of town. He didn't have to worry about alcohol either. That was something he had never tasted.

"Good," Rankin said with some satisfaction. "Maybe my time in here ain't all been in vain if it keeps another poor soul from following in my path."

"Joe, I got to find the sheriff. It's important," Toliver said, remembering what brought him here in the first place.

Rankin looked closely at the fidgeting Toliver. "What's the problem?" Suddenly Grayson Toliver seemed torn between the need to leave and the desire to tell someone what the Utes had done. Rankin tried to ease his discomfort. "Hell, Toliver, you may as well drag up a chair and fetch us something warm from the stove. Then you can tell me what's ailin' you. You ain't likely to find James before he gets back so stop your squirming." Toliver's shoulders slumped downward.

"Thought you said he was eating breakfast?"

"Could be, could be," Rankin replied thinking of his brother. "On the other hand, James may have gone home to the little woman or off visiting a businessman er two. Just no tellin'." A look of resignation came over Toliver's face and he shuffled back down the hall to get them coffee. He had to tell someone. He needed advice and there was still the matter of his dog, lying there dead in the cold.

"While you out there, throw another piece of stove wood on the fire. Them brothers of mine don't give a whit if I come down with pneumonia er not, they so cheap with wood. And I'm the one cut it down, busted it up and hauled it down here in the first place. Expect, by God, they'll do their own cuttin' from now on or else freeze their asses off," Rankin fumed. He shook his head, still unable to believe his own kin would keep him locked up on Blacky Stillwell's flimsy say-so.

Grayson Toliver was finishing up his story when the outer office door opened and they heard heavy boots thump across the plank flooring. Toliver jumped up and ran down the hall, leaving Joe Rankin nursing an empty cup and musing over the Utes' obviously desperate act.

Sheriff James Rankin listened to Grayson Toliver tell his story for the second time, rolling the chewed toothpick from side to side of his mouth, his face a mask of study.

"And you've notified the Army?" Jim Rankin asked.

"Well, I did—I mean, I tried," Toliver said, fumbling to explain himself. "When I get back to the office, I'll try again."

"Expect that's your best bet for now," the sheriff ventured, rubbing his hands together before the hot stove. If anything, the temperature had dropped since sunrise and a thick layer of gray clouds were approaching from the west carrying more snow.

"What do you mean, Sheriff?"

Jim Rankin turned his lanky backside to the stove and looked at Toliver with blinking blue eyes. "Nothing I can do, Toliver and you know it. The Utes are the Army's problem."

"You're the law," Toliver persisted.

"That's right, and my jurisdiction ends at the Carbon County line." Jim Rankin gave the Union Pacific man a bleak smile that lifted the corners of his brushy moustache. James Rankin was almost an identical copy of his brother Joe, now confined to a jail cell and no longer speaking to him. Although James had more hair on his head and was a little more raw-boned. Bobby Rankin, the shorter of the trio, looked nothing like them.

"How do you know they aren't still camped nearby. That would make it your problem too."

"If they were, it would, but you don't know Utes. Hell, they probably on the other side of Little Snake River by now." Jim Rankin could see a flicker of doubt cloud Toliver's eyes. "You don't hafta take my word for it," Rankin said, waving an arm towards the cells in back. "Ask Joe. He knows them Utes better than any white man in two states."

Grayson Toliver hesitated for a moment, glancing down the hall where Joe Rankin was being held. Even though he couldn't see him, Toliver knew Joe was listening to what was being said.

"I best get back to the office and see if Fort Steele is on line yet. Still got the eight-ten due anytime now." Toliver moved to the door as a strong voice floated down the hall and filled the tiny office.

"Sorry about your dog," Joe called from the back. Toliver started to speak, but a flashback of his dog lying there in a pool of blood, closed his throat. He simply nodded at Jim Rankin and hurried out into the cold.

Jim Rankin came down the hall and stopped before his brother's cell. Seated on the cot once more, Joe Rankin ignored his brother's presence.

"How we doing?" Jim asked, standing there with his hands folded across his chest. A half-smile creased his wind-rawed features. It was the hardest thing he had ever done, keeping his brother locked up this way. Some way or other, he had to get through to Joe. Get a grip on his life . . . heavy drinking and womanizing with every skirt that came along was going to get him killed one day.

"What do mean, *we?* Ain't nobody in here but me," Joe said sharply, pretending to look around for someone else.

"Well, at least you're talking to me again." Jim Rankin dropped into the chair Grayson Toliver had recently occupied.

"No thanks to you I can still talk," Joe shot back. "The ague don't kill me, expect that slop you been feedin' me will."

"Is kinda cold down this way," Jim allowed, giving his brother a wide grin. "But they don't come no tougher than you."

"That what you think, is it? Ain't Port Weems squared it with Blacky yet?" Joe asked, changing the subject.

"Seems your new friend went straight home after he left here. Nobody's seen him in town since," Jim replied. "Don't reckon he's packed up the missus and left Rawlings, do you?"

"Ought to have known that loudmouthed skinhead wouldn't keep his part of the bargain once he was clear of jail." Joe Rankin's expression became hangdog. He turned to look at his brother with fire in his eyes. "Dammit, James, you gotta let me out of here. It goes against the grain, but you tell Blacky I'll square up with him soon's I get the money. Gotta get back to the livery before I'm ruined and my own horses won't know me."

"Checked on the livery first thing this morning. Snooky is doing a commendable job while you're away. He's probably gonna want a raise after this though," Jim said, grinning again.

Joe only shook his head, his face growing sad. "Snook Rains ain't got the sense to bridle a horse much less make change. Won't have a customer left when I get out . . . no, correction, *if* I get out."

"What do you make of the Utes?" Jim asked professionally since he was legally bound to conduct an investigation.

"Wouldn't know," Joe said, assuming an air of indifference.

"Like hell," his brother retorted. "You much as live with them most times. Probably ain't a squaw safe around you."

"I don't live with them. I merely wager a few hard earned greenbacks when they race their ponies." Joe looked through the steel bars at his brother. "You should try it sometimes. It relaxes a man and Lord knows you need relaxing."

"What do you mean by that?" Jim Rankin asked, rising to the bait.

"You hang around the house pestering your wife too much. Ride down with me this spring to White River and I'll show you a good time. We can place a few bets . . . talk a little philosophy. Do you a lot of good."

"That all you ever think about, having a good time?"

"When at all possible," Joe replied, brushing at a piece of wool lint stuck to his big moustache.

"Man can't get ahead that way."

"That you or the little woman talking?" Jim Rankin seemed to swell twice his size and Joe hurried on now that he had a burr under his brother's bottom. "Know she ain't got much use for my lifestyle." Joe smiled crookedly at his brother. "I'm a bad influence on you and Bobby but you ain't likely to catch me tied down to one woman for life, no sirree."

Jim Rankin stood up abruptly. "There's no talking to you."

"Not if it don't include you unlocking that door," Joe shot back. Sheriff Jim Rankin headed back down the hall and his brother called to him as he reached the doorway. "Where's Bobby?"

"Should be along directly. He's bringing your breakfast."

"Jim!" The broad back of the Carbon County Sheriff stopped in the doorway and turned back, waiting for his brother to issue a parting shot.

"Quinkent and the others . . . they were starving."

"They broke the law," Jim Rankin reminded his brother.

"Tell that to dying children who ain't got food for their bellies. No man—white or red—will stand for that too long," Joe whispered reverently.

"I guess not," Sheriff Jim Rankin said lamely after the silence grew long between them. He was thinking of his own two children, their bellies full, safe and warm at this very moment. "I guess not," he whispered again, too low for his brother to catch. He was still obliged to investigate the break-in. He stepped into the cold, pulling his hat down tightly on his head as he trudged up the street to the snow-draped depot.

CHAPTER 6

The trailing dead branches of evening primroses scratched at the curtained window of the imposing structure like a cat begging to be let in from the cold. And it was cold, here on the open plains in the shadows of the Rocky Mountains where the Cache la Poudre River cut its way east across the arid, broken land. Screaming winds sailed down from Long's Peak and raced across the treeless landscape to slam into the little Union Colony of Greeley with the speed of a Union Pacific locomotive, piling huge drifts of snow around the unprotected buildings.

Inside the imposing, two-storied adobe house at the corner of Plum and Monroe Streets, a thin-shouldered man with close-cropped graying hair was bent over a huge eight foot wide cherry desk, reading a letter through for the third time. He still was not quite satisfied with its wording and he picked up his pen once more and started yet another draft. Of all the letters he had ever written, and there had been countless thousands in the last fifty years, this one, quite possibly, was the most important of his life, for if it succeeded, it would pave the way for a new life. A new life he and his family so sorely needed about now. The fact that in some ways the letter represented a method of having to eat his own words never bothered him past the first few minutes. What counted most now, was achieving what he so desperately needed. If this letter did not accomplish its intended purpose, then a few hard-given apologies paled considerably in the present financial quagmire in which he was drowning. Not only was his personal life in crisis but he had lost the ability and the confidence of Greeleyites as well. He had heard the rumors accusing him of financial irresponsibility and for putting on airs as a man of superior intelligence. These snide remarks hurt him deeply and over time had its effect on him physically in his stooped posture and stumbling gait. Gone from his eyes as well was the sparkling enthusiasm of his youth. Avoided on the streets by men who at one time were staunch supporters of his idealist approach to adapt the Fourier Phalanx here on the lonely, windswept plains, he preferred the quiet office of the *Greeley Tribune* which he had founded more than eight years before. He still owed the estate of Horace Greeley one thousand dollars he had borrowed to start the newspaper.

As Founder of Greeley, Nathan Cook Meeker had poured his heart and soul into Union Colony as well as his money. And from the beginning things had gone poorly. More than fifty colonists took one look at the treeless dust-blown landscape and cried that Meeker had misrepresented its supposed Eden-like qualities. There were no "pine groves sheltered by majestic mountains." The nearest mountain was over fifty miles away. If that wasn't enough, Meeker paid the outrageous sum of five dollars per acre for land, sight unseen, from the Denver Pacific Railroad through William Byers, their land agent and founder of the *Rocky Mountain News*. Most of this land, all twelve thousand acres, proved to be virtually useless and Meeker was forced to purchase additional lands, including a section that Byers had sold him that wasn't even owned by the Denver Pacific.

Even humble beginnings were nothing compared to the one big heartache for which Meeker suffered constant ridicule. Without one shred of experience, Meeker had plunged into an irrigation fiasco that would eventually cost the colonists of Greeley one hundred times what Meeker had estimated. Even the imported fruit and nut trees Meeker ordered from back east soon expired in the dry climate. He was further blamed for the lack of rain and the successive grasshopper plagues that destroyed much needed crops. And on a bleak day just a week ago, he had received an ultimatum from Charles Storrs, the attorney for the Greeley estate in New York. In the letter, Storrs stated they had no option but to forward their claim against Meeker for collection. To stall Storrs, Meeker had quietly sold the only forty acres he possessed from the settlement of Greeley and forwarded the small amount as partial payment.

Such were the affairs of Nathan Meeker on this cold December day.

Meeker laid aside his pen and picked up the letter from Senator Henry M. Teller, admonishing him for his outspoken and frank criticisms of Senator Jerome Chaffee through his newspaper articles, and suggested he write the Senator a personal letter to appease him. Meeker had fought Chaffee over establishing a School of Mines at Golden, hoping Greeley would be chosen instead. It was this letter of apology to Senator Chaffee that Meeker was working on when Arvilla Meeker came in carrying a tray of hot tea.

"I know you must be tired, Mr. Meeker," his wife said, placing the tray on the large desk. She pulled her sweater together. "It's cold in here." Nathan looked up from the letter and smiled at his homely wife of thirty-three years, his love for her evident in his eyes.

"Tea would be fine just now," Nathan said, laying aside his pen. "I can't seem to find the right words anyway."

"It will come. You've never been at a loss before," Arvilla said, pouring them both tea. Nathan closed his eyes for a moment and massaged his temples. When he opened them again there was despair hidden in their depths.

"I've never been in such need as this before," he said quietly. Even to Arvilla, it was hard for him to admit his shortcomings.

"If it's God's will, you will prevail," Arvilla responded. Nathan reached out and touched her cheek, the skin once soft and pliable was now leathery and aged to a dark brown by the harsh climate.

"Dear wife how I love you."

"And I you, Mr. Meeker. Oh, I almost forgot," Arvilla said, taking a letter from her sweater. "This arrived just a few minutes ago." Nathan Meeker took the letter and looked at the Washington D.C. postmark. "It's from Judge Belford," Arvilla added gently after reading the return address. She hoped somehow its contents would be uplifting for her beloved husband, yet fearing the opposite.

Nathan tore open the letter and read it first to himself and then to his wife. His voice was steady and did not betray the dejection he felt inside by its contents. The letter was short and direct:

Dear Sir,

It would afford me great pleasure to assist you in procuring the appointment you desire but I feel it impossible at this time. No removals will be made except for cause. An appointment might be gotten as soon as matters quiet down a bit. Should you think of something, let me know. I will assist you with all my power.

James B. Belford

Like Chaffee and Teller, Judge Belford had been sent to Washington as Colorado's first Congressman in the elections of 1876. Meeker had written both Teller and Belford for assistance at General Bela M. Hughes urging. The genial Hughes was made an honorary General, by his uncle, who was Governor of Kentucky. It was Hughes who had promoted Ben Holladay's Overland Stage routes as well as the Denver Pacific Railroad. Hughes believed in Meeker and admired him for his editorials against President Grant.

Nathan looked up from the letter at his wife as he finished. He laid it carefully next to the letter from Senator Teller.

"Well," he finally said after a few moments had passed, "although not encouraging, Teller nor Belford didn't flat out say it couldn't be done."

"If you wish to be Indian agent, Mr. Meeker, then I have no doubt you will," Arvilla said, finishing her tea.

"How am I able to instill such confidence after all I've put you and the children through?" Arvilla Meeker collected their cups and returned them to the tray before answering.

"What has happened here at Greeley is not your fault alone. There were others, strong-minded men who sought the same things, yet received none of the blame. It isn't fair you are singled out."

"I accept the good with the bad, dear wife. After all, I am the one who encouraged people to give up their homes back east and come here to this place. They cannot be held responsible for my shortcomings and failures to provide water for their crops. The last few years have been tough on everybody . . . especially you, Arvilla. Had I taken more time with you and the children, perhaps son George would still be alive."

Arvilla shook her head. "George would have died back east as he did here. Consumption can't be cured." It was a statement of fact, yet Nathan saw the anguish on her plain face just from thinking of their dead son. And here he was, trying to move them even deeper from civilization by asking for a job as agent of the White River Utes. A thread of doubt grew deep in his chest. And then he thought, what else could a man of sixty do to provide an income for his family? He was a writer, not a muleskinner or hard-rock miner. And with their savings dwindling away, Meeker had no choice but to pin all his hopes on the Indian agent's job. After Arvilla left, Meeker went back to the letter to Chaffee with renewed spirit.

"How could you let yourself be talked into doing such a thing?" the pretty-eyed woman asked the muscular, lean-faced man who lay across the bed with hand behind his head, staring up at the ceiling. The man had removed his shirt in the heated room, warmed by the bright sunshine pouring through a glassed window. The petite woman stood before the prone man with hands on her small hips, waiting for his answer.

Major Thomas "Tip" Thornburgh shifted his eyes to his hazel-eyed wife and gave her a mischievous grin. His eyes roamed down her well-formed figure.

"I don't really know how it happened, dear. One minute, we were just standing there having a drink and the next minute some of the men were boasting how good a shot I was and . . ." he said, reaching for her.

"And you can get that look out of your eyes, Tipton Thornburgh," Lida said, backing away from his reach, although her own voice betrayed the truth.

Tip Thornburgh sat up and patted the bed beside him. "Come, sit down, Lida." A special light came into his eyes.

"Only if you promise to be good." Lida edged closer to her broad-shouldered husband of eight years. His naked torso, layered with hard muscle that lay across his flat stomach like knotted ropes, caused her heart to flutter in her chest.

At thirty-five, Major Thornburgh looked every bit the rank he carried. Since graduating from West Point in '67, twenty-sixth in his class, he still carried his tall lanky frame with easy grace and gentle disposition, adding muttonchop whiskers to his countenance to compliment his black eyes and curly black hair. Thornburgh, born in East Tennessee, ran away from his mother and joined the Sixth Tennessee as a private. Later he fought with General Sheridan's men at Stone River and through the efforts of his older brother, Jake, got himself appointed to West Point in '63. Leaving West Point well after the Civil War, Thornburgh held several artillery positions at the Presidio in San Francisco and Fortress Monroe, Virginia. He rode in President Grant's second inaugural parade and it was here that he met Lida Clarke, whose father was in charge of Paymaster Corps. Sometime after their marriage, Lieutenant Thornburgh accepted a position with his father-in-law's Corps and found much to his dismay, hauling money from one Texas fort to another was hardly stimulating to a man of military science. Yet there were consolations. He loved being outdoors and needed the extra pay as a Major now that he and Lida had two children and a third on the way by 1875. In the Texas frontier, Thornburgh honed his hunting and shooting skills and it was here his reputation grew as a marksman. Two years later he was transferred to Omaha to work with his father-in-law and his status as crack shot grew even more.

And now, he had let himself be talked into a shooting contest with perhaps the most renowned sharpshooter in the entire west, Dr. Frank Carver. Carver claimed to be a dentist but no one could provide testimony of ever having seen him pull a tooth. He claimed to be friends with the likes of Wild Bill Hickok, Calamity Jane and the cannibalistic Liver-Eating Johnson, who supposedly consumed the livers of Crow Indians he killed in combat. Carver said he had shot some two hundred and fifty elk and eighty deer in a single fortnight along with the gas lights in the bar of the Waldorf-Astoria just

75

to amuse his friend, General Sheridan. Thornburgh smiled ruefully to himself as Lida took a cautious seat next to him.

"What are you smiling at?"

"Something I heard this morning," he said quietly, slipping a strong arm around his wife's tiny waist. "All the hoopla over this contest with Frank Carver attracted General Crook. Word has it, he plans on being at the match."

"Probably just a rumor started by someone who has bet all his money on Dr. Carver and simply wants to make you nervous so you'll miss your shots," Lida said, snuggling into him. She pulled back after a moment and looked up at him. "You aren't nervous because General Crook will be there, are you?"

Thornburgh looked down into his wife's smiling eyes and laughed at her concern. "Not a bit. If Carver is as good as they say he is, I won't stand a chance anyway . . . Crook or not."

"Well, I've seen you shoot silver dollars thrown into the air too many times. I'll warrant it will be a rocky road to Dublin for Dr. Carver," Lida said resolutely.

Thornburgh laughed and kissed the top of his wife's black hair that hung in ringlets around her face and shoulders. "If there's money enough for betting, Mrs. Thornburgh, I suggest you lodge it with my opponent." She looked up lovingly at her husband and slowly their lips came together in a tender kiss that grew passionate. When they broke for air, they found little Olivia standing in the doorway, watching them closely. At five, their daughter was all eyes. She held to a small blanket that had lived through their oldest son Bobby's early years before Olivia lay claim to it.

"What is it, Sweetie?" Lida asked, getting her breathing under control once again.

"Georgie has my rabbit and won't give it back," the small child said, looking from her mother to her towering father who looked slightly aggrieved by his young daughter's sudden appearance.

George Washington was their youngest child and barely three years old.

"Did you wake Georgie from his nap?" Lida questioned Olivia who looked back with her father's large eyes and shook her head. Thornburgh released his wife, stood up and reached for his shirt. Lida grabbed up Olivia and hurried out to find George and the stuffed rabbit. No explanations were needed between them. Parenthood, at times could be trying.

Thornburgh slipped on the double-breasted frock coat and buttoned it up before turning to admire himself in the mirror. He had to admit, in regimentals he looked rather dashing and properly military at the same time. He stopped by the door and lifted the Army issue Springfield carbine and checked the breech action. The single shot carbine, like the heavier Springfield rifle carried by infantrymen, employed .45-caliber metal cartridges although backed by only fifty-five grains of powder as opposed to the rifle's seventy. Even though he was offered a Spencer repeater upon his arrival at the Army of the Platte, Tip Thornburgh preferred the Springfield for its greater accuracy at long range and the fact it was less prone to misfires. And the old Springfield rifle had a maximum range of thirty-five hundred feet—twice that of a Spencer.

Sometime later, Major Tip Thornburgh left his residence, after kissing his wife and children good-bye, crossed the Platte and rode the short distance to town. Although cold, the day was awash with brilliant sunshine, and already, crowds from outlying ranches and farms were swelling the normal population to overflowing. Saturday was the high point of the week in any town or city, but today was especially so. It was the day the Army officer would pit his skills against the renowned crack-shot, Dr. Frank Carver, and Omaha was proudly making as much of the event as a land speculator trying to pawn desolate prairie land to newcomers.

Omaha near the end of '78 was as modern as any city back east with its wide streets and rows of neat brick buildings where business and commerce flourished. Even beyond the Union Pacific tracks where the bawdy houses, saloons and gambling halls tended to congregate, the shanty log hut structures had given way to clapboard buildings, keeping nothing of its humble beginnings. Omaha consisted of one tiny log building in '54 and a population of six. A short three years later, the town boasted a population of over three thousand and choice lots were selling for four thousand dollars each.

Thornburgh debated whether to go by Department Headquarters but changed his mind when he met Major Clarke on the crowded street.

"Well, son-in-law, ready for the big event?" Major Robert Clarke was a popular old Army man and Thornburgh liked and respected him, notwithstanding the fact he was Thornburgh's father-in-law. It was said, but Thornburgh never knew for sure, that Clarke was a cousin of General Sherman and therefore, through his efforts had been able to jump Thornburgh from Lieutenant to Major over one hundred older lieutenants and two hundred fifty captains.

"Ready as I'll ever be," Thornburgh said, trying not to take notice of the gawking faces of the crowd that passed by them. A large white banner with red block letters stretched across the main thoroughfare, proclaiming the event. For the first time, Thornburgh felt a slight case of jitters that radiated outward from his gut. What if he failed after the first few shots? The town had been promoting the upcoming event for the last week and some people, he had heard, were traveling from as far away as Chicago. To have the event fizzle in front of such large crowds would be personally embarrassing to him and to the United States Army.

"Doc Carver's been buying drinks and covering bets all morning long. Rumor has it, he's favored two to one over you lasting thirty minutes." Major Clarke looked keenly at Thornburgh. "What do you say?"

"I'd say, up to now, Frank Carver's covered everything he's said and made it stick. The man stages these sporting shoots for a living, don't forget. I'm going to do my best, nothing less," Thornburgh said, thinking again of the people who had come from long distances. He only hoped he didn't disappoint them as well as his family.

"That's the spirit!" Clarke thundered, slapping his daughter's husband on a hard shoulder. "Even the old man will be watching, so by thunder show Doc Carver your metal." Thornburgh didn't have to ask to know who Clarke was referring to: General George Crook. He felt the nervousness spread into his chest. He had to get his emotions under control, otherwise, Carver wouldn't need the full thirty minutes to tag him out.

"Lida and the children coming?"

"I've made arrangements for a carriage. That's all young Bobby has talked about."

Major Clarke looked closely at Thornburgh and lowered his voice. "You want a shot of Guckenheimer to steady the nerves? Keep a bottle in my desk for just such special occasions."

"Best not," Thornburgh said. "I'll be in more need of it afterward."

"Son, you beat old Doc Carver, we'll break the seal on a bottle of expensive champagne I've been saving."

"Just keep the Guckenheimer at hand, just in case I don't."

"Hell, that ain't no way to talk, Tip. I've seen you shoot and believe me, Doc Carver is in for a big surprise."

Major Thornburgh placed the box of ammunition on the table provided, and checked for the last time, the Springfield's action. It was smooth and flawless as it should be. He had spent the better part of three hours last night tearing it down and meticulously cleaning each piece before reassembling and oiling it well. He was as ready as he was ever going to be.

A uniformed officer stepped away from a knot of men nearby and came over to where Thornburgh stood, laying out his cartridges in neat rows. The man unfolded a copy of the *Weekly Herald* and placed it on the table so Thornburgh could read the bold print proclaiming the historic event. Thornburgh smiled to himself. Already the newspaper was calling it historic. He doubted that outside his family and a few close friends, the memory of the event would last beyond tomorrow before slipping into oblivion.

"Well, what do you think of being the center of attention?" Captain Daniel Overbay asked his friend. Overbay worked also for the Paymaster Corps and had graduated a year ahead of Thornburgh from West Point. Overbay's noticeable limp was the result of a Confederate bullet that had splintered a bone in his foot during the battle of Antietam.

"Not much. Especially if I lose miserably," Thornburgh said quietly.

"Aw hell, Tip. That ain't going to be the case and you know it. You're the best damn shot we got in all the Army. And me and the boys stand behind that with our money."

Thornburgh smiled faintly, "What's got me worried. Together they watched as a buggy drove up bearing boxes of the glass balls that would be used in the contest. A young boy of fourteen scrambled down from the wagon which had drawn up a short distance away from the Platte River and the spectator stands built specifically for the contest. The boy began unloading the boxes of glass balls, stacking them to one side as instructed by the man driving the wagon. Once the boxes were unloaded, the driver moved the team some distance off so as not to spook the animals once the contest started. The man walked back to where Thornburgh and Overbay were standing.

"You want to take a few practice shots, Major? I'll have my boy, Jamie, toss a few for you." When he saw that Thornburgh was hesitating, he added, "It's for my boy as well. Needs to throw a few to get the proper height and distance squared away. What do you say?" Thornburgh looked around at the jubilant crowds filling the stands. A roped off section was reserved for dignitaries who had not yet put in appearance. He wondered where Dr. Carver was. Probably was his way of rattling the nerves of his opponent.

"Go ahead, Tip, bust a few for the boy. Crowds wouldn't mind it either," Dan Overbay urged.

Thornburgh looked at the expectant father. "Well, guess it wouldn't hurt none." The man's face beamed and he turned to the boy who was standing thirty yards away.

"Chunk a ball up when I give the signal, Jamie," he shouted. He turned back to Thornburgh who had loaded the Springfield and was casually holding the carbine in one hand by his side. "You ready?"

"Guess so."

Dan Overbay stepped away from Thornburgh to give him plenty room. The crowd fell silent.

"Okay, Jamie, let one fly," his father shouted.

"Blow it all to hell," a drunken voice shouted from the throng. All eyes were riveted on young Jamie who crouched low and suddenly flung a bright green ball skyward from an underhanded position.

Thornburgh watched as the spinning glass ball caught the rays of the afternoon sun. Bright flashes of green light burst from the turning ball like fireworks on a Fourth of July night. He waited with the weapon still held next to his side until the ball approached its greatest arc before quickly raising the carbine to his shoulder. The explosion rocked the stands and all eyes were glued to the glass ball as it few into a thousand pieces. A foot-stomping roar of approval rose up from the stands.

Dan Overbay stepped up grinning and thumped Thornburgh on the shoulder. "Carver better look out."

Thornburgh laid the warm carbine across the table after jacking the spent shell from its breech.

"Wanna shoot another?" the man asked. Jamie stood by in a ready crouch, waiting for his father to give him the sign.

"Expect we better wait. Don't want the crowd to get too worked up. Besides, I miss one now, it may sully them, take away some of their fun."

"Well, I see your opponent coming so I'll get back to the boys," Dan Overbay said. His parting words didn't do much to soothe Thornburgh's rising apprehension. "Just take your time, Tip. You'll not miss." Thornburgh looked around at the growing number of people lining the streets and caught sight of Dr. Frank Carver, dressed as flamboyantly as the first time they had met, five days ago. Today, Carver was dressed from head to toe in a white linen suit and matching wide-brimmed panama. To Thornburgh, Carver looked like a white elephant. Escorting him was the mayor and a few other dignitaries who all looked to have been enjoying more than just Dr. Carver's company by their flushed faces. Carver came up and extended his hand to Thornburgh. In the other, he carried a gun encased in fringed leather and beadwork.

"It's good to see you again, Major." Carver's face was smiling but his intense blue eyes were busy appraising Thornburgh's condition.

"And you, sir," Thornburgh said a little too stiffly. He had to try and relax. Thornburgh took a couple of deep breaths.

"Been looking forward to this all week, Major. You know, it's not very often I'm faced with such a worthy opponent." His smile was easy-going and seemed genuine to Thornburgh who felt himself beginning to relax.

Thornburgh smiled back at Carver. "That remains to be seen. I'm simply honored to compete in a match against such a skilled shooter as yourself." Carver beamed. He untied the rawhide string holding the flap over the sheathed rifle.

"If you gentleman will excuse me," the mayor said, rubbing his hands together, "I'll step over to the box and announce the event."

"I see you're shooting the old Army issue Model '73," Carver said, looking at Thornburgh's carbine. "Most officers I know are carrying the Spencer seven shot repeater."

"It's the one I'm used to," Thornburgh said simply.

"It's a mighty serviceable weapon, the Springfield, but—" and it was here that Carver slowly pulled the gleaming rifle from its case. The brass on the weapon glinted in the sun like a newly minted double-eagle.

"Sixty-six Winchester. Figured you'd be shooting something a little newer yourself," Thornburgh said.

Frank Carver smiled. "Like you, I'm rather used to this old 'yellow boy'. It's served me well the last fifteen years." He began loading the rifle with .44 rim-fire cartridges.

"Are you gentlemen ready?" the mayor called from the raised stand.

"Shall we begin, Major?" Carver said, jacking a shell into the chamber.

CHAPTER 7

News of the Ute break-in sent curious citizens down to the depot for a closer look at the warehouse in spite of the light snow that was falling. Among the inquisitive throng was the diminutive figure of Rawling's first citizen, James France, who made up for his shortness by growing a thick beard that reached to his knees. The bug-sized France had opened the first store here back in '68 and grubstaked many a hopeful miner headed south to Bugtown and Poverty Bar below Hahn's Peak district situated between the Elkhead and Sierra Madre Mountains in Colorado. In addition, France cashed vouchers for lonely soldiers from Fort Steele and after the agency was established at White River, he held Interior Department contracts for hauling Ute supplies.

But James France wasn't there to ogle the break-in. His presence was purely business. Since he held the lucrative government contract to keep the Utes supplied, France viewed any negative acts by the Indians as adversely affecting him personally and financially.

France pushed his way through the crowd and entered the depot. He spied Grayson Toliver talking with a group of townspeople and motioned him over. Toliver said a few more words and broke away, coming over to James France. France didn't bother with niceties, but launched immediately into Toliver.

"Warned you this could happen." France's hazel eyes fairly snapped in his small head.

"Mr. France, I—"

"U.P. can't withhold twenty-five thousand pounds of rations and a year's annuities from poor starving Indians for two years and expect them to do nothing." France may have been small in stature but his booming voice was clearly heard by all those present. France was sufficiently worked up over the Ute situation.

Toliver gave France a distressed look. The whole morning had been a strain for him. The army at Fort Steele had refused assistance and it took Union Pacific officials in Omaha talking with General George Crook to get them motivated. A detachment had been promised from Fort Steele within the hour. To top that off, the eight-ten was sitting six miles out of town where Sugar Creek crossed the tracks with a train load of irate passengers. Part of the trestle had given way and Toliver had spent the last hour putting together a work crew, buying lumber and renting a wagon from Snooky Rains to shore up the damage. Nobody wanted any part of the work in this weather and Toliver had been forced to pay double wages. He only hoped his superiors approved the expenditure. And he still hadn't buried his dog.

"I'm doing all I can to correct the situation," Toliver said very carefully. A throbbing headache was building behind each eyeball and he didn't need James France chewing on his coat as well.

"Union Pacific could have corrected it two years ago," France shot back. "I blame them and Commissioner Hayt for this mess. If he paid more attention to the Utes' requests instead of running his bank and gathering Republican votes, none of this would have happened. What did you expect the Utes to live on for two winters while your damn railroad ignored their pleas for help?"

Grayson Toliver stood there, open-mouthed under the short man's verbal assualt. How could he convince France in light of what had just happened that he had been pleading with Omaha for months to release the annuites to the Utes so something like this wouldn't occur.

The door swung inward and a snow-covered soldier stood there with a grim look on his face. Both men turned to stare at the big soldier.

"You Toliver?" he asked, pinning France with an icy stare.

Grayson Toliver stepped around the little man, glad for whatever respite was offered. France had a way about him that ground people down and Toliver figured he was ground down far enough for one morning.

"I'm Toliver," he said.

"Private O'Malley. Just wanted to see the fool who's sending us out in this damn snowstorm to look for a few skinny-ass Indians."

"You've called in the Army?" France asked amazed.

"Had no choice. Sheriff Rankin won't handle it," Toliver replied doggedly.

"Ha! James Rankin ain't crazy! Nobody in his right mind would go—" another thought struck him, "how much did they take anyway?"

Toliver looked sick and his eyes found the floor and stayed there. "Best estimate is, they carried off about seven hundred pounds," he mumbled. James France looked from Toliver to O'Malley.

"Seven hundred pounds," France repeated, not believing his ears.

"The Union Pacific would send men out in this weather to track Utes down for a dab of supplies? Supplies that rightly belong to them? I can't believe it."

O'Malley's eyes seemed to be on fire. "The U.P. ain't sending the Army no place, mister. My orders came direct from headquarters."

"Oh! Do tell," France said, stroking his long beard. "And just who do you think is in cahoots with the Army, O'Malley? I'll tell you," France said, rushing on now he was sufficiently worked up all over again. "It's them snot-nosed politicans and Army brass who's got their hands into the Union Pacific's pockets that's who."

O'Malley tried staring down the little man from his lofty height and failed. James France was like a bantam rooster with his spurs sharpened for just such an occasion. O'Malley looked beyond France at Toliver.

"You runnin' the railroad here, er do I keep listening to this pint-sized pair of lungs vent his spleen." France grew even redder and opened his mouth to really give the Army a tongue lashing, but Toliver stepped around France and completely blocked the little man's vision of the big trooper.

"Unfortunately O'Malley, I'm the U.P. dispatcher today. What can I do for the Army?"

"You can find me a scout, Toliver, that's what you can do. Ain't none of me boys been south before."

Toliver looked blank for a moment. "Don't the Army have their own scouts?"

"We do," Patrick O'Malley said with a sigh. "None are kept on during the winter, man."

Grayson Toliver turned to James France. "Hasn't Joe Rankin done some scouting for the Army? I heard he's friends with the Utes."

France laughed. "You'll never separate Joe from a warm woman and a bottle. Not in this weather."

Grayson Toliver smiled for the first time that morning. "Right now, Joe Rankin has had neither for some time." It was James France's turn to look blank.

"I'll get my coat and we can go talk to Joe if you want," Toliver said to O'Malley.

"Let's get on with it. As we speak, my men are waiting in the snow with their asses frozen to a saddle." They left James France standing there, stroking his beard and looking worried over this new affair with the Army.

Joe Rankin listened patiently while Grayson Toliver explained what had happened that morning and finished by asking him if he wouldn't guide the Army detail for the Union Pacific. Private O'Malley stood there stiffly with his arms folded across his burly chest, not saying a word.

"Who's paying me, U.P. or the Army?" Rankin asked, looking from Toliver to the broad chested private.

"I've been authorized to pay scout services as per usual rate," O'Malley spoke up. His displeasure of the situation dripped from every word.

"Them's summer rates, this is winter," Rankin said curtly.

"That's the pay, thirty-seven fifty a week, take it or leave it!"

"Ain't interested," Ranking said mildly and turned to sit back down on his cot.

Toliver spoke up quickly. "How about if the Union Pacific pays you another twenty a week." He was desperate and knew his superiors would expect him to handle the situation.

"Price is three hundred flat," Joe Rankin said from the cot without looking their way. The exact amount he needed to clear himself with Blacky Stillwell if Port Weems failed to come up with his own share. And knowing most skinners, Rankin figured he would be stuck with the whole amount . . . at least until he located Weems.

"Three hundred!" O'Malley exploded. "Ain't no way the Army's anteing up that kind of money for no scout."

"Then, you best get to ridin', Private. Them Utes has got a good six hours head start."

"Wait a minute," Toliver interrupted. He could see things slipping away. "The Union Pacific will make up the difference, provided you get results." Toliver had no idea how this would play back in Omaha but right now he didn't really care. The Union Pacific needed Rankin more than the three hundred.

Rankin stood up, smiling. "Results I got no problem with. Just tell me what you want done once we catch up to them."

Grayson Toliver stared at Rankin for a full minute before saying anything. He had not thought beyond this point. As a matter of fact, his thinking had been rather poor all morning and it bothered him greatly for he considered himself a methodical thinker and planner.

"Bring them back here . . . I suppose."

"You suppose," Rankin said sarcastically. He hated dealing with someone as outright rank green as Toliver, but if it got him out of jail and squared him with Stillwell, he figured he'd muddle through. Least 'til he had Weems in his sights.

"What would you suggest? I mean, my superiors will expect some type of action."

"Oh, I expect we'll get action once we catch up to them," Rankin said, eying the tight-mouthed trooper. "What is your orders, O'Malley?"

The big Irishman looked through the steel bars at Rankin with unwavering eyes. His dislike for the scout was growing. "Overtake the heathens and bring 'em back . . . dead or alive."

"I see," Rankin said. It appeared Toliver wasn't the only green chap who knew little or next to nothing about Indians.

O'Malley shifted from one foot to another, uncertainty crowding his leathery face. "Anything wrong with that?" he demanded.

"Oh no," Joe responded lightly, "expected as much from the Army."

"What's that suppose to mean?" O'Malley demanded.

"You ever fight Indians, Private O'Malley?" Rankin queried.

"Douglas is an old man, Mister Rankin," Toliver cut in. "And so are most of the others in his band. Douglas has been visiting me regularly now for weeks. They are weak and hungry. Surely they won't fight."

Joe Rankin shook his head and smiled ruefully. "I might be better off in here after all." Both men looked at him like he had lost his mind.

"Rankin, is there something you ain't telling us?" O'Malley said coldly. He was a second away from walking out of the jail, Union Pacific or no Union Pacific.

Rankin looked from one man to the other. "This Indian, Quinkent, the one you call Douglas, he is not alone. There were rumors Captain Jack, Nicaagat, as he is called by his people, has over a hundred lodges encamped along the Little Snake, fifty miles south of here. They too are starving."

"So?" O'Malley said.

"Just this. Whether you know it or not, the Utes makes a formidable enemy and a fierce warrior in a fight. There's a reason the Comanche and Sioux leave them be. How many men you got outside, O'Malley?"

Private O'Malley cleared his throat. "Seven, eight counting me."

Joe Rankin laughed uproariously. "Eight. There's eight of you?" he said incredulous.

"The Major—that is Major Thomas figured it was enough," O'Malley said defensively.

"Well, I'm telling you it ain't near enough if shooting starts and with Captain Jack doing the leadin', I can guarantee it."

With burning eyes, O'Malley stared hard at Rankin. "Are you

91

gonna do the scouting for us or not? We got no more time to waste."

"Just wanted you boys to understand what you're up against is all," Joe replied smoothly. "Somebody tell Bobby to unlock this damn door and we'll get to it soon's I throw my tack together."

Relief flooded Grayson Toliver's face. "Appreciate you helping the Union Pacific with this matter," he replied as O'Malley stepped back into the office to fetch the jailer.

"Wouldn't go heaping any praise on me just yet, son. Even if we do manage to get a few of them hollow-ribbed Indians back here without a fight, how's it gonna look to the press?" Rankin moved his hand through the air as if was holding a newspaper and reading the headlines, "Union Pacific slaps irons on starving Indians! How's that gonna fly back in Omaha?" Rankin grinned, throwing off the blanket as O'Malley came back with the jailer.

A new look of worry spread across Grayson Toliver's face as the impact of Rankin's words sunk home. Maybe he had better talk to Omaha again before things got out of control.

"I've been trying to tell them to release the annuities," Toliver replied, barely above a whisper.

Rankin stood up and shook out his leather coat, giving the U.P. man a bleak look.

"What you shoulda done, boy, was give Quinkent and Captain Jack what was rightfully theirs in the first place and none of this woulda happened."

"So people keep telling me."

"I see you smooth-talked someone into going your bail," jailer Bobby Rankin said to his brother as he came over and twisted the key in the lock. Bobby stepped back with the door in his hand, grinning at his brother.

"Bobby, you and James better hunt a hole before I get back," Joe Rankin said, stepping clear of the cell.

"You threatening an officer of the law?" Bobby Rankin asked, his sense of high spirit still in place.

"Ain't the law's got to worry. It's a couple sorry relatives better look out," Joe said half-serious.

"Maybe I should check one more time with my office in Omaha. Just to make sure this is still what they want to do," Toliver interjected. He was worried more now than ever by what Rankin had said. He could end up being the laughing stock of Rawlings if the press decided to make a big deal of this. Might even be fired.

O'Malley's jaw dropped and he looked at the Union Pacific agent with bleak eyes. "You do whatever makes you happy, Toliver, but I got clear orders and by God I intend to follow them to the letter." He turned to Joe Rankin. "Let's ride."

When they gathered on the stoop in front of the jail, Joe Rankin ran a professional eye across the troopers hunched over in their saddles. Their faces said it all. None wanted to be sitting here in a driving snow about to head out across frozen country to face God knows what. Thirteen dollars a month didn't pay for this kind of treatment. Standing at the hitch rack was a big chestnut sorrel, with bedroll and slicker tied behind a saddle. It was Joe Rankin's horse.

"Somebody was all fired sure of himself," Joe remarked, looking around at Toliver and O'Malley.

"Weren't them," Bobby Rankin spoke up with a big grin on his face.

"I been that bad a prisoner you'd turn me loose in all this snow and cold?" Joe asked.

"The worst we ever had," Bobby quipped.

A sharp whistle cut off any reply Joe Rankin was formulating. Black smoke smudged the gray skyline to the east.

"It's the eight-ten!" exclaimed Toliver, heading for the depot on a dead run. O'Malley stepped into the saddle and looked back to Rankin who hadn't moved.

"Dammit, Rankin, let's go!"

Joe Rankin looked up at the Private with glacial blue eyes. "One thing we need to get straight, O'Malley. Out there, I'm in command. All of you will do as I say, no questions asked and you might just live through this. Understood?" A cold silence stood between the two men for a few minutes before O'Malley spoke.

"We'll do what you say as long as it don't interfere with anything military," Private O'Malley said, grudgingly. Rankin nodded and moved over to his horse. His brother followed and handed him his rifle.

"It's fully loaded, Joe. You'll find a box of shells for it in your saddlebags." And then he leaned closer. "Be careful out there," Bobby whispered. Joe took the large caliber, .50-95 Winchester from his brother and shoved it into the boot beneath his saddle.

"Don't worry, little brother," Joe said, pulling himself into the saddle, "way it's been snowing, doubt if we'll get much past the Little Snake . . . passes'll probably be blocked by now."

Jailer Bobby Rankin stood there a long time after the riders had disappeared into the swirling mists, worry for the safety of his brother etched deeply on his face.

CHAPTER 8

Nicaagat listened intently as one of his scouts reported back to him. They had stopped by a frozen stream surrounded by dense trees to build a fire and cook some of the provisions they had taken from the warehouse in Rawlings. Here, among the pines, the wind held to their tops, creating a soothing sound to the hungry Utes who warmed themselves before the spruce fire, their bellies full for the first time in many days. A light sifting of snow drifted down between the green boughs as the men smoked real tobacco and talked in lone tones. Nestled in the broken foothills of the Sierra Madres, Nicaagat had been sure no pursuit would come. He stared up at the mountains to the east that formed a curtain of snow dotted with dark green spruce and fir while his scout continued to appraise him. Behind him, the long narrow ridge of the Atlantic

Rim formed a wall that ran for twenty miles southwest of Rawlings. Winter was fast closing this portion of the narrow valley at Bridger's Pass. Soon it would not matter, Nicaagat concluded. The *Mericatz* dared not venture into the mountains during the hard winter moons. They would turn back soon. Heavy snow clouds were now building to the west. They must hurry on to the Little Snake with the food. These things he thought as he listened absently to what Sowepk was saying. The others gathered by the fire only a few feet from Nicaagat and Sowepk were privy to snatches of conversation yet they pretended not to hear, out of respect for Nicaagat. In time he would inform them of what Sowepk had to say.

Quinkent came silently through the trees towards the fire, holding his rifle loosely in one hand. Not one to sit idle while he felt *Mericatz* followed their trail, Quinkent had been out doing his own checking while the others ate and smoked. And now he was cold and wet and very hungry.

Wordless, Quinkent moved over to the steaming pot and helped himself to the contents. He did not look at Nicaagat or his scout. That Sowepk had sought out Nicaagat and not him, was insult enough. Quinkent would not dignify their presence by so much as a glance. Besides, Sowepk told nothing Quinkent didn't already know. Nine men followed them. Less than two hours ride. Eight of them dreaded *swerch*, soldiers from Fort Steele. The one leading these soldiers wore a set of fine light colored buckskins. This *Mericatz*, Quinkent knew for he had visited them on occasions to bet on the pony races at Smoking Earth River. He was always loud, like most *Mericatz*, and drank too much while eyeing their women. Quinkent did not recall his name, only that he was a tracker and scout for the hated *swerch*.

Quinkent drank greedily of the thick broth, waiting for Sowepk to finish. His tale was too long. They had camped here now for over four hours, to rest their horses and eat. Quinkent had hotly opposed their stopping until they were safely across the Little Snake, yet the others had sided with Nicaagat, complaining of hunger and the cold. Quinkent had stopped short of calling them little children fearing the insult might be too much under the present circumstances. Now they would be forced to deal with the soldiers and the trapper.

Having taken the short route back to the Little Snake, it was Nicaagat's claim that any pursuers would take the easier and less mountainous route through what the *Mericatz* called Alamosa Gulch to Muddy Creek.

Nicaagat hurried over to the fire at Sowepk's first mention of the soldiers. The others quickly stood and put the fire out with kicks of snow. Quinkent stood by impassively while several of the men paced nervously back and forth, checking their weapons and looking in the direction of the soldiers as if they were already coming through the trees.

"We must stop the *swerch* so the others can get the food back to the village," Nicaagat said, his dark eyes snapping.

"We stop too long," Quinkent said loudly. "Now the soldiers come to punish us for taking these gifts without their permission."

Nicaagat's eyes burned with anger and he tried staring down Quinkent, who gave no ground to the younger warrior. Everybody knew it had been a fatal mistake to stop now. Saying these words added nothing but sickness to a man's heart.

"These things belong to *us!*" Nicaagat spat out. "Not to the *Mericatz!*"

"Why do they follow us if they were ours to take?" Quinkent said simply.

Nicaagat did not respond, instead, he turned to Sowepk. "You and Cojoe will keep watch on these soldiers. Do not let them near the Little Snake. We will drive them north if we have to."

Quinkent shook his head, "Nicaagat speaks of risking a war with the *Mericatz*. We should only follow them for a time. Like all *Mericatz*, they will grow tired of the cold and no warm food for their bellies and give up."

"If they cross the Little Snake, we will do what we have to do," Nicaagat said with finality.

"You do not speak for all *Nüpartka*. If the *Mericatz* continues across the Little Snake there will be a council to determine what to do!" Quinkent shot back.

For a long moment Nicaagat looked as though he was ready to kill Quinkent. Abruptly, he turned away, mounted his horse and quickly left the camp. Others scrambled to catch up their own ponies to follow their leader.

Wordlessly, Sowepk and Cojoe looked at Quinkent and silently departed north. Quinkent surveyed the still camp and kicked more snow on the fire where a tendril of thin smoke escaped upward. The men were growing careless and the camp showed it. Discarded, opened tins of tomatoes and peaches littered the snow. It reminded Quinkent of coming upon a *Mericatz* camp one spring. The thought was not pleasant to hold in his head and he mounted his own horse and headed southwest with the others.

Joe Rankin paused to blow his running nose and scan the upper reaches leading to Bridger Pass. The frigid air fairly crackled with the sounds of horses and men. A thick line of snow clouds clung to the ridgeline of the Atlantic Rim. They were in for more snow and a lot of it, Rankin concluded. The pass would be hell on both men and horses if they were to linger for long here.

"What's the problem, Rankin?" Private O'Malley bellowed in the increasing wind. Tiny flakes of ice-tinged snow pelted the small group.

Rankin looked over his shoulder at the big Irishman hunched over in his saddle against the sudden wind and stinging ice. The others lined up behind O'Malley like snow-covered stumps, unmoving.

"No problem, General. Just a storm coming."

"Dammit, Rankin, get on with it then before we all freeze to death."

"Your funeral, General," Rankin said, nudging his horse forward. He had to admit, he couldn't recall having done anything as dumb as this in the past. Except maybe where women were concerned. But even then, he was in no danger of losing his life by riding around in a snowstorm. An irate husband he could handle, or he had so far, Rankin concluded, thinking of Port Weems.

As they neared the summit, the storm broke over them with a furious roar. The trail before them was lost in the swirling madness of white. O'Malley's horse bumped into Rankin's.

"Stay close," Rankin shouted in the screaming wind. The air was thick with flakes the size of silver dollars. Rankin continued, moving more or less on instinct, searching for the depression he knew was just below the summit. He stumbled onto it by accident a little while later and directed O'Malley and his men to crowd in behind the thin line of spruce that offered some respite from the blowing snow. Huddled next to the wall of the Atlantic Rim, they rode out the storm as best they could.

Rankin positioned the horses between them and the open pass to block the wind and driving snow. Half-frozen, the soldiers merely hunkered down with their blankets pulled over them for warmth. With the snowstorm, the temperature had actually risen. A fortunate thing, Rankin concluded two hours later after the storm had blown itself out and he was tending to the animals. One of the army horses had died in its tracks, muzzle deep in the snow.

"Suffocated," Rankin said matter-of-factly, brushing the snow from the other animals.

"Damn!" Private O'Malley cursed as he freed his own horse from a six foot drift of snow. "What do you want to do now, General?" Rankin said, looking around him at the new layer of snow. He guessed in the last two hours, at least three feet of snow covered the ground. Going would be even tougher than he had anticipated, at least until they got down the other side of the pass.

O'Malley glared at Rankin, "Dammit, Rankin, these are private stripes and you best start remembering that!"

"Don't need to tell you a horse carryin' double ain't gonna make it up this pass much less down the other side."

"Know that," O'Malley snapped. He turned to his men. "Charlie, looks like you gonna hafta ride double with Morgan. Think you can make it back to the Fort?"

"Believe we can," Charlie Loomis said, looking at Morgan.

"Just remember to keep this sharp ridge on your left," Rankin added. "Shouldn't have no trouble."

"Okay then, mount up and report back to the Major. Tell him we are still in pursuit of the Indians," O'Malley said, mounting his own horse stiffly. He looked down at Rankin still standing in hip-deep snow.

"You coming?"

"I'm coming, but I still think this is crazy to keep after Indians already lost to the mountains."

"You don't know that for sure," O'Malley shot back.

Rankin mounted his horse and looked over at O'Malley. "I do know that and what's more, O'Malley, *you* know it."

"Ain't my job to think," O'Malley responded doggedly. "Army tells me when to get up and what to do before I go back to bed each day."

"That's what I figgered you'd say," Rankin said with a sigh. He reined his horse away from the protected lee and slogged slowly upward through the belly-high snow. With the summit less than a quarter mile away, he figured it would still take them better part of an hour to make it. As it turned out he was wrong. It took nearly two hours and the horses were exhausted by the time they reached the wind-swept pass. The snow was less than a foot deep here at the pass as Rankin guided them down the opposite side at an easy pace once the horses were given a few minutes rest.

"Looks like the storm kept to the other side of the pass," O'Malley remarked. The going was easier now and Rankin kept them moving steadily downward until they intersected Muddy Creek. Calling a halt, Rankin let the horses drink from the half-frozen creek while the men set about making coffee and breaking out rations. At best, they had two, possibly three hours of daylight left, Rankin figured. Not enough time to make it to the Little Snake where hot food and shelter awaited them.

"What is it, Rankin?" O'Malley said, pouring himself a cup of coffee. "You look like you're going to be sick."

"Just thinking of the hot food and warm blankets we going to miss tonight at Charlie Perkin's." In actuality, Rankin was thinking more of the half-breed Snake girls Charlie kept next door in a hotel.

"Just wrap that three hundred dollars around you the Union Pacific and the Army's paying. That ought to keep you warm enough," O'Malley said, grinning evilly.

"A sight warmer than the thirteen you gettin'."

O'Malley's face sobered. "Rankin, I don't much like you or your kind."

"And what kind is that, O'Malley?" Rankin asked, coming over to the fire where he stretched his hands out to warm them.

"The kind that bleeds people for their services. The kind that keeps girls down on the Row."

"Man's got to make a living and you troopers need a place to spend that thirteen a month." Rankin bent down and poured himself a cup of coffee. When he stood back up he looked at Private O'Malley across the rim of his cup as he brought it to his lips.

"As for my services, I ain't making a killing scouting fer the Army. I get a fair wage, that's all. Damn few know this country like I do outside them Utes we trailin'. That's why I'm here, remember? You come looking for me."

O'Malley, never a great thinker, buried his head in his coffee cup. Rankin looked around at the other six troopers who were as green as they come and looking for him to provide their care.

Rankin put to words what he was thinking. "Anybody been out here more than six months or seen a real Injun?" The young troopers looked at one another and then back to the tall scout.

"Excuse me, Mister Rankin," a young shave-tail of a boy spoke up. "Name's William Sprague, from Pittsburgh. I served with General Crook for most of eight months during the Sioux campaign before coming to Fort Steele."

"Got a good feel fer Indians, do you, boy?"

William Sprague colored for a moment. "No sir, leastwise, not like you have." And then his face brightened. "Did meet this Captain Jack we are trailing though. He was General Crook's pet scout."

"Nicaagat? Danged Crook's hide!" Rankin exclaimed. "That Ute knows too much about white men ways. His type's the worst kind to deal with."

"Why do you say that?" O'Malley asked, momentarily forgetting he wasn't speaking to Rankin.

"Nicaagat, the one you call Captain Jack, was raised with a good Mormon family in Utah. Chief Walkara sold him as a child with Brigham Young's blessings to this Mormon family who taught him English and put him to work driving an ice wagon around Salt Lake City. Didn't take Nicaagat long to figger all white men were crazy. He ran off and joined the Uintah Utes. Married a Yampa Ute gal named Tatseegah and finally joined up with the White River Utes while old Nevava was still chief. Knows our customs, our ways of doing things. Hell, even hear tell, Nicaagat is a better military man when it comes to planning a battle than most generals."

"Ain't no Indian that smart," O'Malley said with conviction.

"Don't go betting your life on it. Nicaagat's one slippery rascal and has close to a hundred lodges under his command. Mark my words, if trouble comes from the Utes, it will be from his direction."

Suddenly a trooper jumped to his feet and fired his rifle at something behind Rankin. The startled scout thought for a second the trooper was aiming at him.

"Indians!" the trooper shouted. Everyone scrambled for cover. Rankin dove behind a cluster of rocks almost on top of where a startled Indian was crouching.

Sowepk sprang for the big trapper with his knife. Rankin barely had time to jerk his own weapon and parry the thrusting knife aside. Out of sight of the others, Rankin grappled with the strong Indian among the rocks, their sounds muffled by the snow. Rankin knew the startled Ute had been there only to scout them out, not to attack. As they struggled, Rankin spoke softly to Sowepk.

"Rankin, where the hell are you?" O'Malley shouted. Unnerved by the commotion, he and the other troopers were hugging the ground and seeing Indians behind every rock. They heard a horse whinny behind a screen of trees.

O'Malley whirled around, "Two of you check the horses," he ordered. "They make off with them, we done for." Two troopers crept cautiously forward on their bellies and disappeared among the trees. O'Malley went back to searching the rocks and cursing Rankin under his breath. The bastard probably high-tailed it first sign of trouble, he figured.

Suddenly an Indian appeared several yards away and O'Malley snapped a shot in his direction. Immediately, Rankin appeared as well, wearing a disgusted look. The scout walked over to the fallen Indian.

"Rankin, you crazy, get down!" O'Malley shouted.

Rankin looked over at the shaken trooper. "What for, there was only two of them, here to scout us out, not to make war."

Slowly O'Malley gained his footing, yet using caution to do so with his rifle ready at the first sign of trouble. The other troopers stayed where they were.

"How you figure that?"

"Simple, I asked him."

O'Malley looked at Rankin as if the scout had suddenly taken leave of his senses.

"You asked him?"

"I do know Ute, O'Malley." Rankin sheathed his knife and rolled the dead Indian over with the toe of his boot. Sowepk stared up at Rankin with sightless eyes. O'Malley had hit the Indian in the neck and gouts of freezing blood lay on the snow.

Rankin looked at O'Malley who had come over to stare down at the first dead man he had ever killed.

"Played hell, O'Malley. Sowepk here, is Nicaagat's right hand scout. He ever gets wind who sent him under, you better get ready for a night visit."

O'Malley was pale as the snow, looking first at the dead Indian and then around at all the blood. It seemed there were gallons. O'Malley swallowed hard, hot spit rising in the back of his throat.

"You got anybody covering the horses?" Rankin asked.

O'Malley nodded his head silently, not yet trusting his ability to speak for fear of getting sick.

As if in answer to Rankin's question, the two troopers sent to guard the horses, stumbled back into camp breathing hard, their eyes wide with fear. One had a bloody head and had lost his rifle.

"What happened?" Rankin asked quickly.

"Ran into an Indian trying to steal our horses," the first trooper said, panting hard. Rankin saw that the trooper with the bloody

104

head was William Sprague from Pittsburgh. "Billy tried to stop him, but he got clubbed over the head. Before I could get a clear shot, he was gone. Took our pack mule and two horses with him."

"Damn! Looks like we'll be eatin' snow from here on out, boys," Rankin said, shaking his head. He turned to O'Malley who seemed to still be in shock.

"Tole you to keep them horses close by like I did mine."

"There was better shelter over there," O'Malley responded, trying to get his thoughts collected.

"Lucky thing you boys caught him in the act, elsewise, you'd all be walking back to the fort, instead of just two."

O'Malley stared long and hard at the scout. "We ain't turning back."

"What are you going to use for food? All you got is a half-empty coffee pot. Ain't gonna make it far on that. And with two men ridin' double, won't be long it'll kill them horses."

O'Malley looked worried. He walked back to the fire more of the need to get away from the dead Indian than to warm himself.

"What about this . . . Perkin's place? They got any horses the Army can buy?"

"Doubt ole Charlie has any to spare. Extra horses are too tempting with Utes around case you ain't noticed." It was Rankin's turn to grin evilly at the perplexed private.

O'Malley's shoulders shrugged just a bit as he stood there looking into the fire. Silently, his men came over and stood next to him at the fire. Someone cleaned Sprague's head wound and dressed it.

"Before you get too down on yourself," Rankin finally added, "we didn't stand much of a chance before we left the jail. That dead Indian, you killed, told me over a hundred and forty lodges lined the Little Snake; combined forces of Nicaagat's and Quinkent's people. What are we gonna do facing that many Utes? Not much and you know it. Hell, by the time we get to the Little Snake, they'll be gone . . . into the mountains. You think snow is deep here, just wait 'til you get in them mountains." Rankin paused to catch his breath. He hadn't talked like this in years. "Another thing you ain't considering in all this, O'Malley. They are starving. You ever try taking away something from a man who's got nothing left to give up?"

O'Malley remained silent, still staring into the fire. The other troopers did likewise.

"Let me tell you, then," Rankin continued. "First the babies start dying. Mothers ain't got no milk left to nurse 'em. Then the old people are left behind in the snow. I know, it may sound cruel, but they ain't much good to the tribe noway when food is scarce. And then the children, the future of the tribe cry out for food, grow weak and die." Rankin paused for effect, looking at the face of each trooper. "After that, why all you got left is people with so much pain don't nothing matter anymore."

O'Malley raised his head and looked at Rankin. "You beginning to sound more like a Ute than a white man. Maybe you should join up with them." His voice was contemptuous.

"Expect they'd treat me a whole sight better than the way we been treating them. All you got to do is open your eyes, O'Malley. They didn't take a damn thing that wasn't already theirs. What would you do under similar circumstances and your family was at death's door? Damn right! You'd act no different, Union Pacific be damned."

"Anybody ever tell you, you jaw too much, Rankin," O'Malley snapped back, before marching out of camp.

Rankin surveyed the troopers left by the fire. "Only trying to get him to see the grief facing us, we keep going."

None at the fire could find fault with what Joe Rankin was saying.

CHAPTER 9

Quinkent looked out across the Smoking Earth River at the pair of spirit birds that had stayed beyond the season. They rested quietly next to the frozen bank among the thin reeds of winter. Their red eyes watched him intently, their heads held at perfect angles to their black and white bodies while they studied the tall man in the red and blue blanket across the frozen distance.

Through the summer and late season of Cherries Ripening the spirit birds had filled the nights of Smoking Earth River with their haunting calls, floating low across the river, soft, yet pleasing to the troubled soul of the man who now breathed deeply of the frigid air. Having been born in the season of the Calling Loons, Quinkent's earliest visions as a boy had been heavily influenced by these beautiful spotted birds. These spirit birds, as he called them, became his talisman and even now as an old man, the image of the loon marked his *carniv*. His *piwán* had even managed to incorporate the bird's likeness into the leather shirt he wore when things were not going well. And things were not going well for the People of Smoking Earth River. Not for two winters now. And Quinkent had worn the leather shirt everyday without fail. Through the baking summers when no rain came to cleanse the air of the foul dust that rose on great wings of heated air, choking man and animal alike, Quinkent persevered. He prayed earnestly to the Great Spirit, Sunáwiv, to end the drought. Even through the harsh winters when the winds howled liked dying men and children cried out for food, Quinkent persevered. But nothing he did seemed to matter. His People were still starving and he alone was responsible.

That was why he ultimately listened to Nicaagat and took the stored things that were meant for his People. Maybe Washington would understand the need for his actions, his responsibilities to the People.

Already one of the hard, late, Snow Moons had come and gone and the *Mericatz* had not come. Quinkent's head still hurt from Nicaagat's words, urging them to take what they could. The wounded soldier left in the snow caused his thoughts to be scrambled deep inside him until he felt sick at such thinking. The People thought they had done the right thing and Nicaagat was praised for his leadership in times of starvation.

To think of Nicaagat now caused Quinkent to feel even sicker and he freed such thoughts from his aging body. His time as *tawacz viem* was drawing to a close, this he knew for he had seen over sixty winters and his People were no better off than when he first became their chief. He had failed in his mission as their leader to provide properly for them. Yet he knew Nicaagat was not the one who would provide and care for the People over the many seasons necessary to become a proper chief. Nicaagat lacked the depth of understanding and patience to be a *tawacz viem*. Times had changed drastically for the *Nüpartka* and they faced new challenges. Who would send their messages to the white chief in Washington and deal diplomatically with the new agent when he came to Smoking Earth country? These things worried Quinkent greatly, and the knowledge Nicaagat would disappear when things no longer went his way. But Quinkent expressed his concern to none of the men of his band, even his most trusted allies, for Nicaagat was not above using any and all things against him. That was the way of Nicaagat, like Old Man Coyote. It was simple and plain for anyone to see if they just took the time to look inside the man.

A limb snapped somewhere close along the bank, startling the loons who rose swiftly from the river, circled once in the still blue air and settled on the far shore once more.

Quinkent wondered why they had not left with the other birds of autumn. Perhaps, one was injured and its mate would not leave the other behind. Their survival could not be assured through the intense Snow Moons of hard winter if they remained here on Smoking Earth River, yet Quinkent drew comfort from their presence.

His smokey eyes lifted from the river to the approaching figure of his *piwán* who came to him with her blanket pulled tightly against the frigid cold. The smoke from many cooking fires clung low to the river like a thin blue cloud over a tall mountain, the smell familiar and comforting to Quinkent. His People still ate from the supplies they had taken from Rawlings, yet it would not be enough to last until the night thunder came. This too worried Quinkent very much . . . and the *Mericatz*.

Singing Grass stepped close to Quinkent, drawing comfort from his presence. There was no need for talk between them and they stood there watching the ball of sun sink slowly beyond the standing mountains to the west, lighting vivid fires of reds and yellows in the cooling skies.

Quinkent drew his strength from the river and it was his custom to visit this lovely place each day to watch the evening begin and to hear the loons calling to one another. Few of the People ventured to intrude on Quinkent's quiet time of thinking and reappraisal of the day, except on occasion, his *piwán*.

"I did not mean to cause the spotted birds to leave," Singing Grass finally said softly.

It was some time before Quinkent even acknowledged she had spoken. And when he did speak, his voice was more like that of a patient father than that of a husband.

"You must learn to walk softly, like the deer," he chided.

Singing Grass looked up at her husband whose stern countenance melted when his eyes found hers. His arm reached out from beneath his blanket and pulled her close.

"I am not one of your warriors to order around," she said, snuggling close for warmth.

Quinkent merely grunted and looked back to the darkening river. He no longer commanded warriors, just old men and children. The young men rode with Nicaagat. He only hoped the women would not be called on to fight the *Mericatz* once the passes were clear in the spring.

"Nicaagat has asked for a council with the elders," Quinkent said after a long pause.

"Do not worry husband, your strength still lies with your wisdom. You have never failed to guide the *Nüpartka* with honesty and humility through all these difficult years since the *Mericatz* came to our mountains. The council fires will only reflect the truth you speak against Nicaagat."

Quinkent shook his shaggy head slowly. "This time, I do not know. The others, even those of our band, sees with blind eyes. They hear only what is being said, and the things that are not, they ignore."

"They will listen," Singing Grass said reassuringly.

"This time, I am not so sure. They only see the *Mericatz* did not come to punish us for taking the supplies and for wounding one of their bluecoats. They listen only to Nicaagat's words and think they are true. Because of him, their bellies are full once more. These things they see and feel. Nothing more is important."

They watched in silence as purple hues formed along the mountain peaks and raced down their timbered flanks to flood the valley floor. Even as darkness descended across the lovely winter valley, the snow reflected enough subdued light that things were still visible around them.

In thought, they moved as one toward the beckoning fire of their *carniv*. With the sun now gone, the air grew colder and snow protested loudly beneath their moccasins as they walked back to camp, leaving the river in an icy fog from bank to bank.

One of the loons cried out through the mists and Quinkent stopped, looking back over his blanketed shoulder at the river he loved. *They knew he was leaving for the night. Were they calling for him to come back? Or were they telling him things would be all right.* Singing Grass pulled at him, urging him forward. Quinkent turned once more towards camp and to the bright fire where supper was waiting.

Canávish had two sons, Saponse and Tatitz. Two boys heading fast into manhood, yet clinging to child-like ways. Like most boys their age, they were boisterous and tended to talk and laugh when they should be listening to what others were saying. There was a lot to teach them about the People, their ways and customs, yet Canávish could not bring himself to chastise the boys when they crowded around the fire after supper with dancing eyes and loud laughter, asking him to tell another story. For all he could tell them, a man must learn of wisdom from inside and outside of himself. Canávish could not teach his sons great wisdom. If a man tried to do this thing, his words would quickly be tangled like briars and nothing would be understood. Like a boy slowly developing inside the body of a man, wisdom would only come from within, not from other men.

It was like when Canávish received the power of *Quigat*, the bear, in a vision after talking with *Sunáwiv*. There had been no need to tell others of his new power. Nor could he tell them what it was like to talk to *Sunáwiv*, for his voice came from neither the sky nor the earth, but from all over. Soon there was no need. The People knew Canávish had received the power. The power to see a small piece of the circle of life, like that left by a *carniv*, yet knowing there is more to the great circle, the sacred hoop of his People, that others could not see who had not talked with the Great Spirit, *Sunáwiv*. That was wisdom, from inside and outside. He said nothing of his thoughts to his two sons, waiting until his *piwán*, Tsashin, joined them by the fire for their family council. Tsashin, whom the *Mericatz* called Susan, was the sister of Ouray, who was a man of great power and made chief of all the People by the *Mericatz* in Washington. Tsashin was, like her brother Ouray, half-Apache. Tall and strong, she stood even with Canávish. Only her sons were taller.

Without saying a word, Canávish picked up his pipe and filled it with sweet tobacco from the buckskin pouch, beaded yellow, blue and white by Tsashin. It had been a long time since any of the *Nüpartka* had smoked such fine tobacco other than the *quap* they were forced to smoke when there was nothing else.

Canávish took his time as the boys watched him go through the ritual of lighting the clay pipe with a piece of smoking coal from the fire and offering it first to the four winds and then the sky where the Great Spirit resided. The pungent smell of trade tobacco quickly filled the *carniv* and the two boys breathed deeply of its fragrance. Their father had not yet offered them the pipe yet they were close enough to manhood to know better than ask. Only when their father felt they were ready would they be included in the ritual.

Tatitz could wait for his father no longer. "Father, tell us once more of the buffalo and the hole in the ground from where all things are provided."

Canávish took into his lungs a huge cloud of smoke and held it for some time without acknowledging his son's request. Slowly, Canávish lifted his chin and released the pent-up smoke, upwards into the *carniv*, his face a serious study. Both brothers looked at one another and back to their father who seemed to be in deep thought with his eyes closed. Without being told, both boys settled down and remained quiet, yet both knew this night of storytelling would not be the same as before.

Canávish brought his chin down and opened his eyes. The two brothers stared at him with huge eyes. Without comment, Canávish extended the burning pipe across the fire to his sons.

When Tatitz realized what was being offered, he nearly dropped the pipe in the process. Gingerly, he brought the pipe to his lips and took a tentative pull. He held the smoke only in his mouth, afraid to inhale for fear of coughing and displeasing his father. Quickly, Tatitz handed the pipe to his brother who did the same. They released the smoke together which was quickly taken up by the smoke from the fire. Tatitz licked his lips, tasting the harsh tobacco for the first time and liking it.

Only when the pipe was safely back in Canávish's strong hands, did he speak. His voice was soft, yet carried a hard edge like some-one trying to teach others the proper way to string a bow or skin a deer. Usually it was the grandfather who instructed the young men through the old stories, of the inside and outside world, and how the land was balanced by each season. Since Canávish was *m'sut t'quigat*, shaman, he had the power to instruct his sons. He spoke aloud his secret name and called out so *Sunáwiv* could hear him.

"As the moon rises this very moment over the mountains to the east, this is the night I choose for you to become men. From this time forward, you will put away childish things and listen carefully around the council fires. You will listen to the things I tell you, of the ways of our People and how it is. Hold close to your heart the good things I tell you now for a day will come when men will not speak the truth and you must be able to know the difference. To see what is in the heart, not what is in the head."

Again, Canávish offered the pipe to Tatitz who accepted it with chest puffed out, his face reverent. Both brothers this time inhaled the pungent smoke, proud they did not cough when it was released.

Canávish began without preamble, the boys giving him their full attention. Sitting quietly next to him, Tsashin looked across the fire proudly at her two sons while listening to her husband.

Canávish began with the oldest story of all. How the People came to be. How *Sunáwiv* made the world from nothing and darkness into light, trees, mountains, animals and finally, the People. He told his sons of *Sunáwiv-ta'watz*, the son of the God, *Sunáwiv*, whom even the *Mericatz* knew about. He spoke of *Sunáwiv-ta'watz's* death and that the old people knew who had killed him but would not say.

Canávish talked late into the night while the fire faded away to nothing but red coals, cooling the *carniv* and bringing blackness to its insides. The eyelids of Saponse and Tatitz became heavy and finally Canávish sent them to their robes. It was a long journey to manhood and the trip could not be completed in one night. They would need time to understand what he had told them. Time for the man to grow within their heads so to see clearly.

And he had yet to speak to them of war.

CHAPTER 10

Tip Thornburgh sat on the edge of the bed holding one of his shoes in his hand and staring at the far wall. A short time later, Lida came into the bedroom after seeing the children were asleep. She saw the look of dejection on her husband's face.

"Dear Tip, how perfectly sad you look sitting there."

Tip Thornburgh roused himself and looked at his pretty wife standing before him with a smile on her face. He dropped the shoe to the floor, letting out a long sigh.

"Did I disappoint you as well?" Tip asked, bending over to unlace the other shoe.

Lida laughed, coming over to take a husband's head in her soft hands. She turned his eyes to meet hers.

115

"Silly question. You could never disappoint me. You performed magnificently." She kissed his eyes, nose and then mouth.

"I don't know about being magnificent, but I gave it my best. Which is rather lame to a man who's just spent a month's wages backing me." Overcap and the rest of the regiment would be on short rations until payday for they had bet to a man on Thornburgh.

"They must look at it as providing three hours of clean entertainment. It was absolutely exciting for the children to see their father perform so."

"And what about you, dear wife?"

Lida kneeled before her husband and removed the remaining shoe from his foot, offering up another smile. This one filled with hidden promises.

"I was proud to be your wife today. You were wonderful. Everybody thought so."

"There might have been one or two there who didn't think so much of me. Like General Crook. Your father told me afterward, even Crook placed a wager in my favor." Tip Thornburgh shook his head wistfully. "Expect it will be a long time before I get another assignment the way I let the Army down."

"Nonsense, Tip. The General would never resort to such things. He seemed to enjoy the match as much as the other spectators."

"That may be so, dear Lida, but it is a hard fall indeed when your commander is there to witness your descent." Tip helped his wife to her feet and began removing his uniform. It had been a long and emotional day, followed by a healthy portion of his father-in-law's Guckenheimer whiskey to ease the pain of defeat. Even Frank Carver's kind words at the conclusion of the match, praising Thornburgh's accuracy with the rifle, did little to relieve the sting of defeat. The last three missed balls played over and over in his mind. Had he taken more time and not misjudged the miscreant wind that kept shifting across the open field, he might have had a chance against Carver. When the match had finally ended, Tip was completely worn out and his uniform stained with sweat while Dr. Carver looked as fresh as at the beginning.

Thornburgh unbuttoned his pants concluding Carver should be as cool as a cucumber. Shooting glass balls was his occupation. It was what he did best. Lida had already removed her outer garments and slipped between the covers, waiting for her husband to come to bed. Tip had one pant leg off when there was a soft rap at the outer door.

"Who on earth?" Lida said, sitting up in bed. Thornburgh looked at his wife and shrugged his shoulders as he hastily pulled his pants back on. As he started out of the bedroom, he grabbed his shirt and threw it on and picked up the burning lamp. Tip opened the door and found Major Clarke standing there in the cold.

"Sorry to have bothered you at such an hour," his father-in-law responded first, stepping quickly inside. "I'll only be a moment. Didn't wake the children, did I?"

"No, they are still asleep." Thornburgh quickly closed the door against the cold.

"Well, I knocked as softly as I could."

"Everything's fine. Are you here to see Lida?"

"No, no. Only want a word with you and I'll be gone."

"Want to sit down, Bob?"

"That's okay," Clarke said, twirling his hat in his hand. "This will only take a minute." When Thornburgh did not respond, Clarke went on. "That was an outstanding performance you gave today, Tip. I really mean it. So do the men. They were behind you one hundred percent, win or lose." Thornburgh nodded glumly, not really wanting to be reminded of his defeat at such a late hour, especially by his father-in-law.

Major Robert D. Clarke's bearded face formed a huge grin, his eyes sparkling in the glow of the lamp Thornburgh held. There seemed to be a mysterious air about the man, Thornburgh admitted to himself upon closer inspection.

"The men weren't the only one impressed with your skills with a rifle, Tip. General Crook spoke with me personally after the match how impressed he was with your shooting ability. So impressed, he asked me to stop by tonight and tell you he wants to see you immediately after breakfast." Bob Clarke was still smiling.

"You holding something back, Major?" Thornburgh probed.

"Can't say. General Crook's orders. But I will tell you this, there's a mighty good chance you will like what Crook has to say." Clarke's mysterious air deepened.

"Dang it, Bob, your aren't leaving until you tell me what's going on even if I got to get Lida out here to work on you," Tip threatened.

"No, no, please," Clarke laughed, reaching out for the door knob. "I must go now. Sleep well, Tip." And Major Clarke slipped through the door, leaving Tip Thornburgh standing there looking dumbfounded at Clarke's behavior. He finally shook his head and returned to the bedroom.

"Was that father's voice I heard at the door?" Lida asked. She sat propped up on several pillows with a thick book in her hands.

"Him all right." Thornburgh quickly removed his clothing and slipped between the covers.

"There's nothing wrong, is there?" Lida asked, her eyes growing wide.

"Everything's fine," Thornburgh responded quickly, seeing his wife was becoming upset.

"What was it then?"

Thornburgh took a deep breath and closed his eyes. "Funny thing. I don't really know. Only that General Crook wants to see me first thing tomorrow."

Lida dropped her book and sat up straight in bed. "What do you think he wants?"

Thornburgh slowly opened his eyes and looked into his wife's pretty face. "Probably wants to demote me after today's match."

"He wouldn't dare!"

Chuckling, Thornburgh reached for his wife and pulled her close.

"Tip Thornburgh, when will I ever learn? And get those cold feet off me."

Thornburgh laughed even harder and held Lida tightly to him. She flailed her tiny fists against his hairy chest to no avail. Finally she quieted down and snuggled close.

"Why do you think you're being asked to report to headquarters?" Lida finally asked.

"Have no idea," Tip replied, kissing the top of his wife's head. "Most likely nothing more than routine business unless the General's wanting to plan another hunting trip. He seemed to enjoy the last one immensely." Lida pulled back just enough to see into Thornburgh's eyes. "I think it's more than that. Why else would father make a point of coming by so late to tell you?"

"I must admit your father seemed rather like the cat that ate the mouse tonight. And he refused to see you."

"That's because he knows I can see right through him. I would have gotten the secret from him easily."

"That is if he had a secret to tell," Thornburgh said dryly.

"My father *knows* something."

"Guess we'll know soon enough," Thornburgh said, leaning over to dim the wick until it gave out only the slightest cast of yellow in the room. Tip kissed Lida's hairline, then her eyes and finally her full lips.

"You were wonderful today," Lida whispered between kisses as she settled back against her pillows. Tip followed.

"Question is, how will I measure up tonight," he said in a husky voice.

Lida smiled and pulled him to her. "I think just fine."

Major Tipton stood before General George Crook's office a few minutes after eight the next morning. He was in full dress uniform and his boots gleamed in the early morning sun. Taking a deep breath, Thornburgh opened the door and stepped inside. The first person he spied was Crook's adjutant, General Robert Williams.

"Good morning General," Thornburgh said, snapping to attention and giving Williams a smart salute. Williams responded with a casual wave.

"Hello, Tip. Care for some coffee?"

"No thank you, sir."

"Here on business then?"

"General Crook is expecting me," Thornburgh replied, looking at the closed inner door leading to Crook's office.

"He's in, fact is, I just left him. Go right in, Major."

"Thank you, sir."

Thornburgh opened the polished walnut door and stepped inside. Crook was bent over his desk studying a sheaf of papers.

"Good morning General," Thornburgh spoke up.

"Oh, Major, thought that was General Williams come back in. Come, come, please sit down." The two officers shook hands.

George Crook settled back in his chair, his keen eyes taking in Thornburgh's lanky form. Like Thornburgh, George Crook was as lean as they come. A fearless Indian fighter of many campaigns, it was against the Apaches in Arizona that Crook earned his star which eventually led to William T. Sherman calling Crook "the greatest Indian fighter and manager the Army of the United States ever had." Still, Crook was the most decent and humane of the many officers and saw the Indians as humans rather than the savages others thought them to be, especially Sherman and Sheridan. Sporting a magnificent forked beard, Crook was as eccentric as he was decent, neither drinking nor smoking or even partaking of coffee. Those that knew him had never even heard him so much as swear. Crook's only quirk was his love of publicity which was further enhanced by newspaper correspondents who accompanied his every move. Regardless, Crook was loved by the men who served beneath him.

"I must say, I enjoyed the match yesterday. You gave a good accounting of yourself and made the army proud."

"Thank you, sir," Thornburgh managed to say without seeming to be embarrassed by Crook's full attention.

"Major Clarke tells me you've grown rather bored of your position in the Paymaster Corps," Crook said, changing directions.

For a moment Thornburgh was flustered and unsure of what to say. He had no idea his father-in-law shared such conversations with their commander.

"Well, sir, what I mean is . . . the job is an important one and I'm grateful for all—"

"It's okay, Tip. I've known you were bored with the job before you were reassigned here from Texas," Crook interrupted. In spite of himself, Thornburgh found himself coloring at being the focus of attention.

Crook continued, "Would you be interested in a field assignment again? Not with the Paymaster Corp, I might add," Crook hastily added.

Thornburgh set straighter in his chair, his heart racing. He tried his best to remain outwardly calm.

"Yes sir, I would," he found himself saying.

"Good," Crook said, rocking forward in his chair to scan through the papers on his desk for a minute. Thornburgh could barely sit still as he waited for Crook to find whatever he was looking for.

"Ah, here it is." Crook pulled a single sheet of paper from the stack and sat back with it in his hand. He looked over at Thornburgh after scanning its contents.

"I'll not hold you to your request for field assignment until you've heard the location."

"Location that bad?" Thornburgh asked.

Crook grinned as an orderly brought in a pot of coffee. "Please, help yourself, Tip."

Thornburgh's nerves screamed for Crook to get on with it, yet he politely accepted a cup from the orderly who, once done, quietly left the room. He tried sipping the hot liquid with his hands betraying his building excitement.

"Henry Thomas thinks so." Thinking quickly, Thornburgh instantly matched the name with the location without Crook having to tell him.

"Major Thomas," Thornburgh said the name. "Commander of Fort Fred Steele."

"That's right. Henry feels he's getting a little too old for field duty and would be interested in a job with the Paymaster Corps. How would you like to trade places with him?"

Thornburgh nearly dropped the full cup of coffee in his lap. It was a full minute before he could speak while Crook's eyes twinkled with merriment.

"I'd like that just fine, sir," Thornburgh finally managed.

"Thought you would, but what about Lida and the children?"

"I'm sure Lida feels the same as I do, sir. She knows how much I like the outdoors."

"You must know, Tip, Fort Steele is not much of a fort these days since the Union Pacific tracks were completed a few years back. You'll find little Indian activity outside of routine patrols, keeping the peace among miners and such."

"Still, it should be interesting," Thornburgh said, finishing the last of his coffee.

Crook stood up and Thornburgh followed. Crook extended his hand.

"Congratulations, Major. I'll put the orders in for your transfer immediately if that is your wish."

"It is, sir," Thornburgh responded, gripping the shy man's hand. "And thank you, General."

"Better wait and thank me six months from now. That Red Desert country may get to you after a while," Crook warned.

"We'll manage, sir." Thornburgh brought himself to attention and snapped a smart salute. He was at the door before Crook stopped him.

"Nearly forgot, Tip. We are hosting a ball for the new officers that arrived here a few weeks back. Please remember to bring Lida tonight."

"We wouldn't miss it." And then Thornburgh found himself standing outside Army Headquarters still dazed by the sudden turn of events. He failed to see the smiling-faced Bob Clarke standing there on the stoop.

"You accept?"

Thornburgh had trouble focusing on his father-in-law. When he did, he clapped the older officer on the shoulder, grinning widely himself.

"You old rascal. How long have you known Crook would offer me Fort Steele?"

"Yesterday," Clarke said, continuing to smile. "George and me decided to hold off 'til after your match with Dr. Carver."

"It's a good thing," Thornburgh confessed. "I couldn't hit a horse with a shotgun right now."

Clarke laughed. "You better get on home and tell Lida."

"That's where I was headed." Thornburgh paused. "You think Lida will be all right at Fort Steele?"

"Lida will do fine there, Tip. She'll be happy as long as you are. Now run along and tell her the good news."

Thornburgh nodded, thanked his father-in-law for his help in procuring the position and hurried off.

Major Robert Clarke watched his favorite son-in-law take the footbridge across the river with long purposeful strides. When he pushed open the door to headquarters, Clarke had no doubt Major Tipton Thornburgh had taken his first steps that would eventually lead to a general's star. The old major couldn't help but feel just a tinge of pride for his daughter having selected such a fine man for a husband.

CHAPTER 11

To everyone's surprise, it began snowing hard as darkness approached and the temperature continued to fall. Joe Rankin pulled his felt hat further down on his head in the bitter wind. Going had been slow the last two hours as the animals suffered even more than the men. Rankin had the two men without mounts riding double rotate to other horses every half hour to conserve their strength.

"Dammit, Rankin, how much further?" Patrick O'Malley asked through the screaming winds.

"Another three hours if we lucky."

"You call this luck?" O'Malley said sourly.

"Better than being dead as that Indian you killed." This silenced O'Malley who dropped his head and hunched his shoulders against the bitter cold.

Had they not been on Muddy Creek, Rankin would have given up and settled in for a cold camp until morning. But he knew with inexperienced troops, he was better off getting them out of the weather before they froze to death. But what really kept Rankin going was thinking of Maggie Baggs. Since they had just passed Blue Gap Draw, Rankin figured they would make the Little Snake before nine that night.

Ten minutes later O'Malley bellowed for Rankin to hold up. He looked back and in the dim light, Rankin could see a dark object lying on the snow. He turned his horse around as O'Malley was giving orders to have the man picked up and placed back in the saddle.

"What happened?" Rankin asked.

One of the troopers who was busy helping the fallen man back into the saddle answered for the others.

"Musta been that head injury. Sprague blacked out and fell off his horse." The two troopers had Sprague under both arms, trying to get him to stand but his legs were not responding. Finally, they threw him over his horse like a sack of potatoes. He appeared to be semi-conscious and his head lolled from side to side.

Rankin rode over and lifted the wounded man by both shoulders and slid him across the saddle while another trooper held the horse steady.

"Got to get him someplace warm soon or Sprague will lose his feet, or worse, his life."

"How much further?" O'Malley asked, his lower lip shivering has he spoke. They were all nearly frozen and exhausted by the ordeal.

"Ten miles, maybe less. Just stick tight to me in this snow storm. Anybody go wandering off now won't be found 'til next spring."

The soldiers seemed to heed Rankin's warning and crowded their mounts until they were nose to tail to one another. A trooper name of Bannister rode beside the wounded Sprague and held him in the saddle.

An hour later as they were fording Deep Creek where it emptied into Muddy Creek, Rankin's own horse stumbled on the ice and broke through the thin crust covered by two feet of snow. Rankin was immediately wet clear up to his chest and he cursed bitterly at his own round of bad luck as well as the luck of this entire expedition. Once on the opposite bank, he dismounted and checked his horse by running his hand over the animal's legs and belly. His hand came away with blood on it.

"Dammit to hell!" He checked the horse more carefully and found a six inch gash on the left fore-leg. The bleeding had stopped almost immediately in the sub-freezing temperature. Numbed by the cold, the horse seemed to be in no pain.

"Can you ride him?" O'Malley asked through chattering teeth.

By now, Rankin was shaking hard from the dousing in the cold creek. He answered by mounting up and riding away without a word.

In thirty minutes they reached the Baggs ranch and never was there a prettier sight to the worn out, half-frozen soldiers. Situated on the Little Snake at Muddy Creek, George Baggs ranch was a showplace even in winter. The sprawling main house of fine logs sported a huge stone fireplace at one end of the structure, a large kitchen-dinning area and three huge bedrooms clustered together at the far end of the hall. The outbuildings were as well constructed as the house and there was always fresh meat hanging from a pole to feed visitors. George Baggs had come to the beautiful little valley of the Snake with a herd of cattle back in '73 after he had gotten Chief Ouray's permission to cross Ute lands. Maggie, his common-law wife came with him, causing quite a stir by her buxom good looks and her inclination to bestow favors on passing miners, lonely cowboys and anyone else that suited her fancy. George seemed not to know or care too much.

Chilled to the bone, George Baggs had Rankin remove his

leathers and slip into a pair of his trousers while Maggie Baggs scurried around refilling bowls with hot soup each time a trooper emptied it, gathering stares as she went. They were gathered about the great stone fireplace where a roaring fire was kept going to thaw frost-bitten hands and feet.

As he began to thaw, William Sprague screamed from the pain that knifed through him as his feet gained new life.

"Rub 'em, Bannister," O'Malley ordered. "Do it gently, or else you can do more harm than good." Bannister knelt beside Sprague who was in agony and began rubbing his splotchy feet covered in white areas.

Rankin came out of the bedroom and accepted a bowl of soup from Maggie Baggs. He gave her his best smile and she returned it while George was busy examining the condition of the troopers.

Rankin ran an approving eye across Maggie's buxom famous figure widely known in this part of Colorado and Wyoming. In fact, to honor her famous endowment, a nearby peak was aptly named Maggie's Nipple.

Rankin took his bowl of soup over to where Bannister sat massaging Sprague's feet.

"Gonna lose some of them toes," Rankin said matter-of-factly. "Soon as he has complete feeling, soak them in a pan of warm water for an hour or two."

"Rankin, as far as I'm concerned, as soon as we are able, we're returning to Fort Steele," O'Malley said, from his seat by the fire.

"Do tell, General."

"Don't push me, Rankin," O'Malley warned.

"You boys want a little something to take the kinks out of your joints," George Baggs interjected, bringing out a couple of whiskey bottles from a side shelf. He turned to his wife. "Mag, how about fetching a few glasses from the kitchen for the boys." Maggie Baggs flounced out of the room with every weary-eyed soldier watching her departure.

"Joe, would you give me a hand?" Maggie called over her shoulder.

"Durnit, woman, can't you see, Joe is too wore out to move," George said exasperated. Joe Rankin was up from his seat by the fire like a live coal had gotten down his pants.

"Aw, I don't mind, George. I'm so stiff I need to walk around some since falling in that creek." Envious eyes followed Rankin from the room, while George Baggs seemed oblivious to the effect his wife was having on the young troopers.

"Private O'Malley, just what are you doing out this far from the fort in this weather?" George Baggs asked, setting the bottles on a small table near the fire.

Like the others, O'Malley had his eyes on Rankin and was only half-listening to what the rancher was saying.

O'Malley's response faded out of Rankin's earshot as he left the room. He walked through a spacious dining area that was larger than most cabins and into the kitchen near the back of the sprawling ranch. He caught sight of Maggie Baggs taking glasses out of a side cupboard and he angled over in her direction. Upon hearing his approach, Maggie turned and gave him a warm smile.

Joe Rankin never stopped until he had the big-breasted woman wrapped tightly in his arms. He planted a kiss on her full lips and it was a moment before they disconnected.

"My Lord, Joe, but you are a pleasure to see this cold night." Maggie continued to hold Rankin, stroking first his face and arms and pressing herself into him.

"Only thing kept me going after my horse broke through the ice and I took a wetting, was seeing you," Rankin said thickly. He kissed her again, harder this time and with more urgency. They broke from their embrace, breathing hard.

"Been a long time, Joe, honey," Maggie breathed in his ear.

"Too long," was Joe's short comment as he continued to hold the woman. Her huge breasts pressed into him hard, sending all the right signals through his body.

"Heard tell, you been spending time with Mike Sweet," Joe asked cautiously. With Maggie, one never knew how she may react to such prying.

Maggie lifted her head from Rankin's chest and looked up at him. "If you came around more often, I wouldn't need the services of Mike," Maggie replied sweetly. In spite of himself, Rankin laughed loudly, squeezing her behind with both of his big hands.

"I swear, Maggie honey, they ain't a gal like you this side of Chicago. Guess that's why I love you so."

It was Maggie's turn to laugh, "Joseph Rankin, we both know where you stand on love, so don't go lying to me. You got the fever bad as I do."

Rankin kissed the top of her head. That was what he liked about Maggie, she was frank, open and honest when it came to sex and a man could just be himself with her, no pretenses.

"We best get these glasses back to the boys or George may get a little suspicious."

"Oh, pooh. Half the time, George is more concerned about his livestock than he is of my needs."

"Well, honey," Rankin said, scooping up several glasses, "we'll see what can be done about your needs later." He gave her a toothy grin and a quick kiss.

"Maybe," Maggie said, noncommittal.

They returned to the living room where George Baggs still held the floor. The young soldiers looked more interested in sleep than listening to the rancher. O'Malley eyed the couple sharply, settling on Maggie Baggs with an appreciative look. Rankin caught the frank appraisal.

"Pass out the glasses," George Baggs ordered, "these boys are in need of a little something to put starch in their shirts again." It was true, the troopers looked about played out and even O'Malley was looking rough around the edges; his blood-shot eyes appeared to have recessed even deeper into his skull.

As Rankin and Maggie passed out the glasses, the rancher came along behind pouring a healthy slug of whiskey into each one.

"Drink up boys, only way to shake them deep chills got a-hold of you right now," George Baggs said, standing before the weary group, smiling and holding what was left in the bottle.

O'Malley tossed his off like any good Irishman, acknowledging with professional pride the quality of the rancher's liquor. He sat the glass on the mantle and turned to face the rancher.

"Me boys and I thank you for your hospitality, Mister Baggs, and if you will show us where we might bed down 'til mornin', we'll be no further bother to ye."

"Been no bother. Got a couple spare rooms down the hall there. Rest of you welcome to bunk out right here in front of the fireplace."

By now Sprague's feeling had returned with a vengeance and he laid on a good portion of George Baggs' whiskey to numb the shooting pains in both feet. Several of his toes, stretched towards the roaring fire was already beginning to blacken. Trooper Bannister continued to bath his frostbitten feet with warm water, trying to prevent as much tissue damage as possible.

"Thank you kindly, Mister Baggs, and you, Missus Baggs," O'Malley replied, giving the woman a hungry look.

"Joe, you know where your room is," George Baggs said. "You been here before." To O'Malley, Baggs said, "You welcome to the other one. It's just down the hall." O'Malley nodded.

Baggs looked the rest of them over, "You boys, try to sleep some. Plenty of firewood near the end of the porch when you run out in here. Use all you want." With that he left the room with Maggie in tow. The woman left, but not without giving Rankin a parting smile.

Rankin came over to stand by the fireplace where O'Malley was busy watching Maggie Baggs leave the room. Rankin smiled to himself. Maggie had a way about her of turning even a religious man to thinking carnal thoughts.

"Fine looking woman, don't you think, Private?"

O'Malley looked sharply at the scout to see if he was being made fun of in anyway. Rankin seemed honest enough.

"Aye. For once, you didn't lie. Never seen a woman with bigger titties."

"Maggie Baggs is pretty all over," Rankin breathed as he emptied his glass of whiskey.

"That so?" O'Malley responded. "Expect a man like you would know. Don't being married mean nothing to you, Rankin?"

The scout smiled as he refilled his glass with Baggs' whiskey. "It would if I was the one married, but I ain't." O'Malley merely shook his head. He turned to his troops.

"Butler, you and Slim bring in the bedrolls. Been a long day and we got a longer ride back to the fort tomorrow, so you best get some sleep."

The two troopers stepped outside into the howling winds that were bringing more snow from the west. Every man there felt the stab of frigid air shoot across the room as the two troopers closed the door behind them.

"My room is first door on the right, O'Malley, case you wonderin'. You can have the one next to George and Maggie." Rankin grinned at the trooper. "Listen close and you might get to hear a little nocturnal activity. They say old George is a randy one."

"Rankin, you're one sick man." Having said that, O'Malley turned his back to the scout and faced the roaring fire with his hands outstretched.

What seemed like hours later, Rankin was awakened from a deep sleep to find Maggie between his covers. Without preamble, they embraced, followed by frantic shifting of clothes and hurried coupling. Maggie was a demanding lover and it required two couplings to satisfy the rancher's wife.

Breathing hard and completely drained of strength, Rankin lay on his back with the woman pressed to his chest. He trailed a tired hand slowly up and down Maggie's silky back as she pressed her huge breasts closer into his chest. Maggie moaned with satisfied pleasure.

"Lordy, woman, but you are a handful," Rankin whispered in her ear.

"Better than anything you got back in Rawlings, Joe Rankin and don't you go forgetting it."

"Ain't nothing back there kin hold a candle to you, Maggie honey, I mean it."

"Then why haven't you asked me to Rawlings?"

Rankin thought for a moment before answering. Truth was, the thought had crossed his mind a time or two, but he still had the good sense not to act on such impulses. Maggie was one of those rare women that could never be satisfied with one man for too long. From the rumors he had heard, Mike Sweet was already giving George Baggs a run for his money in that department. Only time would tell how that would shake out.

"Because, you and I are a lot alike, Maggie. We both have similar needs. Wouldn't be two months and I'd be forced to shoot some lover hanging around you. Besides, I figger you and Sweet are running pretty tight just now."

"Mike is adorable but he's not up to your standards, Joe."

"In what respect?"

Maggie giggled, ran a soft hand down Rankin's lanky frame and into the nest of hairs between his legs. She heard him suck air into his lungs.

"Maggie, you are one brazen woman," Rankin whispered, turning his head to meet Maggie's full, upturned lips.

O'Malley and his men had been up an hour before Rankin stumbled out of his room, looking like he had gotten little sleep. Rankin looked exhausted and his face and eyes showed it. O'Malley took in his general condition and couldn't help taking a shot at the scout.

"Appears you getting too long in the tooth for night rides in snow country, Rankin. Too much of the good life sittin' around that cast iron stove down at the livery playing cards and foolin' with them whores down on the Row."

Ranking didn't immediately answer until he had poured himself a cup of coffee and came over to stand with his back to the fire. He was dog tired. Maggie could be mighty hard on a man when she wanted to be. It was near daylight before she had slipped from his bed to return to her own with George.

Rankin cast a side-ways glance at the smirking trooper. If only he knew the truth. He took a long swallow of coffee.

"Trouble with you, O'Malley, is you don't know what's real and what's not."

O'Malley glared at the scout. "What in hell is that suppose to mean?"

Rankin was just too tired to argue with the big Irishman. "You wouldn't understand, O'Malley." With that, Rankin wandered off to the kitchen, leaving Private O'Malley fuming.

After breakfast, with Maggie giving Rankin satisfied looks across the table, the scout suggested the Army might ride up river a few miles and talk with old Jim Baker. Could be, he knew something of the Utes that passed this way.

It was obvious O'Malley wanted to start immediately for Fort Steele, yet knew what Rankin said made sense, especially when he turned in his report.

"Let's get to riding then, Rankin. That's what the Army's paying you for."

"Wrong, O'Malley. Most of this one is on the Union Pacific."

"Well, maybe so, but if talking with this Baker will do any good, the Army's interested."

If anything, it was colder than the day before, and saddle leather creaked and groaned in the frigid clear air while the sounds of horses' hoofs breaking through the frozen crust of snow echoed sharply across the narrow valley. Rankin led the way up river with O'Malley and one other trooper tagging behind.

"Who is this Baker fellow anyway?" O'Malley grudgingly asked Rankin.

"Don't tell me you ain't never hear of Jim Baker, now?"

"Well. I haven't, so tell me."

"Old Jim Baker is about as smart as they come," Rankin said, grinning at Private O'Malley. "Man knows how to live. Got a couple Snake sisters living with him, seeing to his needs and such."

"Might have figured coming from you."

"I swear, O'Malley, don't you like wimmen?"

"I do!" the Army trooper shot back. "But Indian women just seems a little too uncivilized."

"Maybe back there in Dublin or wherever the hell it is you come from, it might, but out here a man's got to take what's available to him. You try livin' out here all winter in the cold and snow without a woman to keep you warm and put food in your belly, you just might have a different view of the world 'fore long."

"What about this Baker then," O'Malley said, changing the direction of the conversation. "How well does he know the Utes?"

"'Bout as well as Uriah Curtis or myself," Rankin replied proudly. Old Jim drifted out of Denver's fleshpots back in '73 and built himself a cabin here on the Little Snake. That's after a full life of fur trappin', scoutin' fer the Army out of Fort Laramie and guiding emigrant trains west. Knows Utes first-hand and what's more he's one of the few white men they trust."

When they came upon the snow-covered cabin, woodsmoke was pouring from the chimney.

"Looks like old Jim is to home," Rankin said, getting off his horse a good twenty yards out. O'Malley and the trooper got down as well.

"Hello, the cabin!" Rankin shouted. Turning to O'Malley he explained, "Can't be too careful 'round Jim. Liable to shoot first and ask questions of the next of kin afterwards."

They stood there in the glare of an overhead sun that did little to warm things and watched as the door to the cabin slowly inched open.

"Who are ye?" Baker bellowed through the cracked door.

"Joe Rankin, Jim. I got the Army with me." It was a moment before the door opened wide and they saw a man motion them forward. In his other hand he clutched a big rifle.

"Nervy jasper," O'Malley said to Rankin as they walked their mounts forward.

"Man don't get old as Jim without taking a few precautions."

They were all standing inside the warm cabin with cups of hot coffee laced heavily with whiskey before O'Malley got a good look at their guest. Baker was everything he had imagined a mountain man to be: grizzled faced, long red hair and with a full set of leathers the color of aged mud. The only thing that didn't seem weathered and old about Baker was his twinkling sea-blue eyes. When Baker sat down by the fire, his wives, Monkey and Beans hovered near his shoulders, stroking his curly locks. O'Malley was fascinated by the two women's actions.

"I know why the Army would be this far south from the fort in the middle of winter, Joe, but what I cain't figger is, what got you out of town?" Baker asked.

"Money is what brought me out here, Jim," Rankin said, looking over at O'Malley. "And not much of it Army's either."

"Oh, whose then?" Baker asked.

"Union Pacific."

Baker laughed, slapping a big hand on one knee. "Durn railroads. Glad to see somebody taking advantage of 'em."

"Mister Baker," O'Malley interjected, wanting to get down to the subject at hand, "we understand you know a great deal about Indians, especially Utes."

The old mountain man surveyed the army private for a full minute, the only sound being the crackling of the fire. When he did finally speak, he addressed Rankin instead.

"You responsible fer these soldiers?"

"Guess in a way I am," Rankin admitted. "But it wasn't my idea to go traipsing around these mountains in a snow storm looking fer Utes."

"That idea was yours, then?" Baker addressed O'Malley.

"Well, no . . . what I mean it was the Major's—Major Henry Thompson—that is, Commander of Fort Fred Steele. We were to give chase and bring back those Indians who had broken into the warehouse in Rawlings and stole some supplies."

"Took supplies, did they?" Baker asked, looking around for his pipe. As if reading his mind, Monkey and Beans quickly brought him his pipe and tobacco.

"Yessiree, they did," O'Malley said in his most official voice, "and the Army would be most obliged if you could tell us anything of who might have been the ones involved or where they might have gone."

"They would, would they?" Baker said, puffing on his pipe. He blew a lung full of smoke into the room. "Mighty interesting."

"What is?" O'Malley asked.

"Why this whole affair, Private," Baker said, grinning. "How is it the Army is so keenly interested in capturing the culprits who was only stealing their own food, yet never bothering to pressure the Union Pacific into releasing these subsidies for two years now. Tell me that, Private O'Malley?" Baker's blue eyes were snapping under his bushy eyebrows.

"Ain't the one to ask such a question. I only do what I'm told, just like the men under me."

"Ain't good enough, soldier. These Utes are starving. Lest you forget, we've had a drought all summer long and hunting has been extremely poor. They need those supplies now more than ever, not sometime in the future after some general decides it's time to release them!" Baker's voice fairly thundered in the tight space.

O'Malley looked at Rankin for assistance, yet all he got from the scout was a toothy grin. O'Malley's face grew red with anger.

"Do you know those Utes who stole the supplies in Rawlings or not?" O'Malley asked through clinched teeth.

"Expect I do," Baker said, calming down once more. He pointed his pipe at Rankin, "So does Joe."

"Well, then, would you know where we might find these Indians?" O'Malley said, finding it hard to continue.

"Could be anywhere out there, Private. If you askin' did they stop by my place, the answer is no. You might try askin' Charlie Perkins though. He does a lot of tradin' with Utes." With that, O'Malley stormed out of the cabin, with the trooper at his heels.

"You coming, Rankin?" O'Malley roared.

"Sorry for the interruption, Jim. Just tryin' to humor the Army."

"Come back in the Spring, Joe and we'll ride over to White River and do a little horse racing."

"Would suit me fine, Jim." Then he turned back at the door and spoke to the two women in their native tongue. They both giggled and threw their arms around their husband. Rankin closed the door behind them. He squinted up at O'Malley in the bright sunlight.

"What was that you just said?" O'Malley said, plainly mad now.

Rankin caught up his bridle and mounted his horse. "Nothing you'd understand, O'Malley. You want to mosey upstream a few miles to Perkin's store?"

"Wasted enough time already. Got to report back."

"Suit yourself," Rankin shrugged, turning his horse around. "We best ride then 'cause there'll be more snow before the day is out."

The silence between soldier and scout was brittle and cold and they were nearly back to Baggs ranch before O'Malley spoke.

"You know, Rankin, you ain't been all that cooperative. A few words to the right people in Union Pacific and you might not get your money. You did promise results back there while you was still sitting tight in jail."

Rankin pulled his horse to a stop and O'Malley rode past him before he could bring his own mount to a halt. Rankin cantered over to the private.

"O'Malley, up 'til now we been tolerating one another best we could. Neither you or I asked for this assignment. Under the circumstances, I done what I could. Got no control over the weather, ner green troopers. But what you are suggesting could heap a lot of grief on both of us. You, because I'd be forced to gut shoot you, and me, for not gettin' the money I'm due and in need of just now." His words were clipped and as cold as the surrounding snow-covered rocks. There was no smile on his face when he said this.

O'Malley was startled by Rankin's frankness. He had heard a little of the scout's reputation and knew he was not making idle threats.

"Never said I'd tell anyone," he said, gruffly, trying to gracefully back out of the situation.

"Just make sure when you turn in your report, you be real careful only the truth is told." With that, Rankin kicked his horse in the flanks and left the two soldiers gawking after him.

"What the hell is eating him, anyway?" O'Malley said to the silent trooper. When he received no answer, he put the spurs to his own horse and loped after the scout.

CHAPTER 12

Nathan Meeker studied the piece of yellow paper with trembling hands, the only outward sign of the building excitement within his slender frame. Suddenly, he laid the paper on his huge desk and wiped his eyes with the back of his hand, looking around at his neat office. How many times had he prayed here for something like this to happen? And now that it had, Arvilla and the girls were not here to share in the excitement.

Nathan paced around the room, his mind busy with the implications of what the message held for him and his family. He stopped before his desk and picked up a pen to jot down a few notes and found his hand still too unsteady to write. His mind raced onward.

The first thing he must do was to quickly send a wire to Ralph in New York, thanking him for his assistance and to secretly pass along to Bob Mitchell, private secretary to Carl Schurz, how grateful Meeker was for his personal intervention with the Secretary of the Interior. And there were others who needed to be thanked as well, Meeker mused, picking up his pen to list their names so he did not overlook anyone.

With a flourish, he wrote the name of I.G. Cooper down in bold letters. Cooper, an old colleague from Meeker's *New York Tribune* days, began pulling journalistic strings on Meeker's behalf with people like Zeb White, close friend of Carl Schurz, and Whitelaw Reid, another close intimate. Meeker, himself, had written both these men concerning the possibility of receiving an Indian agent position. Meeker wrote their names down as well below that of Cooper.

He laid the pen down and began rummaging through a sheaf of papers on his desk until he extracted the wire he was looking for from the pile. He reread the wire from his son, Ralph, dated May 23, 1877.

> Dear Father:
> Make your application to Secretary Schurz direct in plain language. Give your knowledge and experience as a matter of course. Obtain what signatures possible from the leading people of Colorado. My friend says that when the document is ready, F.V. Hayden will see Schurz personally. I feel Hayden is the best man. As you say, he will do it.
>
> Yours,
> Ralph

There had been no word from this friend of Ralph's for nearly two years when just last week, Meeker had begun receiving private reports from both Colorado Senators Chaffee and Teller of the sort usually issued only to political henchmen or to someone about to get a government job. Meeker glanced over at the *Congressional Record*, sent to him by Senator Teller with his speeches marked. Speeches that ridiculed Schurz's conservation schemes for Western Lands and his suggestions for treating all Indians with abstract justice. Teller, the most powerful senator in the Western US, had complained loudly and often to the Senate that Secretary Schurz held to an Easterner's unrealistic approach to dealing with Western problems, to wit: Indians.

Meeker reached over and flipped the thick book of record open to one of Teller's passages. Was he trying to tell him something? Perhaps, if Meeker ever got an Indian agency, he might be wise to heed the advice of Henry M. Teller. Both Teller and Chaffee's names were added to his growing list.

Meeker returned to the pile of correspondence and found the note he had received ten days earlier from Henry Teller, informing him that he had visited the Commissioner of Indian Affairs and had nominated Meeker for the agency at White River as the agent there had recently resigned. Teller went on to tell Meeker of his confidence in him to make great improvements in the condition of the Indians there and how they could be taught to farm and raise cattle. Further, the salary was to be fifteen hundred dollars a year, plus a free house and garden.

Meeker laid aside the note, thinking how the salary was not very much, but even with the sizable debt he still owed Horace Greeley's estate, there should be no problem in paying off the loan within a year.

But not until today did it finally sink in that he had been appointed to the White River Agency. The wire from F. V. Hayden lay face-up on his desk and Meeker couldn't help but read it through once more, thinking how desperate he had become over the winter months for such news. The wire was his salvation. No longer would he have to endure the open ridicule of the other Colonists in

Greeley who blamed him for all their troubles. Arvilla and the children could once more hold their heads up proudly knowing that he had a government position.

> My Dear Friend:
> Your name had been sent to the Senate for the White
> River Agency. I spoke to Mr. Chaffee about your
> confirmation and he said there would be no difficulty. I
> shall see other Senators from time to time, though I
> think you will be safe. I congratulate you much. Mr.
> Mitchell, a friend of Josie's and private secretary to
> Secretary Schurz, took an active part for you. I shall keep
> a close look-out.
>
> Sincerely,
>
> F.V. Hayden

Meeker thought again back to Hayden's trip through Greeley some four years earlier. The great government geologist had stopped by to examine the coal beds around Greeley. Meeker breathed a sigh of relief for having been there to tour Hayden around the countryside. He added Hayden to the list of names, sat back in his chair and closed his eyes, feeling his heartbeat racing at his temples. Very soon he would be off on the grand adventure to White River. The extravagant imaginations of his youth flooded his thoughts. Maybe Arvilla was correct. Maybe the Lord had planned his failures just to test his courage? To prepare him for a final brilliant success as an Indian agent. His mind leaped ahead. With all his experience in handling sophisticated white colonists, he should have no trouble in managing simple savages. He would win their love and confidence and raise them out of the misery they were now living by teaching them the wonders of modern society. Once that was accomplished, he would be called on by the President of the United States to perform the same miracles for the rest of the unhappy red men. Afterward, he would be made Commissioner of Indian Affairs for life by the grateful nation. His reverie was broken by a noise in the outer parlor.

Meeker opened his eyes, grabbed up the wire and raced for the front of the house as fast as his spindly legs could carry him.

Arvilla was busy removing the pin from her hat that had been fashionably out of date for four years. She turned away from the hall mirror, holding the hat in her hand. Arvilla saw the look on Nathan Meeker's face.

"Whatever is the matter, Mister Meeker?"

Meeker danced up to her, his hazel eyes flashing excitement. An excitement Arvilla had not seen in her husband's eyes for a very long time. Meeker took Arvilla by both arms and twirled her around the cramped living room nearly upsetting a lamp in the process. He was laughing and crying all at the same time. Arvilla became somewhat concerned, not knowing whether to laugh or to cry along with him. Had her husband finally taken leave of his senses?

Finally, Nathan Meeker came to a halt, out of breath, yet smiling broadly at his perplexed wife.

"Mother, you cannot believe what came today," Meeker said, holding out the wire for his wife to read.

Arvilla took the wire from her husband, smoothing her clothes as she quickly read Hayden's wire. Nathan watched as a flush filled his wife's pale cheeks.

"Oh, Mister Meeker! Thank God." Arvilla clutched the wire to her chest with both hands while looking up at her husband with large expressive eyes.

"It isn't God I must thank," Meeker returned. "I've already started a list of the people I want to personally thank for their assistance in my securing this post."

"Rest assured, Mister Meeker, God had a hand in it," Arvilla stated resolutely. That was the one major disappointment in Arvilla's long married life, not getting Nathan Meeker to embrace her Christian faith.

"Yes, dear Mother, I suppose he may have assisted in some way I do not know about." Nathan crushed his wife in his arms, kissing her fully on the lips. Arvilla was surprised by the sudden show of intense affection. There had been very little in the past several months with the weight of the world hanging over her husband's shoulders. She returned his kiss, softly at first and then harder, deeper. It was Nathan Meeker's turn to be surprised by his wife's ardor. As if anticipating his question Arvilla spoke first.

"I left the girls in town. They were to stop by the newspaper to see you. We had no idea you would be home just now."

"Nor I," Nathan responded, still holding his wife tightly to him. "I simply felt this great urge to be home."

"The Lord moves in mysterious ways," Arvilla promptly stated.

Nathan laughed, taking his wife by the hand as he guided them towards the stairs. He was not willing to breach that subject further. Right now there was a more pressing matter he wished to attend to.

Smiling like a school-aged girl, Arvilla allowed herself to be led up the stairs and into their bedroom.

More than a month had passed since Joe Rankin had led the ill-fated army patrol south after the recalcitrant Utes. And not much had happened since then, at least not where the Utes were concerned.

The army wisely forgot about the incident surrounding the Utes once the eastern papers got hold of the story. Private O'Malley and the other troops at Fort Fred Steele spent much of the hard winter performing rather dull and senseless routines, while speculating about the new post commander coming to relieve Major Henry Thomas in the Spring.

Joe Rankin returned to the livery business, yet badgering Grayson Toliver nearly everyday for his money. The Union Pacific was more than a little reluctant to pay Joe's scouting wages with all the negative publicity. The fact that the Union Pacific had not been paid freight for the annuities garnered them little sympathy from the eastern newspapers in the face of a bunch of starving Indians. Paying Joe Rankin would be the final act of admitting guilt in the whole affair by the railroad and so far the board of directors in Omaha had refused to honor Toliver's voucher of payment to Rankin.

Meanwhile, Joe Rankin had threatened bodily harm to the young station master if he wasn't paid soon. What made him even madder was the fact Major Thomas refused him entry into Fort Steele when Rankin came seeking his scout's wages for the Ute affair.

Turning to his brothers for help had done precious little in getting what he had coming to him. Sheriff James Rankin merely told his brother that he had no authority over the military or the Union Pacific, which made Joe even madder.

To add fuel to the fire, Blacky Stillwell began badgering Rankin for the three hundred dollars he still owed him for destroying his property. Rankin had explained to the saloon owner that Port Weems was responsible for half the damages. Trouble was, Port Weems had left Rawlings the same day he was let out of jail and had taken his family further west, leaving Rankin with the total bill.

Only after Blacky threatened to have him arrested again did Rankin thunder into his shabby saloon one snowy day, half-soused and dripping death from both eyes. Witnesses said later, Joe laid fifty dollars on the bar and told Blacky Stillwell if he didn't think that amount would cover the damages owed him, then he was, by God, ready to expedite the saloon owner's short trip to hell, commencing immediately.

Blacky Stillwell took one look at the cold-faced livery owner and the Colt protruding from his waist-band and promptly declared the debt paid in full by scooping the money up from the bar. Rankin wasn't satisfied, making the saloon owner sign a statement to that effect.

James France had done more of share in stemming the tide of negative press flowing out of eastern newspapers concerning Rawlings. He had personally made two trips to Washington to plead the Indian affair case before the Senate. Change was slow in coming but after a few weeks, several newspapers ran stories that put a greater emphasis on the good attributes of Rawlings, down playing the Ute affair. There along with France were two of the board of directors for the Union Pacific, absolving themselves and the railroad of any misdoings where the Utes were concerned. Everyone finally agreed it was nothing more than an unfortunate set of circumstances, a bookkeeping error if you will, that had kept the Utes' annuities in the warehouse at Rawlings for two years, rather than anything the Union Pacific had done intentionally. Both the Union Pacific directors and James France left Washington congratulating each other on setting the record straight.

Having read the latest report of France's excursion back east and the resultant findings by the political establishment, Joe Ranking armed himself with a copy of the newspaper and trudged the three blocks south to the Union Pacific station to see Grayson Toliver. He found the young ticket master diligently working behind his steel mesh cage. His eyes betrayed the fact that he was not happy to see the livery owner.

"Afternoon, Mister Rankin," Toliver said cautiously.

Rankin dispensed with the pleasantries and slammed the folded paper down in front of Toliver. His cold eyes glittered with fury.

"Toliver, ain't wasting polite talk over wages due me and promised by you any longer."

"What are you talking about, Joe?" Grayson Toliver's pale face grew even paler.

"This!" Rankin flipped the paper open and pointed to the article. Young Toliver's eyes followed Rankin's finger. "Seems your bosses back in Omaha got the political bigwigs in Washington to agree that the UP had nothing to do with the affair. A clerical error or oversight, nothing more, they said."

Toliver hurriedly scanned the article, not having seen the paper today. Rankin waited for him to finish reading and picked up where he had left off.

"There's no mention the UP hired me to guide the Army or that they were involved in this affair in any way. Hell, the Army's managed to bow out of it altogether."

Toliver looked up at the red-faced Rankin. He could see where the scout would be mad. The slanted article never bothered to mention it was the Union Pacific who had demanded the Army catch the culprits and bring them back to Rawlings for punishment, nor the fact they had hired Rankin as scout and guide for the expedition. It was all one misunderstanding, according to high-placed sources within the railroad and the government. What made Grayson Toliver mad as well was the statement that the annuities had already been released and just waiting for the next White River Indian agent to arrive so the goods could be sent out to the reservation. Nobody in Omaha had bothered to inform him of the changes concerning the annuities. The whole affair made him look like a fool to all the townspeople. He said nothing of this to Rankin.

"Well? You gonna give me a voucher for my money or am I taking my case to the newspapers? Appears to me, those boys back in Omaha may be more than a little willing now to get me out of their hair once and for all."

"Joe, I hired you to guide the army with Omaha's approval. I'm prepared to stand firmly behind my commitments, even if Omaha doesn't." With that, Grayson Toliver brought out the voucher book and quickly wrote Rankin a check in full. After signing the voucher boldly, Toliver used his blotter to remove excess ink.

"There you go," Toliver said, handing Rankin his check through the mesh cage. "Should have done this long ago."

Rankin took the voucher, hesitating. "You figger your bosses back in Omaha's going to kick up a fuss?"

Toliver shook his head. "Don't expect them to. After all, they did hire you and you have every legal right to the money."

Rankin nodded his head, folded the voucher and stuffed it in his coat pocket.

Toliver grinned at the scout, "One other thing, Joe. You best get over to the bank and cash it this afternoon, just in case."

"I'll do just that," Rankin promised. He had his hand on the doorknob when Toliver called after him.

"Joe, I'm mighty sorry I didn't just give you the voucher earlier."

Rankin gave the young ticket master a begrudging smile. "Wish I could get the Army to admit their mistake and pay me as well."

For a long time after Rankin had left the depot, Grayson Toliver sat there staring out at the whiteness and wondering if tomorrow he would be out of a job for what he had just done. A sharp whistle shattered the silence and Toliver got up to slip into his heavy coat to greet the four-ten train. As he stepped into the blowing snow, Toliver made a professional note of the time. It was exactly four-oh-nine.

At four-eleven, Grayson Toliver no longer worked for the Union Pacific.

CHAPTER 13

I t was the time of the Swelling Moon, the *Mericatz* called it April. A time when the Winter Waiting for Spring was deep within the People. When the deep snow was slinking away from the earth, like Old Man Coyote. Already the high meadows were beginning to green while the Smoking Earth River, white with cold snowmelt, clawed its way through the valley where the *Nüpartka* had gathered their *carniva*.

The earth was slowly awakening to the new rhythms of life. The People could feel this new spirit, deep within themselves and soon they put aside the thoughts of hunger and cold experienced during the Hard Winter Moons.

It was also a time for quiet reflections, a time for listening to Spring, for the People waited for the first sounds of night thunder which would awaken the sleepy bear in its winter den and awaken the spirit of *quigat* in the People as well. The night thunder would signal the beginning of the spring hunts for the People, when the earth would be singing with new life. And the People of the *Nüpartka* would be singing along with the land.

Winter was dead, so too, part of the People, yet it was not good to think of these things for *iniputz*, the "ghosts of the dead," would draw close to the People if they were thought about too much.

It was into the thin, yet swelling sunshine, that Quinkent appeared from his *carniv* one day and stood with his blanket across his shoulders, looking out at Smoking Earth River where the swelling buds of alder and cottonwood were responding to the coming spring. Although the full face of the sun had barely cleared Sleepy Cat Peak to the east, a time when most of the men were still asleep in the warmth of their robes, Quinkent found the village a flurry of activity as men sat smoking in groups while their *piwáns* were busy preparing things for the coming spring hunt.

Quinkent could feel the excitement spreading up from the cool earth through the soles of his feet and into his heart. This familiar feeling was comforting to the old chief and he stood there a long time, unmoving, relishing the turning of time when the earth laughed with the People. Although Singing Grass was tending her cook fire only a few feet away, she did not intrude into her husband's thoughts.

Only when the spirit birds called to him from the greening reeds by the river did Quinkent stir from his position and approach his *piwán*.

Singing Grass smiled up at her husband, offering him a cup of weak coffee. Quinkent knelt beside the woman before taking the tin cup from her. Their eyes met.

"You feel it too, my husband?" Quinkent nodded, sipping the coffee. No further words were necessary between them, for it was the same feeling that all the People accepted and acknowledged as part of the unbroken circle of life given by *Sunáwiv*. Only Canávish could explain the bear-power that brought back the sun, shining and hot, each year. Yet the People knew too that Quinkent possessed similar power, for he too had talked with *Sunáwiv* during troubling times. That was why most of the old ones of the *Nüpartka* followed Quinkent as *tawacz viem*, and not Nicaagat, who was not even one of the People and some suspected was part *Mericatz* or Mexican. Yet the younger men of the People always made their *carniva* near Nicaagat.

After Quinkent had eaten his breakfast, he went off to see about his horses, of which he had over one hundred, leaving Singing Grass to continue her work with a new piece of deerskin. Quinkent had managed to shoot the mule deer three sleeps back.

Winter valley where the *Nüpartka* encamped for winter, was called Powell Park by the *Mericatz*. Located a dozen miles downriver from the White River Agency, this valley began where the Smoking Earth River shot through a narrow rock gateway nearly two miles in length and was a favorite place for the People to winter their horses since the weather was usually milder, with less snow. The low benchlands were covered with over ten thousand acres of good grass with a mixture of scrub oak and cedar.

Others were there as well checking on the condition of their own animals in anticipation of the coming spring hunts.

"*Maiquas*," a lean Indian said, walking past Quinkent with a rough-coated pinto in tow. Quinkent returned the greeting without really bothering to see who it was, although he felt sure the voice belonged to Pauvitz. His eyes instead were glued to his own horses now grazing up slope a few hundred yards above the river.

As he moved away from the river, up through the mixed cedar and oak, Quinkent found the air a bit cooler and he tugged the blanket he had fitted around his waist free and threw it across his shoulders, all the while observing his horses as he walked slowly through the herd. The shaggy little mountain-bred ponies had fared much better than the People, Quinkent observed, stopping here and there to feel or scratch one of his favorites. By Ute standards, Quinkent was a rich man considering the number of horses he owned. Only Canávish owned more.

He continued moving through the herd, keeping a sharp lookout for one deep-chested bay that had won much money from the *Mericatz* at last summer's races. The well-muscled little horse was not among the others and Quinkent climbed higher, beyond the scrub oak and cedar, into a brush-choked draw where he knew some of the horses came to get away from the howling winter winds that visited winter valley on occasion. Snow still clung to this protected lee, where the sun did not touch because of its southern trek across the sky.

Almost immediately, Quinkent flushed several horses from within the brushy draw and they loped into the open, their hoofs clattering loudly over the rocks. Two belonged to Nicaagat and a third to Canávish, a long-legged grey-coated horse with an unusually big head. Everyone thought the horse ugly and a great deal of fun was poked at Canávish for keeping the animal. Some thought that Canávish should sell the unfortunate horse to a *Mericatz* so neighboring bands would not think the *Nüpartka* were such poor judges of horses. Tatitz even offered his father one of his own horses if Canávish would only allow him to shoot the animal before he bred someone's good mare. It was a grand joke enjoyed by everyone in the village. But that had been before last summer's races. Now the men of the People no longer laughed, for other than Quinkent's bay, Canávish's ugly stallion won nearly every race and had made the shaman a lot of money from the *Mericatz*.

Afterward, the men of the People came to Canávish wanting to have their mares bred to this ugly horse who could run like the wind. It was Canávish who put on a face of serious study, saying he thought it might be a bad idea. Before long the People would have nothing but big-headed ugly horses and soon none of the other tribes would come to sell or swap their mounts any longer. The People could see the grand joke that Canávish was playing on them. Everyone laughed with the shaman for the *Nüpartka* loved a good joke most of all.

Quinkent stumbled into the rock-filled draw, beating the brush with a long stick he had picked up and calling out to the animal, yet keeping his rifle handy should he flush a deer out instead.

"Aheeee! Aheeee!" His high pitched calls reverberated across the land. After walking deep into the draw, Quinkent turned back, wishing now he had at least ridden one of his horses. He found himself breathing hard and tiring easily whenever he exerted himself. The years were catching up to him and he acknowledged the change with indifference. These things did not matter for he was still *tawacz viem* and as long as he held the position, Quinkent would work tirelessly for the good of the People. His health did not matter . . . only the People.

As he made his way back out of the rough draw, Quinkent thought again of Washington and whether they would send a bad agent this time to look after the People because of what they had done three Snow Moons ago. Would Washington be displeased enough that they would also send soldiers to punish those responsible? These were the kinds of things a *tawacz viem* should be properly concerned about, not worrying about the physical body.

As he edged away from the draw, a thunder of hoofs shook the ground and Quinkent stopped to watch several of the young men, whose job it was to watch over the herd for the People, sweep past, pushing a large number of horses further down river to a new grazing area. One of the youths, laughing wildly, waved to Quinkent as he thundered by him. Already the People had forgotten the numbing cold of winter and the pain of hunger. The night thunder was growing near; all the People could feel it. Quinkent could feel it even more so, standing here on the side of the low mountain. Down below, he had a clear view of the Smoking Earth River and the encampment. Automatically, Quinkent's eyes sought out his own *carniv* among the others. He saw his *piwán* busy scraping at something which he knew to be the deerskin. His eyes trailed further up river to a second set of *carniva* where those that followed Nicaagat lived. To show their differences, Nicaagat would not join the two camps as one. It was his way of saying to the People that he should be *tawacz viem*. To support this idea, a person needed to only look at the number of *carniva* in Nicaagat's camp and then Quinkent's for justification. Yet the People knew only Quinkent had the power to talk with *Sunáwiv*, not Nicaagat. For now things remained unchanged, yet Quinkent wondered how long he could last in the position if he didn't make Washington listen to the needs of the People. Perhaps, not long if the soldiers came once the passes were no longer blocked with deep snow. Perhaps, even sooner if the People listened to Nicaagat at the council of tribal elders today.

Quinkent breathed deeply of the clean cool air and knew he would rather die here in these mountains with the blue sky shining down all around him, than to be locked up on a little piece of land like the *Mericatz* had done to their plains enemies that lived on the flat land east of the mountains. All the People of the Ute bands had heard how sickness came to these people locked up in that place of red dirt and heat.

As Quinkent made his way back to his *carniv*, he knew that before he allowed this thing to happen to the People, he would join forces with Nicaagat and fight the *Mericatz*. Locked up on a little piece of poisoned land was to die a horrible death. With that thought in his mind, Quinkent stopped by his *carniv* to pick up his beaded pipe pouch and to slip on the special leather shirt Singing

Grass had made for him to wear at council meetings. Quinkent was proud of this colorful shirt with its rows of double crosses stitched across the upper breast, signifying the life symbol of the four winds. Among the colors on the shirt was the red for fire, the yellow for bright open sunlight, and the deep blue for the sky, all sacred colors of the People. The last thing Quinkent did before he left for the council was to place around his neck the beaded buckskin suncircles, that which is given from father to son, tied to a string of white weasel fur.

Singing Grass left the place by the fire where she had been working with the deerskin, coming over to Quinkent to lay her hands on his chest. Her dark eyes were like that of a doe, wet and open. She smiled up at him, smoothing his shirt as she did so.

"Tsashin says that Canávish will predict the time of the night thunder at the council meeting today." Tsashin was the *piwán* of Canávish.

"Unh," Quinkent grunted, his thoughts busy with the details he intended to present on how to deal with the *swerch* should they come to punish them for what they had done in Rawlings. All the People were afraid of the soldiers for they had strange customs and chased after their women. It was generally agreed that all *swerch* were crazy and should be avoided most of the time. Yet Nicaagat knew the soldiers and understood their ways, having scouted for the General of the North against their enemy, the Sioux. Perhaps, Quinkent considered, this was why some of the People rode with Nicaagat.

Quinkent left his rifle with Singing Grass and set off for the council meeting, being held in Canávish's *carniv*. It was the only neutral ground where Quinkent and Nicaagat would meet on equal footing. And since Canávish possessed the most powerful of the bear-medicine, as *m'sut t'quigat* of all the *Nüpartka*, it was proper to conduct such a council at his fire.

Quinkent entered Canávish's *carniv* quickly and turned to the right to take his place in the center of the circle, after their traditional greeting of, "*Maiquas.*"

To Quinkent's right sat Canávish while the big-bellied Colorow sat on his left. Nicaagat sat directly across from Quinkent, his beady black eyes seeing nothing, yet seeing everything all at once. Others around the council included Sowówic, Nicaagat's sub-chief, Pauvitz, brother-in-law to Ouray, and Yaminatz, who preferred to live with a small group of the People in the upper Bear River Country and had many friends among the *Mericatz* who had built houses at the stinking springs which they called Steamboat Springs. Present also, was Nativitz, the oldest of the People and now almost blind. Seldom did Quinkent or Nicaagat seek his advice anymore for his mind had become feeble and his words stirred up so, that nothing made sense. Yet he had a right to be there.

After a little while, Quinkent removed his pipe and filled it with tobacco. The others did likewise and soon the air inside the *carniv* was filled with pungent smoke as the men at the council fire blessed the four winds, mother earth and sky. Canávish offered up a prayer using a twisted piece of sage held over the center fire while its fragrance filled the lungs and hearts of those present.

A long silence ensued before Quinkent began to speak using the old language. As *tawacz viem*, it was Quinkent's place to talk first.

"I have been thinking of this thing we did three Snow Moons ago and why Washington will think it bad we took the gifts." Nicaagat stirred, rolled a cigarette with a piece of corn shuck and smoked it like a *Mericatz*. All the while, his black eyes never lifted from the center fire. It was not polite to stare at a man while he was speaking.

Quinkent paused, allowing his words to enter each man's head for the language of the old ones took time to hold near the heart before the truth could be fully understood.

"There was bad feelings between Washington and Danforth.

That is why he left, not because the People had done something bad. Perhaps, now, Washington will send us a new agent who will not treat the People good like all agents should because of this thing we did in Rawlings." Quinkent relit his pipe while he thought of his next words carefully.

"I think I must go to that place and send a message to Washington and tell them how the People suffered. That is what I think I should do. Then Washington will be happy with the People once more and send us a good agent. Maybe, Washington will see this agent has plenty of gifts so our children will no longer cry out in the night from hunger and the old ones will not die. Washington will see how it was wrong to send the *swerch* after us for taking the gifts. Were we not the ones who suffered the loss for this?" Quinkent asked, referring to Nicaagat's soldier, Sowepk, who was killed by one of the *swerch*.

Colorow let out a thunderous, "Unh!" Protocol was not one of Colorow's good points and interrupting a speaker was a known and accepted habit of his.

"This is all I have to say for now," Quinkent said.

Without waiting for the proper elapse of time when a man should be reflecting on what has been said, Colorow spoke up, his sad face grim and deeply lined.

"What you say is true. It is a good idea to talk with Washington, see that we get a good agent this time who will provide our rations like they should," Colorow said, thinking of his already empty belly, even though his *piwán* had fed him well at breakfast. "I will go talk with the soldiers at the fort as well so they will be our friends again."

"Unh," said, Pauvitz, followed by the old one, Nativitz. After this, silence returned to the *carniv* and the men smoked their tobacco for a while. When the proper time had passed, it was Canávish who chose to speak next.

"These words I hear are good and true for they are spoken from the heart, where all powerful medicine must come from if a man is to walk the path of true wisdom." As Canávish talked, he lit another piece of sage from the center fire and swirled it around over his head, first pointing to the sacred four winds as before.

"As is the way of the People, one man can not tell another what he must do for we are all guided by the vision we received from *Sunáwiv* during the time of our vision quest. Further, one man can not speak for another man, for that too is the way of the old ones who have gone before."

Next, Canávish took out some of his *pöorat*, the medicine tobacco, and lit the sacred pipe he kept for special councils. He offered it to each of the men around the fire and only after it had gone the full circle, did Canávish continue speaking.

"It is almost time once more to celebrate with *quigat, Mamaqui Mowats*, the Bear Dance. Like you, I too feel the spirit of Spring stirring in the blood. The spirit of *quigat* beats at my temples and squeezes the heart. I had a vision that only the People should participate in the *Mamaqui Mowats*. There has been much sadness among the People and *Sunáwiv* wishes the time to be one of reverence and prayer. Only the last day shall we celebrate in the traditional way, with feasting and laughter. With his stirring within me, *quigat* will soon awaken in his den. This is the time chosen for the night thunder to return to the Smoking Earth River," Canávish said simply.

Each man at the fire could not help but be moved by Canávish's powerful words and medicine and there was murmuring of "Unh," all around the fire. Even Nicaagat seemed visibly moved by the shaman's words. And now it was his turn to speak. Nicaagat wished it that way for the words that lingered longest beyond a council seemed to be those spoken last. This time he had important news that not even Sowówic, his sub-chief knew about, for Nicaagat had only learned of it two sleeps ago while he was visiting Peck's store down on Bear River.

Usually dressed in his scout's uniform issued to him by General Crook more than two winters ago, Nicaagat was now wearing traditional Ute clothing of buckskin and leggings, except for the silver metal he wore about his neck presented to him by President Johnson as a delegate to the Brunot Treaty Conference in Washington six winters past. Nicaagat was very proud of the metal, yet there were some among the People of the Utes who felt that nothing came of this treaty since a piece of their beloved mountains, the San Juans, were no longer theirs to hunt on any longer. Ouray was chiefly held responsible and for a time there was bitterness between the seven bands over this matter.

"The words gone before are all powerful and true," Nicaagat began. "But to talk with Washington will be useless. Their hearts are not like our hearts for they can not see beyond the stone buildings in which they hide all day. They do not see our suffering, nor care. They are too busy doing what the *Mericatz* calls, work. That is why we took what was rightfully ours. We harmed no one, except the dog that belongs to the *Mericatz* at the place where the train stops. This should be proof enough of our intentions to Washington, yet they send the *swerch* to teach us a lesson. And even though one of my best warriors died at their hands, they were still too weak to track us here in the mountains.

"And they still do not come even though the snows have lifted from the low passes. Nor will they for I have learned a new agent is being sent to look after the People."

Everyone was surprised and it showed. Even Quinkent's jaw dropped open at the news and he wanted very much to rush in and learn who this person was but he forced himself to remain quiet. Even though an old person has shorter days left on the earth, their patience was greater than the younger men. Quinkent closed his

161

mouth once he realized it had fallen open and he waited for the others to quiet down, while the blood beat hard inside his head.

Colorow let out another thunderous, "Unh!" at the news. Only Sowówic seemed upset by the news, and those at the council knew it was because Nicaagat failed to inform his sub-chief.

"Some of you may know this agent. He is the one who is responsible for the place the *Mericatz* calls Greeley. He is called Meeker and in one moon will come here to our country. The presents Washington has been holding for us in Rawlings will be given to this Meeker to bring with him. This I learned two sleeps ago from the *Mericatz* called, Peck."

Quinkent countered, seeing his status as *tawacz viem* slipping away further by the news that Nicaagat carried. He could see the delight in Nicaagat's small black eyes as he spoke, knowing he held something that only he knew.

"How can we believe this Peck. He is a *Mericatz* and everyone knows it is hard to understand when a *Mericatz* speaks and even harder to hold his words for very long." Quinkent knew these things were true as did everyone at the council, yet they also knew this Peck was an honest *Mericatz* who was a friend of the People. All Quinkent was trying to do was lessen the impact of Nicaagat's announcement, but he could see it wasn't going to work this time. A piece of his power had already gone away.

Nicaagat returned Quinkent's fire, looking him this time directly in the eyes.

"These things I have said are true. You are becoming more like an old woman, staying by the fire rather than seeing about the business of the People."

Quinkent was furious and was on his feet before he realized it. If he had brought along his rifle now, he would have shot the little dark-faced half-breed. Canávish stood up and placed his hand on Quinkent's shoulder to calm him.

"You spend more time with these *Mericatz* than any other, yet when Washington wants something, they talk to me. It is my name they know that Washington respects. I was not a willing party in giving away part of our mountains as you were. A *Nüpartka* would give up his life first." Quinkent had become desperate to hold on to his power and he was flinging everything he could at his adversary to downplay Nicaagat's importance at this council.

Nicaagat had gained his feet, as the others, except for old Nativitz, who seemed to not even know where he was or what was going on, only now he was mumbling incoherent words in a high-pitched voice. But the focus lay between Quinkent and Nicaagat.

"Soon your voice will mean nothing to Washington. Your time is passed, like a sigh lost to the spirit wind. And then you will no longer be *tawacz viem*." With that, Nicaagat abruptly left with Sowówic following close behind.

No one said anything. The council of tribal elders was over and Quinkent left feeling sick like a young colt who had eaten too much green grass in spring. His heart was heavy and right now all he wanted to do was stand by the river and listen to the spirit birds until everything inside and outside his world was made whole again. Yet when he thought of this new agent, Meeker, there was something he could not remember about this *Mericatz* that made him feel even sicker for his People. Perhaps, it would come to him as he listened to the spirit birds. They had never failed to soothe Quinkent once these bad feelings were deep inside him.

The others stood outside Canávish's *carniv*, discussing the unusual council that had just taken place. To end a council this way was not good, yet what was done could not be undone. They watched Quinkent disappear from sight behind a thick screen of naked alders. They stood there a long time, looking towards the river.

CHAPTER 14

The night thunder came as Canávish had predicted it would, occurring late in the night on the heels of a thin quarter moon now blanketed by heavy clouds. The thick clouds brought with the thunder a light sprinkling of wet snow that clung to their *carniva* like glue, yet the people of the *Nüpartka* were too excited and busy preparing for the upcoming *Mamaqui Mowats*, the Bear Dance, to take notice of the late spring snow.

The sun was moving higher in the southern sky each new day and warming the earth and the People. They could feel the movement of the earth and the bear as it tried to awaken from the long sleep of winter. It was the People's responsibility to make their own thunder so the bear would awaken and leave its den. The People had been performing this spiritual dance each year far longer than any of the old ones could remember. Each year, Canávish told the ancient story of how the Bear Dance came to the People. Even though the story was well known, it was good to hear it each Spring.

With the upcoming Bear Dance and Spring hunts occupying the men's thoughts as they came together in small groups to talk and smoke, the trouble at the last Council of Tribal Elders was quickly forgotten. The men knew how it was with Quinkent, how he liked to be called *tawacz viem,* how important it made him feel when his *Mericatz* name was sent to Washington. The men of Quinkent's *carniva* and Nicaagat's *carniva* knew these things, but did not mind for, other than Nicaagat, who wasn't really one of the People, it was not important so much to be called *tawacz viem.* Things usually righted themselves given time without the need of a chief and for as long as the *Nüpartka* lived in the most beautiful spot on earth and had plenty of good things to eat, there was really little need for a *tawacz viem.* So they let Quinkent continue being their leader if it suited his needs. Right now they were happy again with the land and soon there would be plenty of meat at the campfires to fill even the oldest of the village. But before that could happen, the Bear Dance must be performed.

While the *piwáns,* little children and old men on feeble legs began gathering new spring foliage and brush from the banks of the river and hillsides in preparation of Bear Dance, Quinkent would leave his blankets early, preferring his own company to the other men. He developed wild mood swings, happy with his *piwán* one minute and plummeting her the next over the slightest perceived wrongdoing. The men knew Quinkent would not stay mad for very long for there was too much happiness among the People during the season of Spring Thunder.

During this time, as the *avinkwep,* the cave of sticks, began to take shape and grow high with cedar limbs, men gathered on blankets nearby to play games with the *Mericatz* cards while others formed long lines along a log to play the old hand game, *nia*, chanting and beating their sticks against the log, while each man kept sharp eyes open for the man who held the marked stick. Nearby, young men of the village raced their ponies on Canávish's race track where fine possessions were won and lost.

Even the *piwáns* found time away from preparing the great feast which was to follow Bear Dance, to form little knots of monte games. During this time, the People played furiously now, for there would be no games during Bear Dance.

The bushes rattled with giggling young girls as they found willing partners after having plucked the man's blanket. A man was required to stay with the woman throughout the Bear Dance. Some stayed together only a little while beyond the dance while others were together through many snows.

It was during this time when the life and spirit of the People were slowing turning inward to the *avinkwep*, that a woman and child appeared before Canávish's *carniv* bearing the sign of *Quigat*. Canávish packed his medicine bundle and with his *piwán*, Tsashin, was gone for five sleeps with the woman whose husband was very sick. When they returned, Canávish was thin and very tired. *Pöwá'a*, the tiny green man who carries the healing power inside a *m'sut t'quigat*, must draw strength from the body, and the medicine singing will always leave a man tired. Tsashin had stayed by Canávish throughout the difficult days and nights of singing and caught the sickness when it came out of the man and slapped it to death, as the *piwán* of a *m'sut t'quigat* must do. Canávish's medicine had been very strong for the man was already out of his blankets and planning a hunt. Such was the medicine of Canávish and the People of the Smoking Earth River were proud the shaman had such power over sickness and evil spirits.

Slowly, as the earth continued to warm itself by the growing sun, the games came to a halt and the men began to construct the *avinkwep* under the watchful eyes of Canávish. First, the men were ordered to construct the "cave" by facing the wide opening of the *avinkwep* toward the afternoon sun in the southwest, for that is the direction in which a bear chooses to face his den so part of the sun will shine into it each day.

As the *avinkwep* began to take shape, other *carniva* of the People, who had been elsewhere during the winter, began turning up on Smoking Earth River. As the *carniva* grew, so did the intensity of the People.

At one end of the *avinkwep,* a group of men dug a round hole and when the hole was deep enough, the men reached with their hands into the hole and scooped out a small cave. When this was done, the singers came with a basket which they placed upside down, closing the entrance to the little cave.

The word went out to the People and soon the men and women of the *Nüpartka* began gathering, forming long lines inside the *avinkwep,* with the men on one side and the women on the other.

Quinkent and his *piwán,* Singing Grass, were the last ones to arrive. Quinkent's thoughts were still preoccupied with Nicaagat's attempt to undercut his authority as *tawacz viem* in the eyes of the People, but he soon forgot such bad thoughts once the singers entered the *avinkwep* carrying the *w'ni thokunup,* a long notched stick, shaped like a jawbone of a great animal. One end of the *w'ni thokunup* was placed on top of the basket, with the other end in a player's lap. The People waited in silence while the player settled himself by the basket. Taking a smaller stick, he rubbed up and down on the *w'ni thokunup,* creating the little thunder sounds that spread deep into the constructed cave, spreading further over the awakening land and rumbling spring air.

The songs of the other singers closed around the first thunder and Bear Dance began.

The line of women moved forward with the throbbing music,

halting before their partners, and then they moved backward two steps. The men followed, carefully covering the spot from where his partner's foot had been withdrawn.

The two lines glided backward and forward three steps with the men pawing the air like bears as they did so. As they drew near, Singing Grass smiled up at her husband who smiled back at his *piwán* as the lines came together and parted. Like the bear who was now awakening from the first thunder of the *avinkwep*, Quinkent felt his old spirit returning to him.

The *machutagogenta*, the two old men whose job it was to keep the lines straight kept a sharp look out for a misstep, cracked a stick against the legs of a man or woman who got out of line. Each time this happened, a great shout of laughter filled the *avinkwep*.

At the end of the dance, the bears were stirring and trying to awaken in their dens and all the dancers went to their *carniva* for quiet talk for there would be no feasting or games this day.

Quinkent spent a long time by the center fire, smoking quietly and barely speaking to Singing Grass, preferring to think of today's Bear Dance as a new start for the People. So far the Spring hunts had been good and many of the young men had killed their share of deer. Huge chunks of red meat sat simmering on the cook fires and none of the People had gone to bed hungry since night thunder. The hot words exchanged at the council meeting had been pushed aside for now. When the warm days of late Spring came, bringing with it this new agent, then perhaps, Quinkent would call another council and have something important to say like Nicaagat had done.

Singing Grass came over to his side and wordlessly began rubbing his wind-chapped hands and face with the skunk oil from a leather pouch she carried in her bundle of household goods. There was nothing better for soothing raw flesh and Quinkent closed his eyes while his *piwán* performed her ministrations on his skin. The oil was vaguely pine-scented and it reminded him of a spruce-fir thicket in early summer when the air is filled with the aroma of the high country.

"You have stood too long by the river today," Singing Grass chided quietly. "Even your lips are peeling." She applied a thin coating before he could say much. Quinkent opened his eyes and looked at his *piwán*. She gave him a smile as she continued to gently rub his red flesh.

Without meaning too, Quinkent found himself speaking of this new agent, Meeker and the release of their annuities.

"Tsashin spoke to me of this." Quinkent felt somewhat disappointed, yet realizing that by now, the whole village must know these things.

"This agent is the one who made a town where before there was only sagebrush. Now there are many *Mericatz* living in this place called Greeley. They cut open the earth with shining knifes and grow strange plants. I saw these things more than five winters ago."

Singing Grass nodded, putting away the skunk oil. "Perhaps, this agent will be good to the People and we will get our presents from Washington like before."

"We will see in time. As soon as a good agent starts doing all the things the People wants this agent to do, Washington takes him away," Quinkent said sadly, thinking of the burly Charlie Adams. Adams and Quinkent had become good friends after Adams nursed Sowówic back to health from a case of blood poisoning after shooting himself while rabbit hunting. That was the same cold winter Adams delivered a number of Ute babies in the warmth of the Agency office. Quinkent also remembered how Ouray had lured Adams away to be the agent at Los Pinos.

Quinkent shook his head, perplexed. He did not understand Washington at times. Why did they not make Uriah Curtis their agent? Curtis, all Utes loved. Quinkent said nothing of this bitter disappointment to Singing Grass.

The People gathered the next morning as they had the first day, except the dancing continued all day. The dancers were a bit more relaxed, even when some of them got out of line or missed a step. Nobody really cared, for the thunder of Bear Dance had now awakened the sleeping bear in his den and he could see, feel and hear what the People were saying. It was during the late afternoon dance that Pauvitz tripped over one of his feet and fell heavily to the hard-packed earth.

The music and dancing stopped immediately and Pauvitz remained where he had fallen, unmoving. Quickly, Canávish came over to Pauvitz with the *w'ni thokunup* and stick to drive away the bad spirits that had caused his fall. Canávish made motions with the instrument to push the evil out of his feet and chase it off towards the sky. Once done, the singing and dancing started again, with Pauvitz taking his place in the line across from his *piwán,* who made a face at him.

Once the dancing was over for the second day, the People were very tired and the center fires in the *carniva* did not burn late that night.

On the third and final day of Bear Dance, the festivities started at daybreak. Rather than go immediately to the *avinkwep,* Quinkent strayed down to the river, feeling the soreness in his legs that always came during Bear Dance. Except this time, the pain pushed up his back and left him feeling really old. As he searched the reeds in the dawning light for the spirit birds, Quinkent thought of how strong Nicaagat danced, even at the end of yesterday. Even now he could feel the tremblings in the earth beneath his beaded moccasins as the dancers started up once more.

Perhaps, he would dance a little later, but no matter what, Quinkent knew he must participate in the night dance—the finest part of Bear Dance. The People must see him dancing and know that he was still powerful and strong. Someone to lead the People as *tawacz viem*.

At sunset, the dancing and singing stopped. As they rested, the People ate a meal. Afterward, all those who had danced and sung during the three days gathered in the *avinkwep*. Huge fires were lit and the dancers made a large circle. Having awakened the bears, who now wandered the forests for food and a mate, the bear spirit was strong once more in the People.

Quinkent became part of the circle with the other men while the women made up the other half of the circle, facing them across the great fire. The great circle of the *Nüpartka* waited in silence and soon Canávish rose from his place and came forward to tell of the ceremony that was yet to come. The People listened carefully so they would know exactly what to do.

Canávish gave a stack of corn husks and his bag of *pöorat*, his medicine tobacco, to the one who played the *w'ni thokunup*. The player chanted a prayer to Sunáwiv, rolled a cigarette and passed the husks and *pöorat* to the next singer in line. After all the singers had offered a prayer and rolled a cigarette, there was a long silence. The prayer was then chanted once again by all the singers together, after which, they lit their cigarettes and blew the smoke to the sky.

Quinkent did as the others and when the dancing resumed, he danced as never before, strong and sure in each step. Twice that night, Canávish filled the handsome beaded pipe with sweet-smelling kinnikinnick leaves, lit the bowl and passed it all around. Each dancer took three puffs, rubbing his fingers over the pipe as though making music from it, and blew the smoke to the sky to ward off sickness that might enter a dancer's chest.

On the following day, when the sun stood at its full height, the dancing stopped. Bear Dance was over and the great feast began.

Quinkent sat before the fire with others in his band as his *piwán* served him food. Their eyes met and Quinkent let it be known ever so slightly that he was pleased with Singing Grass. She smiled, moving away to serve the others, leaving Quinkent to think about his first Bear Dance and how as a young man he had gone with this girl to her father and mother and had drunk from the same cup with her. Many of the young men would do the same tonight. Only then could the young man and girl become *piwán* to each other.

This was also the time for old mates to make new ones and once the drinking cup was passed between them, they went away to make their own *carniva*. Quinkent had made many *carniva* over his lifetime. Even now, near the edge of his village, lived his first *piwán*. Since Singing Grass, he rarely visited there anymore, although he continued to provide her food and other necessities.

Quinkent's thoughts turned to the breaking apart of the village following Bear Dance. The men left to form hunting camps, sometimes great distances to the north with their neighbors, the Shoshoni, to hunt buffalo while other camps spread east into the frowning plains where the enemies of the People once lived. Now the People were free to roam and hunt at will across these lands.

Then a sadness entered Quinkent's heart as he thought of this new agent. Would the agent want to force the People to live on little pieces of land where a man could not breathe clean air and hunt whenever they desired? This agent found his way into Quinkent's head without his even thinking about him now that Bear Dance was finished. It was not something Quinkent liked to hold too long in his head and so close to the heart.

Canávish came to sit next to Quinkent and Singing Grass quickly brought the shaman a plate of food. Quinkent was glad for the company for it took away the bad thoughts. Only, Canávish's words brought them back again.

"What do you know of this agent?" the shaman asked, with his mouth full of food.

"I know nothing," Quinkent responded after a long moment of trying to think again just what it was that bothered him about Meeker. In the end he could say nothing against the agent.

"Did you not tell Washington it was Curtis we wanted as agent?" Canávish pressed.

"I sent my words," Quinkent said simply, the bad feelings having returned. Both Quinkent and Canávish knew that as *tawacz viem*, Washington should have listened, but didn't and a little piece of Quinkent's power was therefore, taken away again. Quinkent could admit this to Canávish for the shaman was part of the *carniva* that made up that band of People who resided on the Smoking Earth River and not on the Little Snake with Nicaagat. Both men knew if they were to survive as a People, it would take great care and patience when dealing with the *Mericatz*. Canávish said nothing more while the two men finished their meal. The silence ended between them once their pipes were lit. As the gray smoke escaped from Canávish's mouth, he began to speak again.

"You must talk with this agent and teach him the ways of the People. That we do not want to do *Mericatz* work. That we do not want to farm or raise the *Mericatz* cattle. We only want to live in peace and go on hunts and race our horses. Only then will Washington not have to send any more agents."

"Unh!" Quinkent grunted, blowing a huge cloud of smoke upward into a night littered with frozen-white stars. He had been thinking of this new agent more each day and the fact that the soldiers had not come to Smoking Earth River as Nicaagat had said they would not. Perhaps, he and this agent would become good friends like Adams or Curtis. Perhaps, he should ride down to this *Mericatz* store on Little River and see for himself. Maybe Charlie Lowery would tell him more than Peck had told Nicaagat. And then he would be the one with important news for the People. Yes, tomorrow he would ride down there to this store. Besides, he could use a little fixed ammunition before he started off on his own Spring hunt now that Bear Dance was over.

Quinkent liked being *tawacz viem* as much as Canávish liked being *m'sut t'quigat.*

CHAPTER 15

Nathan Meeker descended from the Union Pacific early on a May day, full of excitement, purpose and promise. With him was William Post, the former Secretary for the Union Colony of Greeley, who had returned from Yonkers, New York at Meeker's request to work at White River as Agency Clerk. In his mid-forties, Post was more than willing to return to Colorado since he was having wife troubles and the stationary store he operated was boring him to tears.

After an all-night train ride west from Cheyenne, Meeker squinted against the early morning sunshine, yet finding the cool air both bracing and invigorating in spite of the ugly huddle of board shacks and warehouses that represented Rawlings. Post joined him on the platform sporting a rueful smile.

177

"Don't think we'll be spending much time in such a perfectly drab place."

"Correct you are, William," Meeker added, looking around with perfect disdain. "Shall we find the livery and see to the agency stock and wagon? I should like to be free of this place by early sunrise."

"Amen to that," Post added, picking up their bags and following Meeker the short walk down Front Street into town. For a small town, there seemed to be a lot of activity, mused Meeker, observing Chinese miners eating noodles on every street corner. When he stopped to ask one the direction of the livery, the man simply bowed, giving Meeker a huge smile. Meeker and Post continued walking until they found themselves outside of Foote's Saloon. Both men stopped and looked at each other.

Meeker pushed through the door and found the saloon amazingly quiet and rather clean. Several men sat at nearby tables and they watched with curious faces as Meeker and Post stepped up to the bar. Little Van, the cross-eyed bartender moved away from a table he had been serving and came around the bar to take their orders.

"Good day, sir. We wish to ask directions of the livery in this town," Meeker spoke up before Little Van could ask for their orders. The cross-eyed bartender with his black hair slicked back tightly to his scalp looked the pair over for a minute before answering.

"Three blocks down, on the left. I'm Little Van. You gents new in town?" Little Van asked, already knowing the answer.

"Just disembarked from the morning train."

Little Van nodded saying, "The eight-ten."

"Pardon?"

"I said that's the eight-ten train."

"Oh," Meeker replied, not really knowing what else to say. "I'm Nathan Meeker, newly appointed White River Agent and this is my clerk, William Post."

Little Van's eyes opened wide, causing his crossed eyes to seem even more crossed. Meeker was reminded of the fellow who joked he once knew a man who was so cross-eyed, he could see both Sundays. Meeker suspected that Little Van's affliction had to be nearly as extensive.

"You don't say. We been expecting you. Get you gents anything to drink?"

Meeker looked at Post for a moment before smiling. "We are rather hungry, but I'm afraid neither Mister Post nor myself drink."

"Shucks, ain't no problem here. How about I have the cook fix you some steak and gravy with biscuits? That sound okay?"

"Why that sounds just fine, Mister Van."

"Folks around here just call me Little Van," the diminutive bartender responded with a smile. "You fellars grab a table and I'll tell the cook."

Meeker and Post dumped their luggage at a scarred table that looked battle worn. Before they had taken their seats, Little Van was back with a pot of coffee and two cups. He poured them full and set the pot down on the table.

"You have your work cut out for you, Mister Meeker," Little Van said, wiping his hands on his apron. "Those Indians have been pretty restless this past winter. Can't much blame them though, seeing's how they were near starving."

"How's that?" Meeker asked.

A dark-faced, long-haired companion seated quietly at the next table spoke up for Little Van. "Utes broke into the warehouse last winter and helped themselves to supplies."

"This is Johnny Red Shirt," Little Van interjected. "He has been known to take a horse or two when they appeared to be abandoned." Johnny Red Shirt grinned broadly, exposing even, white teeth.

"That must be the incident I read about back east. It could hardly be called stealing since it was their own annuities they were after,"

Post spoke up. Meeker frowned slightly at Post's comments. He could see he would have to educate Post on the rights and wrongs where Indians were concerned. Stealing was stealing, no matter the reason. It was those self-educated people back east that had no idea the situation decent folks were having to endure because of the Ute problem.

"Good morning, gentlemen," a dignified individual in planters hat and white suit said, as he attempted to make a grand entrance, coming to a halt before Meeker's table.

"How you doin', Doc?" Little Van asked Doctor Ricketts, the Baltimore physician who preferred the seedy life in Rawlings and morphine over respectability back east.

"Quite well, sir," Ricketts returned, giving the bartender an exaggerated bow.

"Doc Ricketts, meet Nathan Meeker, come to straighten out the Utes on White River," Little Van said. "And this is his clerk, Billy Post." Doc Ricketts swept his hat from his graying head with a flourish while Post was tempted to explain to their new acquaintances that he preferred being called William and not Billy. He hated the name. In the end, he remained quiet.

"Ah, Mister Meeker, you are a brave soul, indeed. Never would I venture so far into the wilderness surrounded by such heathens."

Meeker allowed a smile to play across his lips. "I don't think either myself or Mister Post has anything to fear from these Utes."

"I do hope you are right, Mister Meeker, I do hope you are right," Doc Ricketts said, leaving them to weave his way through the saloon and to the rear where several Chinese had a smoke shop sat up.

Little Van shook his head, "A pure waste of talent."

"Oh?" Meeker asked.

"For a fact. Old Doc Ricketts been hooked on morphine for several years now. Been going down hill ever since and his health shows it."

The cook brought them a breakfast of tough steak and thick, greasy gravy. The meal went down hard for Meeker, yet he consumed it all, not one to waste money. Post did the same without complaint.

Afterward, they found Joe Rankin's livery just where Little Van said it would be and Meeker introduced himself and Post to the stocky scout.

"Expect you come for the agency wagon and team?" Rankin asked, after looking the new agent over carefully.

"I was told we would have a driver for the wagon who knew how to get to White River," Meeker said.

"Joe Collom. He's down at France's buying a few supplies for himself. Be along directly."

"How well does he know that country and the Indians?" Post spoke up, picking his teeth with a shaved splinter from the side of Rankin's livery.

"Better than most. Joe's gone to ranching near the Ute Reservation. He'll do right by you," Rankin said. Rankin took them around to the side of the livery to check the wagon and to show them the four agency mules he had been feeding ever since Danforth drove them over from White River with his things.

"Been caring for these mules now for eight months, not to mention providing storage for the agency wagon," Joe Rankin said, sizing up the new agent.

A slight smile lifted the corners of Meeker's mouth and he came directly to the point.

"How much does the Indian Bureau owe for this service?"

Rankin pushed his hat back on his head, exposing thinning black hair to the bright sun and quickly came to a decision.

"Three hundred dollars ought to cover it." Rankin thought of Blacky Stillwell and his venture into extortion. Rankin was prepared to settle for less than half that amount.

"Come around to the hotel, Mister Rankin and I'll see you get a voucher for that amount," Meeker said without batting an eye. "Of course, I'll need you to sign a paper saying you accept this payment in full for the services rendered."

"Be glad to," Rankin replied, his spirits soaring. A slender youth came out of the stable with a wheelbarrow of manure which he dumped on a huge pile out behind the livery.

Rankin waved him over once he had emptied the load. Rankin turned to Meeker.

"Want you to meet my associate." Rankin clapped the younger man on the shoulder. "Gray, this is the new agent for them White River Utes, Nathan Meeker. And his clerk, Bill Post. Gentlemen, this is Grayson Toliver, of late the dispatcher for the Union Pacific for Rawlings."

"Is there more money to be made working a livery than as dispatcher?" Meeker asked, faintly curious.

Grayson Toliver gave the men a quick smile and dropped his sunburned face to the ground. He reeked of horse manure and his clothes were rough cut from cheap cloth. Gone were the suits he had worn everyday to work as railroad clerk and dispatcher.

"No sir," Toliver said quietly. And then he looked Meeker in the eye. "I was fired."

"Oh." There was a detectable note of disapproval in Meeker's voice. As he had done throughout most of his life, Meeker was too quick to pass judgement on anyone before all the facts were in. Today was no exception.

"Hold on now," Rankin said. "Mister Toliver, here, was let go suddenly and without just cause." Rankin told the agent of the Ute affair and how the young dispatcher had stuck by his guns and paid Rankin for providing scout. "The Union Pacific bigwigs didn't cotton to all the bad publicity this little affair created in the newspapers and Congress back east. Naturally, they looked around for the scapegoat nearest the fire."

"How unfortunate," Meeker responded, with feigned sympathy.

"So you see, I kinda feel responsible fer the boy gettin' into trouble in the first place. I can't pay him much but it's steady work and honest." Rankin gripped Toliver's shoulder for a moment before sending him on his way.

"You'll be happy to know, Mister Rankin, I have seen to it the supplies and annuities in storage have been released and it is my intention to load the wagon with as much as it will carry before we start out in the morning."

Rankin smiled ruefully. "Expect old Quinkent and his followers could have used them a lot more three months back when they were still fightin' the cold. You can guess what Toliver would say about it considering he's the one lost his job."

"I did what I could as quickly as I could, Mister Rankin. My appointment was approved by Congress less than two months ago, so you see it would have been impossible for me to affect any change last winter."

"Oh, I wasn't blamin' you. It's that danged railroad's fault fer not handlin' it like they should. Ain't lost no love over them Utes, but starvin' a man is the worst kind of death, even fer them."

Joe Collom rounded the corner of the barn with the sawed-off James France in tow. Again, Rankin did the honors, introducing Meeker and Post to the two men.

Meeker didn't seem all that pleased at first with Collom's slight appearance. Collom didn't strike the agent as someone rough enough to be ranching in the wilderness with the likes of savage Indians. Collom was an Englishman, who together with his brother, had sailed across the Atlantic four years earlier and headed west as soon as their feet touched shore.

James France wasted no time in launching into a diatribe about how badly he was losing money on the Interior contracts he held for hauling supplies to the White River Agency at three dollars and a half per hundred pounds. Meeker was taken back by the little bug of a man's tale of woe. Meeker noted, with a disapproving look, the tobacco-stained full beard the little man proudly displayed for Meeker's benefit.

"The Utes are spoiling for any reason to fight and you can't blame them. They damned near starved last winter."

"I've already seen to it the release of the twenty-five thousand pounds of goods and annuities," Meeker interjected when the little man paused to catch his breath. It took part of the wind from his sails, but only momentarily.

"Everything's been out of kilter since before Danforth took over from Littlefield in '74. Danforth didn't have a lick of luck teaching them Utes how to farm and live in houses. To top that, a bunch of 'em rode off to join up with General Crook to fight the Sioux with Captain Jack leading the bunch. Now Jack is a wise one to watch, so be on guard. He knows the language and understands more of the white man's ways than any other Ute, except Ouray. Jack don't favor any peace plan and I'm not sure how much you can hope to change things. Both Douglas and Jack voted for Uriah Curtis as their agent. Hell, Curtis is practically a Ute himself and not liable to push them in any direction other than the one they want to go. They won't like you taking his place, so if you was smart, you and Mister Post would catch the next UP headed east and forget about White River." France took a deep breath. Meeker stared at the little man who was breathing hard from his lecture. A faint trace of irritation played across the agent's face.

"I assure you, I intend to bear down on these Indians and will show them how they all can become rich by farming and raising cattle. Hunting will soon be a thing of the past."

Both France and Rankin's jaw dropped open. Rankin spoke first.

"Ain't noway you gonna get them Utes to give up hunting and settle down fer diggin' in the ground."

Meeker smiled as if listening to an errant child. "Through love, faith and patience, I believe with my experience as head of the Union Colony of Greeley, it will not take long to teach them the wonders of providing for their own independence by accepting our ways of living."

Rankin shook his head and started for the livery. He had heard enough to know that the Interior Department, in their infinite wisdom, had somehow managed to send yet another inexperienced agent to White River. As usual there was never any thought given to trying to understand Ute ways and customs. In this matter, Rankin sided for once with the little firebrand, James France. White River was a keg of black powder, set to go off and Meeker just might be the lit fuse that would send the whole mess up in smoke.

Meeker and Post had finished breakfast the next morning before daylight flooded the vast emptiness. Together, they made their way up Front Street to the Union Pacific depot only to find the door locked. Meeker couldn't help but feel a tiny bit of exasperation.

"I thought the dispatcher was going to be here at six," Post said, shivering in the cold air of early morning. Red streaks to the east marked the location where the sun would eventually come up from the Red Desert floor.

"Did," Meeker replied in a clipped voice. Behind them the rattle of an empty wagon turned them around. It was young Joe Collom, expertly handling the reins of the four black mules with steam issuing from flared nostrils. Collom brought them to a halt before the two men.

"Morning, gentlemen," Joe said, jovially. Both Meeker and Post returned his greeting, standing there with their shoulders hunched against the cold in the dim light of morning.

"Have you by any chance seen Haywood Grant, the dispatcher?" Meeker asked.

"Why no, at least since late yesterday. You want me to go on and pull the wagon down to the warehouse?"

"Guess so," Meeker said, wondering how long they should wait for the UP man. He had plans to be well out of town by full daylight. Now he wasn't so sure.

"I'll ride over with you," Post said, coming around the wagon to pull himself up on the seat next to Collom.

"Be over directly," Meeker promised. He watched the wagon pull away from the depot and ease across the UP tracks and the hundred yards down to the warehouse.

Meeker was startled by the flare of a yellow light from inside the depot. He stepped to the door and knocked. A minute later, Haywood Grant opened the door looking red-eyed and tired.

"Thought I heard a wagon," he mumbled to Meeker. Slept over last night 'cause I knew you wanted to get an early start." He stood there holding a lamp in one hand and the door with the other. "Please come in, sir."

"Only for a minute," Meeker explained, "Collom and Post are over at the warehouse waiting to load up."

Grant sat the lamp down on his desk, scratching himself and looking a little lost. "Gotta find my shoes . . . build a fire."

Meeker's impatience bubbled over. "Suppose you give me the key to the warehouse and I'll have my men start loading the wagon."

Grant squinted at Meeker through sleep-puffed eyes. In his midforties, Haywood Grant had the looks of someone who had led a troubled and rough existence before coming to Rawlings. His deeply etched face was the color of pale pastry. Meeker found himself wondering if the man ever got outside in the sun much.

"Can't do that, Mister Meeker." Grant had turned to throw a piece of stove wood in on a crumpled up newspaper. Opening the damper, he lit a match and quickly closed the lid once the paper caught.

"I don't understand," Meeker said.

"Simple." Grant looked around the room for his boots and spied them beneath his desk. He fished them out and started to put them on after sitting down. "I got to account for every item that goes out of that warehouse. What's more, you got to sign for it."

"Why that's absurd!" Meeker fumed openly now, seeing how the dispatcher was making poor progress in getting underway.

"Might be to you, but I got my orders."

"Those goods have been released to me," Meeker almost shouted. "I got the signed signatures to prove it in my bags back at the hotel."

"Still don't cut no ice with me. I'm accountable until everything has been removed. The last dispatcher didn't do that and was fired."

"That so. Sounded more like to me the Union Pacific laid the blame of this whole Ute annuity affair on the young man's doorstep."

"Think what you like, but ain't no supplies going outta that warehouse 'til I got the *t*'s crossed and the *i*'s dotted. Them's my orders."

Streaks of fire raced across the gun-metal sky, expanding and coalescing until the gray was finally blotted out. Through the distant haze of early morning, the three men standing next to the warehouse watched as a sliver of molten orange lifted above the desert floor.

"That's what I like about the West," Joe Collom said to the others. "We've nothing to compare this to back home." Tight-lipped and angry, Meeker was in no mood to appreciate the beauty of a Wyoming sunrise just now. It had been well over half an hour since Meeker walked over to the warehouse and still Haywood Grant had not put in an appearance.

Post was under no such self-imposed time schedule and he commented for both of them on how wonderful the sunrises were back in Greeley.

"You miss home?" Post asked the young Englishman.

"There are times I do, but mostly I stay too busy enjoying my ranch and hunting in the mountains to let it bother me that much."

"About time," Meeker interjected. All eyes shifted to the figure who came out of the depot and crossed the tracks with a clipboard tucked beneath his arm. The group fell silent.

Haywood Grant walked past the waiting men and unlocked the heavy padlock without saying a word.

"Friendly cuss, ain't he?" Post whispered to Collom.

"Grayson Toliver was much more likeable and social. It's a pity the Union Pacific fired him over something that was not his doing," Collom whispered back as they closed in on the open doorway.

It was much colder in the warehouse than it was outside. Grant found a lantern and lit it.

"Place stinks," Post commented.

"More like rotting food," Meeker said, feeling the anger rising again in him.

Grant held the lantern over his head and the light fell across the scattered boxes of supplies and foodstuffs. Surprised by the light, large rats squeaked their displeasure at being interrupted and scurried to darker corners.

"Knew I smelled rats," Joe Collom said.

Meeker's eyes blazed in the light of the lantern.

"You worried about signing for the goods we remove from here while half the supplies have been lost to rot or damaged by rats to the point they are not useable!" His thin body shook with fury. Haywood Grant seemed to shrink behind the lantern he was holding.

Meeker turned to Post and Collom. "I want this place inventoried. Every box, every sack examined and usable contents recorded. I intend to file a complaint against the Union Pacific through Secretary Carl Schurz, for mishandling government supplies and annuities."

"It was this way when I got here," Grant finally said from behind the lantern, trying to distance himself from any fallout.

"This is gonna take hours," Post warned.

"So be it," Meeker snapped. "I want a full accounting."

"I ain't gonna stay in this stink hole for hours while you go through mountains of this stuff. I got the eight-ten to worry about," Grant bawled.

"Then I suggest that *you*, sir, attend to railroad business while we see to the government's." Meeker's voice was edged with ice and tight with anger.

In the end, Meeker and company was delayed leaving Rawlings until early afternoon, but Meeker had gotten the full list of damaged or destroyed goods and the amount was significant. Before they left, Meeker had sent a full report to Secretary Schurz and purchased a new lock for the warehouse. Next, he deposited the key with James France and instructed the little trader to begin shipments to White River, commencing in three days until all the annuities had been cleaned out of the Union Pacific warehouse.

When Haywood Grant found out about the new lock he was furious and threatened to have the blacksmith cut it off. He settled down rather quickly once Meeker waved a wire beneath his nose, instructing him to take charge of the government property as he saw fit without interference from anyone.

Even so, Haywood Grant's face was as dark as a threatening storm as he watched the loaded wagon roll slowly out of town. What made him even madder was that Meeker refused to sign his bill of laden showing the original pounds of freight shipped.

CHAPTER 16

Major Tip Thornburgh surveyed his bleak surroundings from the railroad platform with a raw wind whipping at his pants. Lida was busy seeing to their belongings and instructing Private O'Malley on how he should load the wagon, while keeping a sharp eye on the children.

"Know it looks rather harsh, sir," Lieutenant Samuel Cherry said, "but give it time. This desert country takes on a beauty all its own."

The merest of smiles slipped across Thornburgh's mutton-chopped face. He turned to face his adjutant. Cherry was a young West Pointer who walked with a slight limp from once having a half-ton cannon fall on him, rather than his friend. From Indiana, Cherry was well liked by the troops and seemed always to have a ready smile for anyone, no matter the circumstance.

Thornburgh lifted his eyes to the half circle of sand ridges that offered some protection from the incessant wind. These ridges were as ugly and oppressive as the aging post. But Thornburgh, like Cherry, was able to see beyond the obvious ugliness of the place. He saw it as a wise career step that would advance him to Colonel, and when General Crook closed Fort Steele as he said he would, he had promised to transfer Thornburgh to another fort where he could have a little adventure. From there, Thornburgh was sure the path would be clear for him to rise to general . . . if he didn't go and get himself killed. Until then, Thornburgh fully intended to take advantage of the surrounding mountains and do some fishing and hunting.

"Oh, I don't think it's all that bad, Sam," Thornburgh replied, his eyes taking in the distant Medicine Bows. As he said this, Private O'Malley came puffing up, stopped before Thornburgh and Cherry, and snapped a smart salute.

"The wagon's loaded, Major. I've taken the liberty of helping Mrs. Thornburgh and the children on board." The two officers returned his salute.

"Thank you, Private —?"

"O'Malley, sir. Your orderly."

"Yes, well I expect it will take a little time to get a handle on everyone's name."

"Excuse me, Major, but I couldn't help overhearing you asking about the fishing around here from Lieutenant Cherry."

"Yes?"

"Well, sir, I know of a few good places I use to take Major Thomas, down in the Sierra Madres."

Thornburgh's eyes lit up. "Fishing good?"

"The best I've ever seen, Major. Nobody's fished there so far as I know, but Thomas."

"Very good, O'Malley. Expect we'll find out as soon as we are settled in." O'Malley looked ready to bust as he drove the loaded wagon and Thornburgh's family to the post while the Major rode into the fort on a beautiful red sorrel that Cherry had brought out for him.

"Captain Payne, your subcommander, is waiting to receive you at post headquarters," Sam Cherry informed Thornburgh.

"Anything noteworthy I should know about Payne?"

Sam Cherry grinned, "Scotty's a good officer, Major. Served under him at Fort D.A. Russell before taking this assignment."

"Sounds fine to me."

"There is one thing, Major."

"What's that?"

"Captain Payne's health is not all that good."

"How so, Sam?"

"Scotty went through some rough times back during the Chief Joseph campaign. Got pneumonia. Winters in Montana can be mighty rough. Spent six months in Paris recovering and I forget how long back East."

Thornburgh's eyes were busy taking in the ramshackle buildings and stone hospital, where biting dust eddied about their corners. Now eleven years old, the post had been constructed to protect Union Pacific construction crews while working across the Red Desert to the next railheads of Rock Springs and Green River. Now there were no longer construction crews to protect nor Indians to fight, Fort Steele was slowly decaying under a harsh desert sun.

The enlisted men and officers were turned out for Thornburgh's arrival and as he approached the Commander's Quarters, the troops were brought to full attention by Captain Scott Payne.

Thornburgh rode up, returned Payne's salute, and dismounted. O'Malley was there to take the reins of his horse. Payne and Thornburgh shook hands.

"Welcome to Fort Steele, Major," Payne said, remaining at stiff attention.

"At ease, Captain," Thornburgh said, slipping off his riding gloves. Payne relaxed to his normally stiff position. Sam Cherry was right, Payne looked sickly and it showed to Thornburgh's practiced eyes. The man looked flabby and ghastly white.

Thornburgh turned to the troops, feeling obliged to say something momentous, but could think of nothing that important to say. Therefore, he simply greeted the men. Following his greeting, he turned abruptly to Payne and asked the captain to dismiss the troops.

The Thornburghs were home.

Over the next few weeks, during that period of adjustment when troops get to know what makes a new commander tick, Thornburgh used this time to learn post routine and flesh out what his own role as chief officer was going to be. It was during this period of adjustment, Joe Rankin came calling.

O'Malley spotted the scout riding in and moved over to intercept Rankin.

"What brings *you* up this way, Rankin? Ain't no whores out here to keep your interest."

Joe Rankin dismounted from the bay, flipping the reins across the hitch post. He gave the private a cold look.

"Been chasing anymore bad Injuns?" Rankin asked, grinning evilly. O'Malley turned crimson as his anger for the independent-acting scout blossomed.

"Who you here to see?" O'Malley demanded, getting down to business.

"Why, I'm here to meet your new commander, Major Thornburgh."

"The Major is much too busy to drop everything 'cause some jasper rides up wanting to yap."

"Don't recall asking your permission, General."

"Damn you, Rankin. One day we gonna have to settle our differences with the mitts."

Rankin feigned surprised. "Why, Private O'Malley, I hold no hard feelings towards you. Certainly nothing that would require pugilistic action." The big Irishman's jaw dropped open as he stared at the slim scout.

"What the hell was that you just said?" O'Malley's fist clinched and unclenched as he rocked back and forth on his heels.

"Fisticuffs, Private, bare knuckles. Surely you understand plain English."

"You make fun of me in front of the men and I'll beat the living tar out of you," O'Malley warned.

Rankin offered the fuming man a cold smile. "You'll never lay a hand on me, O'Malley." As if to emphasize the point, Rankin shifted the big Colt slightly on his hip. "Now step aside." Rankin pushed past the enlisted man, took the two steps in one and opened the door to the Post Commander's office.

Major Thornburgh listened attentively as Joe Rankin unloaded his troubles from last winter and the ill-planned and ill-fated attempt by the Army to bring the Ute culprits back to Rawlings.

"I was promised double wages as chief scout by Private O'Malley. So far, I've received nothing in the way of compensation from the Army."

Thornburgh leaned back in his chair and studied the far wall. He finally turned his eyes on Rankin again.

"You say Private O'Malley offered you these increased wages?"

"Well, not exactly," Rankin said, squirming a little in his seat. "Told him I wouldn't scout in such hostile weather unless I got double wages. Hell, Major, there was snow up to the belly of my horse, and he's a big horse."

"I see," Thornburgh said, yet not really seeing at all. The only thing he did know was O'Malley was not authorized to offer Rankin anything but standard wages, weather notwithstanding.

"I'm here to collect my money," Rankin finished up.

"I will check the report filed by Private O'Malley and Major Thomas. If your services were indeed secured, I'm sure payment can be arranged. At the standard scout's wages."

Rankin was half out of his chair. "Ain't good enough, Major. You can check all the danged records and reports you want. I was hired and that's that. And not at no standard rate, either!"

"Standard rate is all *this* Army will pay, Mister Rankin," Thornburgh said, feeling his temper rise.

"Expect I'll take this matter to a higher authority," Rankin promised, settling his hat back on his head.

"My adjutant will see you get General Crook's address," Thornburgh said, standing up as well.

"And don't bother calling on me for help again, Major. Wouldn't scout for the Army if my life depended on it." With that, Rankin slammed the door behind him, mounted the big bay and left dust lingering over the parade ground as he thundered from the post.

O'Malley watched from the stoop of Hugus's sutler store, grinning. He called back into the interior of the building.

"Looks like Mister Rankin left in a huff." The words were barely out of his mouth before Major Thornburgh emerged and spied the lounging Irishman.

"Private O'Malley! I want to see you now, Trooper. On the double!" The smile on O'Malley's face wilted like a flower under a desert sun.

"Coming, sir!" O'Malley called back. All the way across the hard-packed grounds, O'Malley cursed the day he ever laid eyes on Rankin. Obviously, Rankin had brought him into this mess as well. He figured once Rankin had gotten nowhere with Major Thomas before he left, that would be the end of it. The big Irishman vowed to even the score where Rankin was concerned if the opportunity ever presented itself.

By the time Rankin had gotten back to Rawlings, Nathan Meeker had finally departed, leaving behind James France to stand toe to toe with Haywood Grant over the agent's rights to padlock a Union Pacific employee out of one of its own warehouses. In the end, Grant decided to file a report and wait for instructions, rather than listen anymore to France's high-pitched, strident voice. He hated sight of the little man with the outrageous beard.

Grant had gotten his report out on the wire before the arrival of the afternoon train and was standing on the platform when Rankin rode by. Grant scowled at the livery man. That was another one he hadn't any use for. The worst thing Rankin could have done in Grant's eyes was to hire that young Grayson Toliver. Everywhere he went in town, all Grant ever heard now was how fine a job young Toliver had done for the UP and how sad it was that he had lost his job. All the while, standing there looking at him with accusing eyes as if he had had a damn thing to do with it.

Grant checked his watch, squinting down the set of twin rails that looked to be on fire, the way the late sun reflected away from the steel. Late again. He cocked his head, hearing something and finally realized it was the telegraph and Grant hurriedly returned to his office while the key was a burst of metallic activity. Grant quickly tapped out an acknowledgment that the wire was clear and ready for the message to be sent. He grabbed a pencil and began writing furiously as the key came to life once more. When he was done, Grant tapped out his signal to the telegrapher in Omaha indicating he had received the message. He settled back in his chair to fully digest the instructions from Howard Sipps, one of the directors of the Union Pacific.

Grant read his scribbled note twice before placing it on his desk. What the hell was he going to do now? His first instructions had been perfectly clear: he was to allow the new agent of White River to inventory the supplies and annuities and remove one wagonload. Nothing more. Secure the remainder and deny further entry to anyone, even Agent Meeker. And now here was another wire, telling him just the opposite. The annuities were now the problem of Agent Meeker and to step aside completely.

Grant looked disgustedly at the note again. What the hell was going on here? Was Meeker running the UP now? Next thing he knew, he'd be out on the street like Toliver. Grant sat there for a long time, in utter silence save for the ancient tick of the huge weathered clock, staring at nothing. Later, the sound of the four-ten roused him from his self-imposed stupor and he got up slowly to meet the train. The only thing he concluded while sitting there, was to step back from this whole Ute mess. He wouldn't care if James France stripped the inside of the warehouse of its boards and hauled them away to White River.

Grant opened the door and stepped out onto the platform as the UP came chugging up. He waved at the engineer. What he was going to do was look out for himself. The one thing he didn't want to do was end up swamping saloons or mucking manure from some stable like Grayson Toliver.

"What do you mean, they ain't nothing you can do! Christ, Jim, you the high sheriff, ain't you?"

"Sit down, Joe, willya."

"Don't wanna sit down," Rankin fumed, standing over his brother's desk with hands on hips. "What I want is for you to get up off that ass of yours and ride over there and tell this Major Thornburgh what for."

"Like I done told you, Joe, I don't have jurisdiction over a military post. Besides, didn't Toliver pay you before he was fired?"

"Ain't got nothing to do with what the Army owes me," Joe Rankin said firmly.

Jim Rankin swung his feet from his desk to the floor and stood up. He looked around the room for his hat.

"Maybe not, but you ought to count yourself lucky that the UP paid you anything. And didn't Blacky agree to a lesser amount for damages, seeing's how Port Weems skipped out on his part? Ought to have money to the good."

"Dang it, Jim, the Army owes me nearly a week's wages and all you can do is tell me how lucky I am. And it was me that put the bug in Blacky's ear about reducing the charges."

Jim Rankin found his hat and settled it over his head, smiling at his brother.

"Way I heard it, you didn't give Blacky much choice."

"He coudda pitched a fit if he wanted," Joe said, calming down a little. Jim Rankin slipped into his coat.

"How much did you charge agent Meeker for feed and storage for them mules and wagon?" Sheriff Rankin queried.

"Now that ain't the law's affair. Private business. Besides, I sunk a lot of money into them durn mules. You know how a blame mule can eat twice that of a horse. Hell, everybody knows that." Joe watched his brother buttoning up his coat.

"Where you off to now?"

"It's supper time."

"Wish you'd look after my affairs as much as you do your stomach. And just when are you going to invite me up for dinner? Know I ain't the kinda material you want to socialize with after hours, but think of them kids of you'rn. They being deprived of their uncle and the wonderful things I could teach them."

"That's what worries me," Jim said, grinning from ear to ear.

"Just go on home, get outta here. Expect I'll just write that general in Omaha 'bout my wages."

"You do that, Joe," the lawman said as he was leaving the jail. "By the time a general acts on anything, we'll both be residing in

199

the cemetery." Joe followed his brother out on the wooden platform.

"Kinda what I figgered, too," Joe said, gloomily. "But you just wait, someday that fancy-looking Major is gonna come wanting to hire me. Then he'll learn just how much a good scout's wages really are."

Jim Rankin waved to his brother and started off down the street to home. Joe stood there in the opened doorway of the empty jail, wondering what he should do next. There were always the girls down on Lower Row. Nah. Besides, it was too early for that. He hadn't eaten since breakfast and the rumblings in his stomach reminded him of this. Where the hell, was Bobby? How could the sheriff of a county waltz off, leaving the town without a jailer?

With no one around to supply answers to his unspoken questions, in the end, Joe decided to sas-shay over to the livery, get cleaned up, and treat young Toliver to a night on the town. He could well afford it after cashing the agency voucher over at James France's store that Meeker had given him.

Besides, young Toliver looked to be too uptight most times and Joe had set himself to thinking on it for sometime now and he had finally concluded, Grayson Toliver was a virgin. He had watched the young lad's movements and none of it included womenfolk. Least none that he could see. And Joe decided tonight was the night he choose for Grayson Toliver to become a man. Hell, Rankin concluded, hitching up his gunbelt, he just might indulge a little himself.

Nathan Meeker was in high spirits. The heavily laden wagon crunched over rock with spine-jolting intensity. Meeker ignored the grinding of rock beneath heavy wheels and jostling of body.

He was as excited as any man of twenty, not that of a man nearing sixty-two. He marveled at the countryside, the cool fragrance of the blue Wyoming air and the limpid caliber of the late afternoon sky.

"What are those mountains?" Meeker asked Joe Collom, who held the reins of the sweating mules. After they had finally loaded the wagon back at the UP warehouse, there simply was no room for three men to ride and Meeker had been forced to purchase a saddle horse from Joe Rankin, now being ridden by William Post. The price irked Meeker somewhat, but not for long. Besides, the agency would need a horse and probably more. Collom looked at where Meeker was pointing to the southeast.

"The Sierra Madres," Collom said, scanning the purple forests and broken ridges. "That point there is called Bridger Peak."

"Tell me about them," Meeker asked eagerly. "I want to learn as much as I can about this wonderful country."

Collom turned slightly in the seat to look at Meeker.

"You really like it, then?"

"Wonderful country. Love the grand openness, don't you?"

"Guess so, never thought much about it either way."

"A man should take time to enjoy the beauty around him. That is, after a hard day's work," Meeker added as an afterthought. "The appreciation will be that more magnified. Please, tell me more about this country if you don't mind."

"Don't mind. It ain't like I'm the onliest one who knows about this place." Collom took a quick look back to see how the load was riding and to check on Post. The man didn't sit a saddle too well. Be like him to fall off and they not know it for miles. He was eating a lot of alkali dust thrown up by the wagon and Collom was tempted to tell him to ride to either side of the wagon out of the dust, but changed his mind. Something that simple, any man ought to be able to figure out.

"This Bridger the famous trapper and guide?"

"The one and the same," Collom said, tearing off a piece of tobacco with his teeth. He didn't see the frown on Meeker's face at sight of the tobacco. Collom worked it up some before it was soft enough for him to continue talking. He spit over the edge of the wagon.

"Let's see, over in the distance-you can't really see it yet—is Hahn's Peak. Old Bibleback Brown and Bill Slater started that gold rush back in '69. Brought in a bunch of folks for a time, I'm told. Not much there now."

"What an odd name, Bibleback." Meeker said, looking off in the distance, imagining he could see Hahn's Peak.

"Never heard him called different," Collom said, shooting a golden stream of tobacco over the edge. "Bibleback's got a place down on the Little Snake. Got ole Charlie Lowry down there with him. Charlie is a wonder on the harmonica. Utes are crazy about Charlie and his harmonica."

"He associates with them?"

"Charlie does more than that. When he carries the mail down to White River Agency—which he does on occasions—he lives right in one of their tepees with them." Meeker seemed shocked.

"How could a white man do that?"

"Easy, Mr. Meeker. You see, things are a lot different out in these parts," Collom said, as if trying to teach a young boy the ways of the woods. "Most folks don't think much about it. Some even take a Ute squaw once in awhile. Utes don't seem to mind."

"Tell me about the agency, have you been there many times?" Meeker asked, changing the subject. After all, he was here to change the Indians' way of living, not to join them in their tepees.

"A few, mostly to attend horse races and place a few bets. The Utes love horse racing next to hunting, best of all. How the agency was started, I got from Joe Rankin. Joe knows Utes better than anyone I know. He said that ole Jim Bridger guided a man from Denver, let's see, think his name was Oakes. This Oakes was some sort of famous person, I don't remember why. But anyhow, Bridger helped him establish White River agency in '73."

"D. C. Oakes was his full name," Meeker said. "Met him a time or two while in Denver on business. Oakes was responsible for starting the gold rush to the Rocky Mountains back in '60."

"I didn't know that," Collom said. "Well, sir, he really started something, didn't he?"

"Joe Rankin said this fellow, Oakes, was an agent of the White River Utes at one time."

"That I didn't know." Had he known how life's circumstances would find him here on a trail heading for a remote section of Colorado to look after a bunch of Indians, Meeker decided he would have been interested picking Oakes brains where the Utes were concerned. But a man shouldn't look behind him or he would see all of life's disappointments and Meeker could count more than a few on his part. Thumble Phalanx, for one. After three hard years there, working at every position imaginable, he and his family left when the commune fell apart, with an uncollectible credit of fifty-six dollars. Then there was the store and fruit farm, that failed. But the absolute worst had been when the Colony removed him as their President of Union Colony of Greeley. It still hurt to think of it, even now, which Meeker was doing when he knew he shouldn't.

"You know, you aren't the only agent these Utes have had. Most last a year, some a little more. But in the end, they have all left."

"How many has White River had?"

"Don't know, four, maybe five," Collom ventured, slapping the reins across the glistening backs of the mules.

Joe Collom said something he had been meaning to tell Meeker the minute they had started out from Rawlings.

"Because we're carrying such a heavy load, we'll have to go the easy route. It's about seventy-five miles out of the way but there's noway we will pull across Bridger Pass hauling this much weight."

"Perfectly understandable," Meeker said, still trying to fathom how five agents could have come to these mountains to administer to the Utes and not a one of them successful.

Meeker lapsed into silence, his mind busy with the things he would do once he was at White River and how much the Utes would come to appreciate and love him for what he was teaching them to do.

Hours later, Collom descended through Alamosa Gulch and pulled the heavy wagon to a stop next to Sulphur Springs. It took a minute for Meeker to realize they had stopped and that Collom had gotten down. Collom looked back at the Indian Agent.

"Far as we can go this evening, Mister Meeker. We should hit the Little Snake tomorrow afternoon. George Baggs has a ranch there we can put up at and a wife who is a good cook." Collom stopped short of mentioning that wasn't all Maggie Baggs was good at. He had to bite his lip to keep from telling it.

Post dismounted stiffly and began beating his hat against his clothes. Puffs of red dust flew from his clothing.

"William, how did you make it?" Meeker asked, forgetting in his characteristic fashion that his clerk had been eating their dust since leaving Rawlings.

"Been better," Post croaked, spitting a gob of red dust from his throat. "Dry out here," Post commented, looking out across the rather flat country of low sagebrush.

"We've had no rain since early spring," Collom said, unhitching the mules to lead them down to water.

The only note of excitement that evening came when William Post went out gathering dead limbs to start a fire. A rattlesnake struck at his boot after Post stepped over a low bush. The snake missed only because his fangs got hung up in Post's pant leg. But he screamed loud enough. And Meeker and Collom came running, with Collom holding his Winchester. Without blinking, Collom shot the snake through the head. Meeker had never seen such skill and told him so.

"Joe Rankin's been teaching me," the young Englishman said rather proudly. He looked at the two startled men. "You eat snake?"

"I would rather chew shoe leather," Meeker responded, turning back to the camp.

"Just as well," Collom said, grinning at the white-faced Post, who was staring at the dead snake Collom was holding out by the tail. "Rankin hasn't taught me how to prepare cooked snake yet."

"Thank God, for that," Post said, bending down to retrieve the limbs he had dropped only seconds after the snake encounter. Being careful where he walked, the agency clerk made his way back to camp and never ventured from the fire the rest of the night.

CHAPTER 17

Although he never said it, Nathan Meeker was dog-tired by the time they came up to Baggs Ranch, nestled there in the pretty little valley along the Little Snake River. The sight of substantial buildings and human activity lifted his sagging spirits somewhat.

By now, there wasn't a single place on him that wasn't sore or didn't hurt. The teeth-jarring wagon ride had cooled his boyish enthusiasm for examining the countryside about the time they had nooned in a flat arid spot, surrounded by low bluffs, their tops rounded by the constant wind. The unnamed little creek had been vile to drink from and Nathan found himself spitting the water out when Post and Collom weren't looking. Even the mules drank gingerly of the chalky-tasting water.

Standing now among a screen of greening cottonwoods and willows on the banks of the beautiful Little Snake that fought its way across the tops of upthrusting rocks, Meeker wiped the back of his mouth with his hand after drinking deeply of its twisting blue waters. The aftertaste was sweet and pleasant. Among the branches gorgeous yellow tanagers flashed about while green-winged teal and hawks frittered about the mile-wide valley.

Meeker could certainly see why George Baggs would choose such a place after having left the dry country of New Mexico.

After introductions were made all around, Meeker left Post and Collom to tend to their animals while George Baggs gave the agent a grand tour of the place along with a healthy dose of history.

Meeker was mildly pleased when Maggie Baggs brought them out a pitcher of lemonade to where they sat on the veranda in the brilliantly clear air. He took professional note of Maggie's attributes and found himself wondering how the pug-nosed rancher had managed to snare someone like Maggie and how difficult it must be having such a pretty, well-endowed woman in such lonely country among men of every stripe.

After they had drank their lemonade, George had one of his men saddle four horses, promising to show the new agent around the area before darkness set in. Meeker would have liked nothing better than to stay where he was, yet obliged George Baggs by stiffly mounting his animal while Post and Collom did the same.

Like Private O'Malley, Nathan Meeker got to meet the twinkling-eyed old trapper, Jim Baker. Meeker was fascinated by his two wives and wondered how a man Baker's age managed two women, not that he held with such activities.

The rancher led his visitors further up river to Charlie Perkin's store, filled with every item imaginable. Meeker and Post poked through wooden crates, sacks bulging with flour, cornmeal and oats and a jumble of various equipment, some of it unfamiliar to Meeker. Boxes of dynamite, blasting powder, caps, mining tools and even violin strings cluttered the place. Along one wall, Perkins had a row of new Winchesters and fixed ammunition. While they were poking around, two Indians came in, looked at the white men, quickly settled their purchases with Perkins, and left silently. Collom was busy, talking quietly to the store owner and even bought a few items himself. Collom motioned in Meeker's direction and Perkins fixed his beady eyes on the new White River Agent. Collom brought the storekeeper over and introduced him to Meeker.

"So, you the new agent, huh?" Charlie said, reeking of raw whiskey and stale sweat.

"I am," Meeker said, already passing judgment on the man.

"Hope you and I kin get along," Charlie said, smoothly. "Last two agents and I never seen eye-to-eye you might say."

Meeker took a step backward to fend off the man's body odor. There was nothing pleasant about the man and Meeker knew instantly he wanted nothing to do with him under any circumstances.

"How is that?" Meeker found himself asking the half-drunken storekeeper.

"Simple, you seed them two Injuns that just left? They bought two thousand rounds of fixed ammunition fer their Winchesters. I'm gettin' rich off'en these Utes. Agents before you didn't like my tradin' such things to them. Wanted me to stop and only sell trinkets, beads, and sech foofaraw. Hell, a man cain't make a livin' out here doin' just that! Ain't that right, George?" Charlie Perkins bellowed over at the rancher who was looking through a catalogue. The rancher merely nodded and never looked up. Perkins turned back to the agent.

"See, old Georgie knows. This is rough country and a man's got to do whatever it takes to get by. Jest last week, I killed a man with a beer bottle who come sneaking in to steal from me. Ain't going to stand fer that, no siree."

The storekeeper's burning little eyes looked beyond Meeker to Post who was fingering one of the new Winchesters.

"She's purty, ain't she?" Perkins called to Post. "You boys interested in a little fun?" Perkins asked, the expression on his face changing conspiratorially.

Meeker frowned; he had had enough of this wily old bandit and headed for the door.

"Stop by my hotel," Perkins called to the departing Meeker and Post. He looked at George Baggs. "Hell, George, take 'em over to the hotel and introduce them to the little ladies, will ya? Even give 'em a break on the price, be'ens they new to the country."

The rancher smiled and waved his hand at Perkins before following Meeker out the door. "What was he saying?" Meeker asked.

George grinned, pointing at the adjacent structure. "That."

Meeker turned to see several half-breed girls lounging around the entrance, watching them with dark eyes.

"Half-breed Snake girls. Make the beds, clean your clothes and whatever else you got a mind needs tending to."

Meeker stared openly. Never before had he seen such an illicit operation than what was being run here by Charlie Perkins.

"I can see now that I might have trouble with such temptations so close to the reservation."

"Ain't the only one, but it's probably the worse of the lot," George Baggs said, mounting up. "Captain Jack and his followers frequent Perkins a lot, for guns and whiskey."

"Who?"

"Captain Jack. He's one of the White River Chiefs. I'm sure you'll get a chance to meet him. Kinda independent. Comes and goes as it suits him."

"I'll just have to see what the law can do about this place, as well as keeping the Utes on the reservation," Meeker said, determinedly, pulling himself into the saddle.

"Just wanted you to see what you're up against," Baggs said simply, turning his horse back down trail. "Expect Maggie's got supper ready by now. Know you must be tired, Mr. Meeker. Didn't mean to keep you out this long."

"I'm glad you did."

The next morning, they crossed the Little Snake and continued south across the next divide, moving slowly through prickly pear and greasewood and down into the richer valley of Fortification Creek. To the west lay a string of broken plateaus covered with juniper and serviceberry. The landscape was drab and treeless to the east and so Meeker concentrated instead on the problems he faced with people like Charlie Perkins.

They lunched at the odd-porphyry dike called Fortification Rocks. Across the valley, broad veins of chartreuse aspens intermingled with narrow bands of forest-green conifers, draping themselves across the rocky shoulders of the Elk Head Mountains like a variegated carpet. Spring was defiantly coming to the mountains and Meeker enjoyed the quiet interlude and peaceful scene.

By nightfall, they were camping on Bear River at Himley's Ford. A mile upriver was Peck's one room store near the mouth of Elk Head Creek. The following morning, Meeker insisted they visit this store when informed of its location by Joe Collom.

Meeker found the small store, a cluttered chaos of sacks of flour, coffee and other foodstuffs, amid guns and ammunition. The counterless store had barely enough walking room among the strewn supplies. Meeker found Mrs. Peck nursing her baby. Meeker inquired of her husband.

"He's away on business. I'm the postmistress," the woman said simply. "I call it Windsor. You know, after the grand hotel Windsor they are building in Denver." Her fat-cheeked baby smiled at Meeker and it reminded him of his youngest son, George

Washington, as a baby, and who was now buried in the Greeley cemetery.

"Yes, I do know of it," Meeker responded, humoring the woman.

"Know it don't look nuthing like that," the woman said sadly, "but it helps me feel better just calling it that." She gave the agent a feeble smile and Meeker wondered if the woman was nearing a breakdown, stuck out here like she was, the only female for miles in any direction. He thought of Maggie Baggs and the half-breed Snake girls. What about his own women, his wife and daughter, Josie, who would be headed shortly for White River themselves? Maybe the hardships would prove too much for them as it seemed to be for this poor unfortunate creature standing before him now.

He thought of Mrs. Peck's half-hysterical laugh long after they had put many miles behind them. They lugged upward over Williams Fork Mountains and snaked their way down Deal Gulch to the charming, blue-green waters of Williams Fork Creek.

Joe Collom called a rest for the mules and while he looked after their needs, Meeker studied the surrounding tawny hills, of commendable size and so uniformly gullied, they reminded him of animals standing side-by-side at a circus. Where he stood, the ground was covered with waist-high sagebrush and little else.

"Getting colder," Post commented as he came up to Meeker.

Meeker shifted his eyes to the gray skies now blotting out the sun of early morning. For the first time, he really felt his age—cold and bone-tired. Had this been a good idea? Should he bring his family this far from civilization to live among a bunch of savages? Would he have agreed to come to White River had he not been so desperate to repay the thousand dollars to Horace Greeley's daughters? Even though Meeker never expected to resolve these and other questions that had plagued him for weeks, he also knew without this agent's job, he was doomed to die penniless in a town that had grown to despise him. Just these thoughts caused his spirits to sag even deeper inside of him.

"Joe wants to stop here for the evening," Post continued, remembering why Collom had sent him out to Meeker in the first place.

"Sounds good," Meeker said, dropping his eyes to his old friend William Post. "Could use a fire and something warm to drink."

"I'll gather up a arm-load of wood." Post started to turn away but Meeker stopped him.

Meeker hesitated, "William, I haven't properly thanked you for standing beside me when others of the Colony wanted nothing more to do with me. Know you took a lot of criticism for it and never complained. You are a true friend." For a moment it looked as though the tired-faced agent was going to lose it. Not normally a demonstrative person, this display of affection was something rare for Meeker.

Post was genuinely affected by Meeker's emotional admission and he was momentarily at a loss for words. When he did manage to speak, his voice was gruff and tinged with pride for his friend.

"They were wrong. They expected things to be made easy for them like it was back East. Those are the ones cried the loudest. There were some thought you had done the best you could under the circumstances."

"I don't know, William," Meeker said, shaking his head. "I trusted people when I shouldn't have." He lifted his tormented eyes to Post. "Who would ever thought William Byers, a pillar of Denver Society, would stoop so low as to cheat us over the price of the land?" William Byers not only had charged the Union Colony five dollars for every acre, going at the time for ninety cents, but unloaded an additional six hundred and forty acres on the Colony he had no title to, forcing Meeker to spend extra money buying out the settlers who actually owned it.

"Some men were never meant to be trusted," Post said simply.

Post coached a small fire to life as a steady drizzle fell over the tiny camp. They huddled near the fire which sizzled and smoked, giving off just enough heat to make coffee and fry a pan of bacon while a violent electrical storm crashed around them. They slept very little during the night and pulled out early the next morning under soggy skies, slipping in the clay ooze of Milk Creek Valley as Joe Collom pointed the agency mules south.

For hours, the tiny group remained silent, the only sounds being the straining mules sloshing across the muddy valley.

"Expect we'll noon at Yellowjacket Pass and cook some real food," Joe Collom said, his eyes busy with the laboring mules. They had left camp without benefit of a cook fire, the wood being too wet to bother with.

"How far then to White River?" Meeker asked. He was heartily tired of riding in the jolting wagon and was still chilled to the bone from the thunderstorm. Soured as he was, Meeker was looking to get the trip over with as quickly as possible now.

Collom thought for a moment. "From Yellowjacket we drop down through Coal Creek Canyon. Expect it'll take most of the afternoon to reach White River."

"At least we'll reach the agency today," Meeker said glumly.

They found howling, sharp winds at the summit of Yellowjacket and hurriedly fixed a quick meal, not the one Joe Collom had envisioned, but the weather had changed all that.

Several times during the afternoon, Collom pointed out an Indian, here and there, watching them intently as they lumbered down the narrow canyon past Danforth's coal mine, emerging onto a wide park covered with sage.

"Do you think they know who I am?" Meeker asked, catching a glimpse of horse and rider among the rocks and timber.

"They know all right," Collom said, searching the benchland for sign of Indians. "Just curious is all. Like I said before, they've had more than a few agents since '71. Only difference now, is they'll have to learn a new *Mericatz's* name."

Meeker looked curiously at Collom. "Merry—what?"

"*Mericatz.* It's what all Utes call a white man." Collom grinned, "Learned that from Uriah Curtis. Never seen a white man could talk their language like Uriah."

As the sun hovered above the distant benchlands to the west, Collom sat holding the reins of the agency mules while Meeker stood up on the wagon seat to survey the agency. They were stopped just shy of the White River which flowed below them like a slithering snake.

From horseback, William Post was busy checking out this new place that would be home. Like Meeker, both appeared unimpressed with the two-acre stockade, sitting there neglected on a sage bench.

Meeker finally sat back down and Collom flicked the reins across the backs of the mules. Collom brought the wagon to a final stop inside the compound, setting the brake before jumping to the ground.

"Don't look to be in too good a shape," Collom said, looking around him at the depressing clutter of small buildings that numbered six. They looked ready to collapse under their dirt roofs from the sharp wind that roared around Adams' Point from the river canyon. A poorly constructed corral off to the left held two sad looking mules who watched the group with large silent eyes.

"Where are the Indians?" Meeker wanted to know.

"Down river a dozen miles," Collom responded, beginning to untie the ropes across the wagon that held the tarp in place. "Old Chief Douglas uses Powell Park as his winter quarters. Less snow and more grass down there."

"I see," Meeker said, looking around some more. Post had already unsaddled his horse and turned him out with the two mules who moved to the far side of the corral.

215

"Only white men here are two of Danforth's employees but they up at Trapper's Lake doing a little fishing before they head back to civilization."

"It certainly doesn't look like they've kept the agency up at all," Meeker commented.

William Post joined them. "Got to put a few more poles in the corral before the whole thing falls over." No one said anything.

Without a word, Meeker walked over to the agency office and shoved his way inside the rotting structure. God, could he make a go of this? Certainly his family couldn't be expected to live under such filthy conditions. Arvilla was too old to face such rigors again. What had he been thinking? And what about Josie? Josie was a bright, happy young woman of twenty-two. She might not survive such a desolate place. He felt overwhelmed by sudden fears like a man drowning in a sea of emotion.

CHAPTER 18

It was Tatitz, son of Canávish and Acari, son of Colorow, who had been at Charlie Perkin's that day Nathan Meeker and the others came through on their way to White River. Tatitz had been at Perkin's store buying fixed ammunition for his new rifle that went "chick, chick" and a new bullet appeared. Tatitz had given one of his finest horses for the new Winchester and he was very proud of the gun. He and Acari, who was several winters older than Tatitz and who already had a *piwán*, were going on a long spring hunt to the land where the mountains sank beneath the frowning plains. That had been their intent, yet when they learned from the stinking *Mericatz*, Charlie Perkins, that the skinny *Mericatz* with the smooth face and gray hair was the new White River Agent, Tatitz and Acari decided to postpone their hunt for buffalo and hurried back to Smoking Earth River to tell Canávish and Colorow.

Ten sleeps had passed since Tatitz and Acari had returned with the news.

There had been much talk and speculation among the men along Smoking Earth River as they passed the days, playing their card games and smoking while their *piwáns* did the traditional things *piwáns* were suppose to do: preparing meals, making buckskin clothing and gathering food and firewood. Quinkent spend his time wandering from small group to small group, listening and sometimes stopping long enough to play a hand or two, but never venturing much comment either way on the presence of this new agent and what it might mean for the People.

On the eleventh day, Quinkent had his *piwán* saddle his horse and prepare him a lunch of fried *pana* and jerked meat. He chose this day, for no particular reason, as the day to visit this new agent and see for himself what Tatitz and Acari had told him. Maybe he could learn something from this agent that he could use against Nicaagat during the next council meeting.

Quinkent chose to go alone, an easy ride north along the river on a smiling sunny day of blue sky and rippling waters. The pleasing call of the spirit birds from last night lingered in his memory and mixed well with the dewy morning of blue light and green earth. For well over eight hundred winters, the *Nüpartka* had enjoyed such incomparable spring days that flowed across the sweet high mountain meadows that was their home.

The warm sun felt good to Quinkent, loosening his stiff winter joints and freeing his mind of the painful memories of past hunger. With a full belly and his favorite bay beneath him, Quinkent rode along the river enjoying the morning, his mind, for once, free of the responsibilities of a *tawacz viem*.

Quinkent rode through the narrowing where the Smoking Earth

River cut its way through the Danforth Hills on his left and the Grand Hogback to his right. As he cleared the passage, he could see smoke rising from the old agency post two miles distant and Quinkent felt the slow, steady beating of his heart against his ribs. What would he say to this agent whom he knew to be forceful with powerful friends in Washington? Quinkent thought again of the *Mericatz* village called Greeley. He thought of this man Teller who had much power and hated all Utes. Quinkent only saw that Teller had picked this Meeker to become agent and not Curtis. This was a bad sign, an omen to warn the People that things may not be right for them in the future. But Washington had been his friend and friend to his People. And as *tawacz viem*, it was his responsibility to see these things remained the same.

Quinkent rode up to the agency office, dismounted and tied his beautiful horse to the sagging rail. Like the People, Quinkent found no reason to visit this place, except to receive annuities, or on his way into the Flattops to hunt for black-tailed or mule deer.

Quinkent ignored the lone *Mericatz* who had been working on the corral fence when he rode up. Now he stood, like someone frozen in ice, holding a pole and watching Quinkent tie up his bay. Quinkent knew this *Mericatz* could not be the agent for he had never seen an agent do "work." This *Mericatz* must be someone paid money to work and therefore could be dismissed.

Quinkent strode across the slouching porch and opened the agency door. He immediately saw an old man with a clean face sitting at a desk. The man looked up at Quinkent who did not move or speak. The *Mericatz* laid aside his pen.

"Come in, please," Nathan Meeker said very slowly, all the while gesturing to Quinkent.

Quinkent wanted to laugh at the sight of this new agent, but he kept his features still. Tatitz had been right: this *Mericatz* looked more like an old woman than a man. The *Mericatz* stood up, offering his hand as all *Mericatz* did, even when they knew the other person. Serious talk could not begin without shaking hands with them. This Quinkent had learned many years ago on his trips to Washington.

"I'm Nathan Meeker," the agent said, holding out his hand and smiling. Quinkent shook the agent's hand. The agent continued to smile. A smile which had no part of laughter.

"I've been hoping someone would come along who could show me around White River." Quinkent continued to stare at the smiling agent in silence until the smile turned into a frown.

"Do you speak English?" Meeker asked, the look of helplessness spreading across his narrow face.

"I speak," Quinkent said slowly, knowing it was sometimes hard to understand a *Mericatz* even when a person was listening very closely.

"Thank goodness," Meeker said, relief flooding his face. The smile returned.

"How are you called?"

Quinkent's eyes glittered in the glow of the feeble lamp from the desk. "Douglas," he said, pronouncing it Doug*eris*. Utes had trouble pronouncing their *l*'s.

"Douglas! You are just the one I was hoping to meet. You know, we have been here for ten or eleven days now and I was beginning to think there were no Indians in White River to look after." Quinkent remained silent since the agent had said nothing to respond to. *Mericatz* was like that. It forced a man to wait until something important was said, otherwise, it was always best to remain silent.

Meeker seemed desperate for Indian company and he asked Quinkent if he was hungry. Quinkent shook his head, no.

"If I were to saddle a horse, could you show me around Agency Park?" Quinkent nodded that he would. Without another word, he turned and left Meeker scrambling for his hat and coat.

Quinkent was unsure how much the agent wanted to see, at first, so he took him up river along secret Ute trails, deep into the Trappers Lake area of the flattops via the south fork of the Smoking Earth River. They climbed through cool forests of evergreens and across whitecapped streams, stopping to lunch with Sleepy Cat Peak looking down on them from the north. All the while, Meeker plied Quinkent with questions, some that were answered and others that were simply met with silence.

On their ride back through Agency Park, William Post joined them and Quinkent became even quieter. Meeker noticed the change and regretted having asked his clerk along.

Quinkent took them through the narrows, past the People's *carniva* and as far south along the river until the land became yellow and barren.

It was late afternoon when they returned to winter valley where Quinkent's *carniva* were located. It was here that Meeker seemed to grow excited and he peppered Quinkent with questions as to elevation, snow, wind and grass. Although puzzled why the agent was taking such great interest, Quinkent answered his questions as truthfully as he knew how.

Meeker smiled at Post who apparently was thinking the same thing. Quinkent sat his horse, his face masking his thoughts.

"This would be the ideal spot, don't you think?"

Post nodded, "Sure beats the agency for looks and if you care to notice, ain't no wind constantly blowing dust in your eyes."

"Yes, I think this is the ideal spot," Meeker said, looking around at the lush grass growing along the riverbottoms.

"Will Commissioner Hayt go along with moving the agency?"

"Without a doubt," Meeker said briskly, "once I explain the facts to him. Most of the agency buildings are in need of extensive repairs, some will be needed to be torn down. Besides, this land here is more suited to agricultural purposes. As Hayt reminded me in his last telegram, the Indians must be taught the agrarian way of life. Here"—Meeker swept his thin arm outward from his spare figure—"is land just begging to be irrigated and turned into produce and wheat."

Post glanced at Quinkent who seemed to be indifferent to the turn in conversation. "Hadn't you best get the chief's blessings first?"

Meeker gave Quinkent another smile. "Douglas, you have explained how this place is much better than where the agency is now located for your horses and for wintering. It would also make a fine place to build a new agency and grow crops along the river there. That way, your people would have good things to eat and be self-sufficient." He paused, waiting for Quinkent's reply. Quinkent said nothing, trying to understand as quickly as he could what this agent was saying.

"Don't believe he understands you, Mr. Meeker," Post said after a few minutes elapsed.

"You may be right, William," Meeker said, looking around him helplessly. "What we need is someone who is a good interpreter."

"Moving here is not good," Quinkent spoke up, fearing the park would be overrun with *Mericatz* if the agency was moved and they would lose the peace and tranquility of this place.

"But I told you all the reasons why it would be good for us and for your people as well," Meeker said.

"This place is not agent's. Belongs to the People," Quinkent insisted, thinking of the spirit birds. Would they leave if the *Mericatz* came here?

"I know that," Meeker said, showing much patience. "We are not trying to take it away from you, Douglas. We simply want to make life better for your people and moving the agency quarters here is part of that plan."

"It is no good," Quinkent repeated again, his voice rising.

"Now Douglas, you want to please Washington, don't you? If you allow this move, Washington will be very happy and your people will receive many fine gifts and lots of food. No longer will your annuities be held in Rawlings like they have been. And to prove Washington is your friend still, those annuities have been ordered released and I have instructed James France to start hauling these things out so you can give them to your people."

Quinkent seemed to swell in his saddle, his black eyes dancing with keen interest. This would strengthen his position as *tawacz viem* in the eyes of his People. Nicaagat could do nothing that would be as powerful as this. Only Quinkent made treaties with Washington. Only Quinkent was worthy of leading the People. In the end, Quinkent was cautious with his answer.

"These things you say are good but I see no loaded wagons."

"They are coming, Douglas, take my word for it. Now you go talk with your people and come see me tomorrow." Meeker turned to Post. "Come, William, let's get back to the agency. I need to write Commissioner Hayt about these latest developments and as soon as the others get here from Greeley, we can start dismantling what good wood there is and carting it down here."

Quinkent watched them go. Like most *Mericatz*, this agent and his worker could not ride a horse very well. Soon, Quinkent found himself thinking more about how he intended to convince his people that moving the agency was best for them.

Quinkent rode back to his *carniv* and dismounted. Singing Grass was busy over the cook fires and did not see Quinkent's face. Quinkent had that certain look when he had something important to say to the People. It was reflected in the way he carried himself and he came that way over the cook fire with his *piwán* watching him.

"You are like the fish that has swallowed a cricket," Singing Grass said, handing Quinkent a cup of coffee. Quinkent slurped loudly at the hot liquid, in the ways of Ute men, only louder this time. He drank the weak coffee as fast as he could for he had other things more important to do this night.

"A council of all the People must be called tonight," Quinkent said simply, returning the tin cup to Singing Grass before turning away. So surprised by her husband's actions, Singing Grass forgot about the bubbling meat she was preparing and walked quickly over to Tsashin, who was also preparing the evening meal for Canávish. Singing Grass quickly told Tsashin what her husband was planning.

"I saw the *Mericatz* ride by earlier," Tsashin said, stirring her cook pot. "Perhaps, this new agent will be good to the People and Quinkent is calling us together to tell us."

"Perhaps," Singing Grass said, yet there was much more lurking in her husband's eyes, much more. She did not mention her fears of this to Tsashin.

"My husband is now with Colorow," Tsashin said, thinking she should go and find him.

"I must get back to my pots and finish before the council starts," Singing Grass said, hurrying away through the diminishing light.

Quinkent stood, slowly looking around him at the silent expectant faces of his people, gathered there before the huge fires. Canávish had completed the ritual blessing and sharing the pipe. It was now time for Quinkent to speak.

"I have been with this new agent who is called, Nathan Meeker. He is the same *Mericatz* who was part of the village called Greeley. This agent has come to Smoking Earth River to be our friend and help us." Quinkent paused, allowing this to sink in. Murmurings rippled through the people while young children were hushed to silence whenever they grew restless.

"We must help this agent," Quinkent began again. "He wants to move the agency here along the river." The reaction to Quinkent's last words were immediate, bringing howls of protest from across the sea of faces.

"He cannot do this thing," Canávish said forcefully from his place next to Quinkent who had sat back down now that he had finished his say for now. It was time for others to speak of this serious thing before them.

"The agency should stay where it is," Pauvitz said. "We do not want *Mericatz* coming here except to race their horses." Winter valley was a favorite place during the summers where Canávish and others held lively races, betting on their favorite horse. There were loud cries against moving the agency from the rows of seated men and women. Quinkent listened in silence. Even though he was *tawacz viem*, the people would have the final say. It was his job to see they made the right decision, for all the People.

Sowówic, Nicaagat's sub-chief who had been visiting Colorow, rose from his place next to the huge-bellied Indian. Quinkent's hard black eyes bored into the man as he drew up to his full height. A full-bloodied *Nüpartka*, Sowówic was considered to be a man of power and persuasion. Even though he made his *carniv* with Nicaagat's, he was still independent enough to be heard and respected by all the People.

"I cannot speak but for myself," Sowówic began, "but this man, Meeker, like all the others sent to Smoking Earth River, knows nothing of our ways and customs. They come only to bend our wills to fit the *Mericatz* idea of how free men should live. Only General Adams came with good heart and purpose, but it was the *Mericatz* back in Washington who made him leave."

Many heads nodded in agreement with Sowówic for had it not been for Charlie Adams, some of the children who were now nine winters old would not be alive today. It was Adams who took pregnant women into his agency office, kept them warm in the thirty-odd below weather and delivered their babies. With Sowówic, it went even deeper where Charlie Adams was concerned. Having accidently shot himself in the leg one Christmas, it was Adams who took the dying Indian into his own bedroom and saved his life during two months of nursing him through blood poisoning. Only two *Mericatz* existed in the eyes of Sowówic that deserved respect: Charlie Adams and Uriah Curtis.

"We should tell this agent that we don't want the agency moved. We like it where it is." With that, Sowówic took his seat amid Colorow's heavy breathing and expression of *unh*. Many in the crowd expressed similar sentiments.

Sensing the growing resentment, Quinkent stood quickly and held out his hand for silence. When things had grown quiet, Quinkent stood there for a long moment and with as much dignity as he could muster, looked out across the many familiar faces who relied on him heavily for their welfare.

"There is more I did not say," Quinkent intoned. "This agent speaks to Washington for me. Washington will do as I ask, but only if the People are willing to let the agency move here to winter valley. If we do this thing, Washington will be pleased and our presents will be released to us. Never again will Washington allow our presents to be held up. That is what Washington has promised." Quinkent took his seat and waited for the People to speak. But no one spoke and the silence filled the sparkling night air. Only the crackle of the fires was heard in the stillness.

The decision had been made. The agency would be relocated.

Suddenly, with a snarl, Sowówic got to his feet and left the council with anger on his face. The people knew that Sowówic would ride north and tell Nicaagat of what took place here tonight.

Later, Quinkent lay in his robes with Singing Grass asleep on his arm. He was too restless and emotionally charged to sleep. When the first loaded wagons rolled into the agency with their presents, Quinkent knew his position as *tawacz viem* would strengthen considerably while Nicaagat's would diminish. From the river a spirit bird called his name over and over again for a long time. Finally, Quinkent drifted into peaceful sleep.

Meeker sat at the scarred desk in the agency office with pen in hand while Post added more wood to the pot-bellied stove. It didn't take much, but the nights were chilly here even in late spring.

"William, why don't you go on to bed. I'm going to finish this wire to Commissioner Hayt and turn in myself. I'm so stiff from riding all day."

Post shut the door to the stove oven and hitched up his pants. He glanced at Meeker who seemed abnormally white in the glow of the single lamp.

"You need to come on to bed too, Nathan. That can wait 'til tomorrow."

"I'd rather finish it tonight, William. While it's still fresh on my mind. I'm hoping that some of the others will show up tomorrow or the next day so we can get started with moving this agency." Meeker was referring to the Greeleyites he had hired before leaving town.

"Suit yourself," Post said, putting his hat on and going to the door.

"William, do you think the Indians will object too much to us relocating the agency?" Meeker asked, with pen poised.

Post turned back to look at his friend. Neither of them knew a thimble full about Indians, especially Utes. But Post never doubted that Meeker had his heart in the right place just like he did when he led the Union Colonists to that arid place beside the Cache de Poudre. Now a fair sized town stood where only hopes and dreams were before.

"I think they may. This Douglas fellow seems intelligent enough. I believe he can persuade the others."

Meeker nodded his head and his eyes fell back to the wire he was writing. Without another word, his hand moved the pen across the paper. Post slipped silently out the door. Sometime later, Meeker straightened and leaned back in the chair to relieve cramped muscles. He picked up the wire and read it carefully through from beginning to end.

U.S. Indian Service
White River Agency
May 23, 1879

Edward A. Hayt
Commissioner Indian Affairs
Washington, D.C.

Sir:

I arrived here at White River Agency nearly two weeks ago and have just spent considerable time with their Chief, a wispy kind of man with a peculiar mustache that is two points on either side of his lip. He is called, Douglas. I have no idea as to what he is called by the other Indians. With Douglas and William Post, agency clerk, we explored the country around White River. Where Douglas and his followers are encamped, some dozen miles below the agency, the land there is far more suitable to agricultural undertakings and Douglas has agreed, in part, to having the agency relocate there. I think he must convince the others but I feel this old Indian is wily and will make them see the sense in this matter. Douglas is to report here tomorrow with how they voted. Since the agency location was set by treaty in '73, I seek your permission to relocate it to Powell Park. I have heard rumors of another sub-chief from several whites in the area by the name of Captain Jack who has a

larger following, nearly 100 lodges, who, I'm sure will
kick up a fuss when he finds out what is going on, but
with your approval, there is little he can do but take it. I
will write more later. Hired help should be arriving in the
next few days. My wife and daughter, in early June.

Respectfully, etc.,

N. C. Meeker

Indian Agent

Satisfied with what he had written, Meeker folded the wire,
turned down the wick and went to bed.

CHAPTER 19

It took three sleeps for Sowówic to locate Nicaagat camped deep in the evergreens above Bear River where he and several others were conducting a hunt. When Sowówic rode into camp, he found several deer hung on low limbs with their entrails removed and a stack of deer hides near the fire where one of men had been smoking them to keep fresh for the women who would turn the hides into soft butter-yellow buckskin, prized by Indian and white alike.

It was mid-day, and Nicaagat sat smoking with his hunters following a good morning of deer hunting. Nicaagat's nut-colored face seemed to light up at sight of his sub-chief. Sowówic dismounted at a respectful distance, tied his blown horse to a low limb and hurried over to Nicaagat who took note of his quick steps.

"*Maiquas!*" Sowówic said as he drew near. The others with

Nicaagat returned the greeting, glad that their old friend was with them once again.

Nicaagat took the cigarette from his mouth, motioned for his sub-chief to sit.

"*Maiquas*, Sowówic. You have ridden your animal very hard. He will do poorly this summer against the *Mericatz* horses if you are not careful."

"A new agent has come into our winter valley. This *Mericatz* is called Meeker." Nicaagat handed his friend his leather pouch and papers for which to roll a smoke. Clearly, Sowówic wanted nothing to impede his telling what he knew yet he didn't want to seem like some half-grown man who was not careful with his words and later shamed for not telling only what he knew to be true. Sowówic quickly shook out enough rough-cut tobacco to make a smoke which he lit from the nearby fire. There was fresh-cooked deer meat and his stomach ached with hunger, yet Sowówic would not eat until he had emptied what was in is head about this agent.

"Four sleeps ago, Quinkent made a council and told the People this agent wanted to move the agency down to our winter valley."

"Unh!" several of the men around Nicaagat said loudly.

Yaminatz was more vocal and spoke up immediately. "This *Mericatz* has no power to do this thing."

"That is what Canávish and Pauvitz and others as well said to Quinkent." Nicaagat's dark eyes never left Sowówic's face. "None of the people there wanted this thing to happen."

"Maybe this agent was misunderstood by Quinkent," Nicaagat said. "It takes a long time to understand what a *Mericatz* has said and even then it is hard to hold such thoughts for long in your head. Maybe, Quinkent had trouble with the *Mericatz* language."

Sowówic shook his head, "I do not believe this is so, for Quinkent spoke again after everyone who wanted to speak had done so. He said that this agent spoke to Washington for him and we must do as Washington says. Only then will Washington be pleased and give us our presents. Quinkent said this agent would see that our presents were never held up again if the *Mericatz* was allowed to do this thing."

A studied silence fell across the small group and Sowówic was contented to finish his smoke, knowing that Nicaagat would not be rushed to make a hasty decision.

Finally, Nicaagat spoke. "Perhaps, we should go and see what this agent is doing. Make him understand that we don't want the agency moved into our winter valley."

"Unh!" everybody said. Without further talk, the men began packing the camp while Sowówic wolfed down as much tender deer meat as he could hold. In less than a slight shift of the sun, the hunting camp was packed with Nicaagat leading the small group, in single file, down through the trees to the ribbon of blue that marked the Bear.

Even traveling late into the night, the group did not reach the narrow canyon that unfolded to meet Agency Park for two sleeps. The sun was high overhead when Nicaagat stopped and stared at the strange, empty place where agency buildings once stood. The others seemed just as surprised.

They rode forward and as they drew nearer, they could see scraps of wood and logs lying about. Only parts of buildings were still standing. The anger grew strong inside of Nicaagat.

They heard a splash and turned to see several men rolling logs into the river from buildings they had torn down. One of the *Mericatz* saw them, wiped his hands on his trousers and came over to the waiting group.

Nicaagat knew this *Mericatz* must be this new agent for what Sowówic had said was true. He looked more like an old woman than an old man. He came up smiling and rolling down his shirt-sleeves.

Meeker came up to Nicaagat's horse and began talking rapidly.

"You must be Captain Jack. I have heard much about you. I need your help to make the others understand just how important it is that they be made to know that I am here to offer my help only if they are willing to pitch in."

Nicaagat listened to the *Mericatz* language in a voice meant to be used for little children. He did not like this agent with the anxious face and the smile that was painted there.

"What does he say?" Sowówic asked in the language of the People.

"I think this *Mericatz* may be your grandmother," Yaminatz said and the others burst out laughing over the rich joke used only by the People.

Meeker stood there, the smile on his face growing larger, yet not understanding why.

"Wait over by the river and I will see what this agent wants," Nicaagat said. He would use the *Mericatz* language only when others of the People were not around for he did not like to hold it for long in his head.

Nicaagat stepped down from his horse and stood there facing the agent while holding to his animal's bridle.

"Why do you move agency?" Nicaagat asked in English.

"Because, Jack, the land below the narrows has plenty of level ground to grow good things to eat. Make you people self-sufficient. You can have cows and plenty of milk to drink."

"This is agency," Nicaagat said, forcefully, with a sweep of his arm. "No law or treaty was made to do this thing. The winter valley is used to keep our horses there during the Snow Moons. They need the grass that grows there."

"You don't understand, Jack," Meeker said, with growing impatience. "Washington wants the agency moved. It is for your own good."

"Don't want agency moved," Nicaagat repeated, his brown eyes filled with hot anger now. "How come other agents not move from old place. They satisfied."

"Listen, Jack. I am the agent now. You are just like Douglas and the rest of your people, you must do as I say or the soldiers will come and make you move!"

Nicaagat shrank away from the agent, his eyes narrowing in their sockets. Without another word, he jumped to the back of his pony and galloped over to where Sowówic and the others were waiting in the shade.

Nicaagat dismounted and immediately began to roll a smoke, the anger still with him. It was a few minutes before he could use the old language, the *Mericatz* words still strong in his head.

"I told this agent we did not want the agency moved. It was set by Washington and agreed to by the People; that other agents had been satisfied with the old place. Why couldn't he? Then he say we better like it or else he will send the soldiers and make us move!"

"*Swerch!*" Sowówic exclaimed. No other agent had ever spoken of such things before. The others became agitated as well at the mention of the possibility of United States Troops moving against the reservation. The tragedy at Sand Creek was not too distant in the past for them to conjure up scenes of soldiers putting them in chains and carting them away to live far out on the burning plains where they would sicken and die.

"We should ride down to winter valley and see for ourselves where this agent is putting up these buildings," Yaminatz spoke up. Nicaagat had been squatting in the shade, watching the three *Mericatz* toiling at their tasks. In silent approval of the plan, Nicaagat caught up his pony and started downriver with the others lined up behind their leader in order of importance. Sowówic rode only a few feet behind Nicaagat for his voice was one the People valued greatly at council meetings.

The late spring air, cooled by the incessant winds that blew around Danforth Hills and shot through Coal Creek Canyon, were soon put behind Nicaagat and the others. When they finally emerged from the Narrows where the slash of green marked the meander of Smoking Earth River as it cut its way across the flat valley, Nicaagat paused to survey the oak-juniper hills where nearly two thousand horses were grazing and the valley floor now covered by many *carniva*.

Nicaagat's *carniva* had arrived ahead of the hunting party and his followers were stretched along the Smoking Earth River for nearly a mile, looking like so many white triangles. Still further down river, Nicaagat could see the small group of *carniva* that followed Quinkent.

They rode forward and were greeted by many smiling-faced Utes that waved to them as they filed past. The people seemed to be in a festive mood while tantalizing odors wafted from every *carniv* they passed.

When Nicaagat saw the carniva with Sowówic's sign on it, he turned in that direction so they could unload a portion of the deer meat Sowówic had killed. They were met by Sowówic's *piwán* whose round face grew even more rounded at sight of her husband and fresh meat. Even Nicaagat could tell the woman was bursting with news. Sowówic dismounted and handed the reins of his horse to his *piwán*.

"The people seem glad we are camped once more in winter valley," Sowówic said to the woman who suddenly grew shy around the group of hunters. She gave her husband a shy smile after which her eyes sought the ground in Ute fashion.

"The *Mericatz* are making a new agency."

"Where does all the food come from that is in the people's cook pots?" Sowówic questioned, while the others unloaded his share of the meat. Hunting buffalo had been poor because of the drying winds and no rain where they had been camping two sleeps ride into the plains. Each day the hunters had gone out and each day they returned without sighting any buffalo. The plains grasses of late spring were brown and dying from lack of rain and snapped when walked on. Nicaagat and the others had never seen it so dry this early in the season. With food growing scarce, the hunters returned with Yaminatz to Bear River country to hunt deer. It was here that Sowówic had found them that day.

His *piwán* smiled even wider than before. "The presents came today and the agent gave everybody all they wanted. Tobacco, sugar, flour and even clothes and blankets fill every *carniv*. Quinkent says this agent will give out more presents as soon as the other wagons arrive from the *Mericatz* village of Rawlings."

Sowówic looked up at Nicaagat whose dark eyes betrayed his thoughts. Perhaps, this agent would be good to the People and it might not be too bad that the agency has been moved to winter valley. That is what Sowówic saw in his leader's eyes.

Sowówic could see in the distance, the beginning of several buildings being erected by more *Mericatz*. It was near several of Quinkent's *carniva* and only a little ways beyond where Canávish had his racetrack. That was good, for Sowówic did not want to move any closer to the *Mericatz* buildings. But as he thought this, he saw his oldest son riding away from these men with Henry Jim, an Uncompahgre Ute recommended to ex-agent Danforth by Chief Ouray to act as interpreter for the People. In a few minutes, they came riding up, shouting *maiquas* to the gathered men.

The two young men threw themselves from their horses, wildly excited as boys are who have not yet grown into a man's body.

"Agent Meeker is a good man," Henry Jim said, smiling at the small group. "There is much presents down at those buildings. More than ever before."

"Who are those *Mericatz?*" Nicaagat questioned.

Henry Jim puffed his small chest outward with unabashed importance. He felt honored by Nicaagat's attention.

"Two of those *Mericatz*, you see by the building where the presents are stored are called Clark and Price. The other two *Mericatz* near the river who are hauling logs are two brothers who are called Dresser." Henry Jim said their names slowly so the men gathered there would understand such names that were awkward and hard to pronounce. "The other *Mericatz* are with Meeker at the old place."

Silence filled the space between the men and the river as they watched the white men struggling with the slippery, wet logs as they fished them from the river. In the still, warm air, they could hear the ring of hammers as the other two men worked steadily at constructing a new building some distance from the others.

Nicaagat was reminded of his days as a youth when he was forced to live with the *Mericatz* family who did not treat him well. He recalled how he had spent most days doing *work* for these *Mericatz* who were always too busy to enjoy life. They did no hunting or racing their ponies. Only work seemed to make them happy. It was too much for him to understand, even now.

And then, Nicaagat thought of Quinkent and was unhappy with the knowledge that Quinkent had been there to oversee the distribution of the presents. It strengthened the old chief's position with his own people and with Nicaagat's as well. Nicaagat checked the anger that threatened to come out of him. When this agent came down to winter valley, Nicaagat determined to go see him again and regain the diminished status he perceived he had lost within his own group. He yet did not know how he would do this, only that he must try. He checked his first impulse to seek out Quinkent and learn what news he carried. It would be a sign of weakness, of acknowledging Quinkent as still the more powerful of the two. This Nicaagat would never do.

He turned to address the hunters, telling them to divide the meat that was no longer needed as before the hunt and to come to his *carniv* later, after the evening meal was over. Now was the time to smoke and reflect on the sudden changes coming to winter valley and how to best deal with them and this new agent.

Quinkent had seen the hunters ride in and picked Nicaagat's dark features out of the group. Without thinking, the little points of his mustache were sticking out from his face in a smile. This time, it was Quinkent who had made good on his promises. The People knew without a doubt that Washington listened to Quinkent through this agent, Meeker. Once the presents had been given out, all the people of both bands were very happy and Quinkent's name was mentioned everywhere he went, which pleased the old chief for it would also cause Nicaagat discomfort.

Quinkent had helped select the new agency site with Meeker and now, as he stood near his *carniv* watching the *Mericatz* working, it wasn't so bad. They still had all this other land for their ponies to graze on and run free. Canávish still had his racetrack and all the people were well-fed and happy. Even now, he could hear the laughing cries of children playing between the *carniva*. The earth had tilted back this fine, warm day and had favored the People of the *Nüpartka* once again. He tried to recall the agent's words while he was helping to give out the presents to the People, but they were a long time rising up within him. Nothing any *Mericatz* said was ever easy to understand, yet he recalled Meeker had promised to have his men build him a house to live in. And nearby, Quinkent's *piwán* could grow things in the ground that were good to eat. Meeker also had promised Quinkent his own cow to milk if he wanted. Quinkent did not like the smell of cow's milk; it made him sick like it did many of the others, yet he had said nothing of this to the agent.

Nor did Quinkent say much about the house Meeker promised him. *Mericatz* did not understand. To live in a house you could not move if something bad happened—was foolish. Only Ouray lived in a grand house at Los Pinos Agency, ate food from a table his *piwán*, Chipeta, prepared with *Mericatz* pots and served on plates. This was fine for Ouray for it pleased him to act like a *Mericatz* and drive around in the grand buggy given him to ride in. Ouray had a fine salary of one thousand dollars a year to spend on whatever suited him, while Quinkent had nothing to show for Ouray having signed away the San Juans in the treaty of '73.

Quinkent knew of no other Ute who had prospered as well as Ouray. Nor had the *Mericatz* in Washington lived up to their agreements in providing monies to each of the bands forever. Not even Nicaagat had been given any money. Only Ouray, and it was Washington who had said that Ouray was *tawacz viem* of all the People. It had not come from the People, yet Ouray had powerful allies and powerful friends among the *Mericatz* and, for now, there was nothing anyone could do to change it.

For now Quinkent would bide his time and see how long this new agent treated the People well. When the agent had finished building the new agency, perhaps, Quinkent would ask him for money like what was provided to Ouray. After all, he too was a *tawacz viem* and if he was going to live in a house, he must have money to buy the things that Washington did not give as presents.

Quinkent smiled, thinking Nicaagat would have a hard time replacing him now that Washington was listening to him once more. On this happy note, Quinkent went down to see Canávish, thinking there might be time for them to play a few hands of cards while Singing Grass prepared the evening meal.

CHAPTER 20

For all the earnest efforts Bob and James Rankin had dedicated to redirecting their brother's Luciferous lifestyle over the past few months, it only took the shorter part of an hour to have it unravel before their eyes in the personage of Jenny Weston. The flashing eyed Miss Weston arrived from Cheyenne one warm day on the Union Pacific, sporting the latest in Paris fashion hung on a frame built to look good even in sack cloth. To say that Jenny Weston created quite a sensation in Rawlings was an understatement but what surprised most folks and even his brothers was how fast Joe Rankin made a move on the beautiful woman. Most people merely shook there heads knowingly and continued with their lives, leaving the astonished lawmen to try and figure out such mysteries of life.

What Bob and James didn't know and wouldn't piece together

until later, after the ruckus had finally settled back down, was that Joe's paramour, Jenny Weston, also happened to be very married to a well-known rancher and businessman back in Cheyenne. It was his insane jealously that had driven Jenny Weston into Joe's arms one night while in Cheyenne buying horses and equipment for his livery.

For a few, but stormy, short weeks, Joe and the paprika-haired Jenny settled into a lifestyle that could best be described as tumultuous and newsworthy. Jenny, very aware of her good looks and charm, had more than a few granite-headed miners and lonely cowpunchers vying for her attentions at the weekly Saturday night dance. Fortified by a few stiffs of whiskey, it didn't take much for the miners and cowpunchers to come to blows, sometimes with Joe entering the brawl just to maintain his sense of dignity and balance in the matter. Not that he had much to worry about. Jenny Weston was hook-line-and-sinker crazy over the livery owner. But Jim and Bob Rankin were growing weary of having to break up fights and hauling the drunken culprits off to jail, warning their brother that the tempestuous Jenny Weston just might be his undoing.

What finally brought things to a head was the sudden appearance of Samuel Weston one evening accompanied by three serious-faced gunmen, each sporting a big Colt on their hips and a Winchester in their hands, looking quite capable of ending Joe Rankin's career, his lawmen brothers notwithstanding.

It was in such saloons as Blacky Stillwell's and Foote's and other establishments as well, that Samuel Weston let it be known he was here to reclaim his wife and take her back to Cheyenne and to shoot the low-down scoundrel who was responsible for trifling with her affections.

In the end, Joe Rankin found out just how fortuitous had been the day he offered Grayson Toliver a job, for without the quick thinking ex-UP dispatcher, the Rankin brothers would have been arranging for their brother's funeral rather than hustling him out of town to head off gunplay and protect the citizens of Rawlings.

With blood in his eyes, Sam Weston came into the livery, backed by the three gunmen with every intention of killing Joe. It took the quick thinking Toliver to slow down the hunt long enough to see Joe was safely out of town by claiming the livery owner had gone south to Baggs Ranch to deliver a load of wagon parts for the rancher's windmills. Less than a dozen steps from where the cool-eyed Toliver was facing down the inflamed rancher, Joe and Jenny Weston were locked in a tight embrace in a small room the livery owner used from time to time.

Had Weston demanded to search the premises, Joe would have found himself in poor position to deal with Weston's gunmen.

After Weston departed, it was Toliver who set off to the jail to tell James and Bob Rankin of the affair. Hurrying back to the livery, the lawmen separated their surprised brother from Jenny's embrace, slapped him on a horse and told him to head south and not to show his face in Rawlings again until they sent word it was safe for him to do so.

Joe protested at first, informing them he had never run from trouble in his life, yet his fondness for the demanding Jenny Weston—who frowned on his activities down on Lower Row—was beginning to wear thin, even for him, and on second thought, quickly agreed to follow his two brothers' instructions. It solved the problem of how to disentangle from the woman without her making a scene.

The next day, Sheriff Jim Rankin saw to it that the couple were reunited and put on the next train heading east.

And that was how Joe Rankin came to find himself at White River Agency just as Nathan Meeker was moving into the newly constructed agency house with his wife Arvilla and their twenty-two year old daughter, Josie. Rankin, ever the professional when it came to appraising women, took note of Arvilla Meeker's wrinkled face and the weariness displayed in her eyes. At sixty-four, it was plain to him, she was struggling with the notion of having to start life anew in a strange place, tending to wild Indians.

Josie, on the other hand, although not too attractive in Rankin's eyes, was a slender, blond-haired girl of twenty-two with vivid blue eyes and an alert face that showed her intelligence.

Joe spent the better part of an afternoon helping the Meekers get settled into their new surroundings. While the wagons were being unloaded, Arvilla got busy in the spartan kitchen and had a meal prepared for the men once things were arranged in the house.

Rankin joined the Meekers, Ed Clark, Frank and Harry Dresser, John Titcomb, and William Post at the table. Nathan Meeker provided grace, a long-winded piece on Thanksgiving, for the safe journey of wife and daughter and the assistance of such good men as Mr. Rankin and others.

Joe picked up his fork and began eating, feeling somewhat less deserving of Meeker's grace, considering his real reason for being there.

"Tell me, Mr. Rankin, how are things in Rawlings now that we have finally gotten the Union Pacific to release the annuities for White River?"

Rankin swallowed hard on a mouthful of food before he answered. "They didn't give young Toliver his job back, if that's what you mean."

"Sorry to hear that, but I rather doubted they would, considering they never admitted to any wrongdoing where the annuities were concerned."

"What sort of business are you in, if I may ask, Mr. Rankin?" Josie queried, her face open and more than a little curious of their guest.

Joe Rankin turned on his natural charm, giving the young

woman a smile. "Please, call me Joe. I own a livery. Rent wagons, horses and such. Fact is, I stored the agency wagon and mules for some months before your father arrived to claim them."

"Is that so."

"Well, Joe, what do you think of moving the agency down here?" Meeker asked, with open earnestly.

Rankin took a swallow of coffee and pushed his empty plate aside to make room for his elbows. "I can certainly see your reasons for moving it here—milder winters, more grass and such. But I expect old Quinkent musta kicked up a fuss as probably did Nicaagat."

"Who?"

"Douglas and Jack, the big chiefs around here if you ain't yet got acquainted."

"Oh yes, I know them both. I must admit, there was some resistance to the idea, but once I explained how much more suitable the land was down here for agricultural crops and for raising cattle, they agreed to the move."

In spite of himself, Joe Rankin let loose a howl. The others at the table were a little shocked by his manner.

"Did I say something funny, Mr. Rankin?" Now Meeker was back to the more formal approach and Joe did not miss the obvious elevation in tension centered in Meeker's eyes.

"Nothing you said, really. It's just that you'll find it a hard go trying to get these Utes to grub in the ground like Digger Indians. It ain't in 'em."

"I beg to differ, sir," Meeker rejoined, nearly rising from his seat. "I fully intend to teach these Indians to be self-sufficient and grow their own food without relying on the United States Government to provide handouts all their life."

"Don't mean no disrespect, Nathan, but I been around these heathens a sight longer than anybody in this room and I can tell you

245

with great confidence, getting Utes to stay put long enough to grow a squash will be a major undertaking."

"That is precisely why I am here," Nathan Meeker said icily, with his hands laced together before his forgotten plate of food.

"My orders were made very clear to me before I left Greeley. Keep the Utes on the reservation. Teach them how to grow their own food so they will forego hunting and raise cattle for milk and meat. We plan to build them homes from which they will no longer want to go roaming whenever the notion strikes them."

Rankin stared at Meeker like someone taken leave of his senses. Meeker was in for a lot of grief.

Rankin shook his head, "I sure do wish you luck but I gotta tell you, you ain't the first to try."

"That might be, sir, but where the others have failed, I intend to succeed. I'm sure Frank or Ed, here, can tell you how happy the Utes all are now. There's laughing children running and playing everywhere you go. These people are happy once again."

Ed Clark spoke up to strengthen Meeker's words. "Why you should have seen them when the lady folk arrived here from Rawlings. Musta been a hunert of them, wouldn't you say, Frank?" Frank Dresser nodded in agreement. "Met the wagons clear to the other side of Coal Creek Canyon, a-whooping and racing their horses back and forth with drums beating. I tell you, it was a sight to behold." The others around the table nodded their heads in agreement.

"Things will be different from here on out for the Utes, you will see," Meeker promised, launching into describing scenes of industrious Ute lumberjacks working the millions of acres of pines, Ute orchardists loading their wagons with fruit to sell in Denver and Ute coal workers digging in the abundant beds located on the agency.

"All these things I have planned for the agency," Meeker finished, with obvious pride in his voice, yet slightly embarrassed for having shared such intimate secrets with Rankin and the others present. Secrets he yet had time to share even with Arvilla. His dreams for Meekerland. Things he was glad now he had not said aloud for fear of being cast a dreaming fool. But they would very soon see how things were and after the railroad was brought to Meeker to handle the exports from the agency, Meeker felt confident the Uncompahgre Utes would ask him to teach them farming as well.

After that, he would be assured the position of Indian Commissioner for life as gratitude for services rendered.

Joe Rankin merely sat there quietly with open-mouthed astonishment, biting back a stinging reply since he was sitting at the agent's table.

"That's gonna take a heap of money."

Meeker smile grew even wider and he glanced over at his engineer, John Titcomb.

"On that score, Mr. Rankin, you are quite correct. My engineer, Mr. Titcomb, and I just this very week returned from Denver where we bought nearly twenty thousand dollars worth of supplies and farm implements to push ahead with the grand plan to make the Utes self-sufficient. Once the plowing has been done and the wheat is ready for harvest, it will be accomplished by the new thrashing machine arriving here this fall."

"How you gonna get them to accept plowing of winter valley, not to mention the feudin' between Douglas and Jack?" Rankin said, not forgetting for one moment the realities of the situation.

Meeker allowed a thin smile to crease his usually stern face. He spoke with great patience, having regained control of his emotions.

"That has already been arranged. This agency has employed Mr. Shadrach Price as plowman, and he should arrive sometime this week. Once Douglas and Jack see the economic benefits from all the various enterprises we have planned, they will want to join forces for the good of their people."

Rankin could see it was useless to talk further with the agent on such matters. The man was in for a rude awakening and nothing he could say would make a difference. The Bureau of Indian Affairs better get another man ready to step into Meeker's shoes because, Joe figured, the agent wouldn't last through next winter with the kind of thinking he was doing.

Rankin turned to Arvilla and Josie. "Mrs. Meeker, Miss Josie, I have enjoyed the company and the meal." Rankin got up and reached for his hat and coat.

"You are more than welcome to spend the night at the new boarding house—free of charge—for lending us a hand," Meeker said, keeping his seat. In addition to her teaching duties at sixty-five dollars per month, Josie also had responsibility for running the boardinghouse Meeker conceived for the express purpose of increasing the repayment of his loans owed to the Greeley estate by offering room and board at two fifty per week. Further, to ensure this enterprise paid off, Meeker hired mainly Greeley bachelors as agency staff.

"Thanks," Rankin said, settling his hat on his head, "but I insist on paying, like any other boarder. I might be here a week or two just to visit some of my Ute friends."

"If you insist," Meeker said, not one to push the issue. With debts such as his hanging over him, Meeker needed all he could get. Besides, Rankin would hold the distinction of being the first boarder since the construction of the boarding house was completed by Clark and his crew consisting of Fullerton, Dunbar and Mansfield the week before. Other buildings, such as the storage shed where the Ute annuities were kept, the agency store, a granary where the harvest wheat would be stored this fall, a milk house and dug well had been completed first, along with Meeker's office and agency house now standing at the corner of Ute and Douglas Streets. The Greeley brothers had constructed their twelve-bed bunkhouse at the corner of Ute Avenue and Meeker Street. Below their bunkhouse was the blacksmith shop, agency corrals and hay area.

"Think I'll mosey down to the Ute camp. Sounds like they may be having a good time." Only in the last few minutes had the drums and the singing started.

"As I said, the Utes are happy once more," Meeker said, not missing an opportunity to reinforce his beliefs of what he felt was already taking place at White River Agency under his direct tutelage.

Major Thornburgh turned out to be a lenient commander to the express relief of both officers and enlisted men—granting passes freely to the troops to blow off steam down on Lower Row in Rawlings, suspending drill when the weather was deemed too hot and allowing dances at the post on a frequent basis.

To pass idle time, Lida and the children spent enjoyable moments meeting the two daily passenger trains, waving to the swells of crowds as they passed by. Although she lacked certain comforts of Omaha, Lida busied herself, making friends with other officers' wives and planning social events to relieve the boredom of such a desolate spot.

Thornburgh had found plenty to do at the Post and was still trying to live down the ill-fated junket to Nebraska he had undertaken for General Crook to stop two pitiful bands of Cheyenne Indians lead by Dull Knife, who were escaping northward from Indian Territory. But the supply wagons mired down and Crook's quartermaster had failed to provide the usual Indian scouts and mobile pack train. To make matters worse, Thornburgh and his troops became lost, marching aimlessly over two hundred and fifty miles of sandhills and dry creek beds. The Third Cavalry finally had to rescue them. Even though Thornburgh had been personally humiliated by the experience, he was not harshly criticized for his lack of success since he could not be blamed for transport failure. But Thornburgh felt the keen sting of having let General Crook down and he promised himself that he would not let it happen again.

The only dark moment of their stay at Fort Steele came when Tip and Lida lost their youngest son to a sudden fever. Thornburgh was thankful of the officers' wives who gave Lida emotional support during this crises. Feeling the keen sense of loss as fully as Lida, Thornburgh tried clearing his head by a fishing trip to Battle Lake with General Crook, who had come out for the funeral. Their expedition to the Sierra Madre Mountains could not have been more perfect, with Thornburgh catching fifty-two red-sides in thirty minutes one day.

"Wire just came for you, Major," adjutant, Lt. Sam Cherry said, interrupting Thornburgh's pleasant reverie.

"Thank you, Sam," Thornburgh said, leaning back in his chair to study the message. It was from his older brother, ex-Congressman of Knoxville, Jacob Montgomery Thornburgh. Jacob stated he was coming to Fort Steele to hunt elk that fall and was bringing along with him two important Tennessee banker friends as well.

This bit of news lifted Thornburgh's spirits immediately and he quickly penned a reply to his brother, gave the note to Sam Cherry in the outer office and went off looking for Lida to tell her the good news.

Beyond the post, across the distant mountain range to the southeast, dark smudges of numerous fires marked the blue skyline as the heat of another dry summer got underway. Fires that would figure heavily into Tip Thornburgh's and Nathan Meeker's future happiness and well being.

CHAPTER 21

Joe Rankin stayed just long enough at White River to observe the seeds of doubt sown among the Utes and the general staff of the agency.

With full bellies and more annuities arriving daily from Rawlings via James France's bullwackers, there was little inclination for the Utes to pick up the white man tools and dig a canal like Meeker wanted them to do.

Meeker tried every way he knew how to get Douglas to get behind the project now that John Titcomb had finished the survey work for the Grand Canal the agent had planned to use to provide irrigation water for the wheat crop. Double rations and extra pay were offered to any Ute who would pick up a shovel. To a man, not a single Ute accepted Meeker's offer.

Exasperated, Meeker sent Henry Jim to fetch the old chief. Time was running out and with no rain in sight, every day they delayed work on the new canal was critical to the success of a fall crop of wheat, now standing a foot tall in a lower pasture.

Bemused by Meeker's efforts to get the Utes to work, Rankin was lounging near the agency office when Quinkent came up from his *carniv*, trailed by several Utes Rankin knew. He moved closer to the office in order to hear what Meeker was going to say to the old chief.

Quinkent came as requested but several of the men followed to see what this agent wanted. Meeker was at his desk writing to Commissioner Hayt. When he spied Quinkent in the doorway, Meeker gave him a smile and motioned the Ute inside.

"Hello, Douglas," the agent said. As usual, Quinkent remained silent yet he did shake Meeker's hand.

"Now listen, Douglas, we really need to get this canal started and today, if possible." Still nothing out of Quinkent. Meeker continued, realizing the Ute would say nothing until he was through talking and understood exactly what it was Meeker wanted.

"I think you can be a big help in getting your men to dig this canal, if you only would, so I'm prepared to give any man willing to dig, a brand new Winchester and a box of fixed ammunition. Also, for each foot dug, every man will be paid a grand sum of twenty-five dollars each, more than enough to buy things for their wives and children. What do you say?" A long silence filled the office, heated by a stream of warm sunlight coming through an opened window.

"Men don't want to dig in ground. They think this is *Mericatz* — white men work."

"Please understand this, Douglas, if you are successful in hiring some of your men to finish this canal, Washington will be heap pleased and will provide you and your people with many more good things. You will be chief for a long time." Meeker could see he had struck a cord within the old chief and he pressed the issue harder. "On the other hand, if this work isn't done, I will have to write Washington who will be heap mad and the presents might stop coming, or worse." Meeker left the *or worse* unfinished, leaving Douglas to imagine what the outcome might be if he choose not to cooperate.

"I will talk to the young men. They might agree to work some."

Meeker gave the old chief a big smile. "That will be fine, Douglas. Tell them to see Ed Clark for the necessary tools. They need to start now for we are far behind on digging this canal," Meeker said, trying to impress upon the Ute the sense of urgency. With typical Ute custom, Quinkent turned and left the office without saying another word.

Meeker returned to the letter he was composing to Hayt when a shadow fell across the doorway. The agent looked up to see Joe Rankin standing there, smiling.

"You really think you gonna get them Utes to dig in the dirt?"

"I am indeed, Mr. Rankin," Meeker responded with high spirits. "Just you wait."

"Wish I could but I'm headin' back to Rawlings tomorrow," Rankin said, figuring hot-headed Jenny Weston and her irate husband had cleared out by now.

"I suspect you will see a surprising sight this very afternoon."

Rankin shook his head, "Gave up on miracles long ago," thinking of his child-hood friend and the snakes. Would he ever out-live the nightmare?

Sure enough, just after Rankin had taken his lunch at the boardinghouse, prepared by Josie Meeker and served to him by buxom sixteen year old Flora Ellen Price. Flora Ellen was married to the plowman, Shadrach Price, a dour Kansan who didn't like the looks Rankin threw at the mother of his two children. Flora Ellen seemed oblivious to Rankin's advances, flouncing around the kitchen in hardly enough clothing to cover her straining chest.

Another time, Rankin figured he would have made a play for the young woman, but this impulse was dampened by the very recent memory of Jenny Weston.

Shadrach Price called everyone to the porch of the boardinghouse to come see what he was pointing at. Rankin, holding a slice of pie in his hand, stepped to the porch along with the others.

"I don't believe it," Price remarked. In the distance, where the ditch came out of a thick grove of cottonwoods, were eight to ten Indians, toiling in the dirt with pick axes and shovels. Quinkent was among them, using a shovel and directing the others on what to do.

"Never would of thought it possible," Rankin said quietly.

"Then you don't know my father," Josie piped up, with blue eyes flashing a smile at Rankin.

"Maybe," Rankin admitted, "but I don't see Jack down there with them."

"Doesn't matter. Jack will come around," Josie said with confidence.

But Rankin wasn't so sure about Nicaagat and it was near the middle of the afternoon when he spied Nicaagat and his sub-chief, Sowówic riding over to the sweating Indians. He would have given a weeks' wages to hear what Nicaagat was saying, but the outcome was very clear to anyone watching.

All the young men who had been digging in the ground threw down their tools and walked away with Nicaagat, leaving Quinkent standing there with a shovel in his hand. After a few minutes, he too walked away.

Rankin smiled to himself. He had warned Meeker. Ain't an Indian alive would dig in the dirt like a white man for long, no matter what he was being bribed with. Rankin picked up his bedroll and strapped it across the back of his horse behind his saddle.

Had he not made up his mind to ride at least as far as George Baggs' ranch tonight, he would have liked to stay longer and view the ruckus Meeker would undoubtedly kick up. Instead, he turned his horse in the direction of Coal Creek Canyon. There was always Maggie Baggs.

Josie and Flora Ellen called their goodbyes from the porch of the boardinghouse. Absently, Rankin gave them a wave without looking back, his mind already filled with the sweet image of Maggie. Ten miles out, he stopped and chatted for a few minutes with the mail courier, Black Wilson, inquiring about the town and if the livery was still standing.

"Never knowed you to skedaddle outta town over some woman before," was Black Wilson's first comment when he pulled up in the shade of a giant alder, growing along Coal Creek and waited for Rankin to draw close enough to hear him.

"Durn you, Black, you ain't never been twisted up with the likes of Jenny Weston either. How's my livery?"

"Grayson Toliver is doing a fine job. Much better than you ever did, I suspect."

"He's a good boy," Rankin admitted, thinking he would need to give Toliver a small raise when he got back.

"How's White River?"

"Expect you'll fine things heating up some." And he told the mail courier of the mounting tension between Meeker and the Utes over the many fires burning throughout the Parks and Bear River country and the canal Meeker was forcing them to dig.

Black Wilson shook his head. "Expect this might be my last trip. They know Meeker writes to Washington about them and neither Douglas or Jack likes it one bit. They see me as someone who carries these lies back and forth and I wouldn't be at all surprised to see a bunch of Utes stop me from coming to the agency anymore."

"Most of the grief is coming from Meeker," Rankin said. "Thinks

255

he's gonna make white men outta savages and everything will be just fine once they put away their horses and take up farming."

"Trouble with Meeker, he ain't no farmer more'n them Utes," Black commented. "You talk with some of them Union Colonists over to Greeley and they'll fill both your ears full of Meeker and the sorry job he did there. Paid ten times over for the land, let the crops die for lack of water because the canal wasn't finished and fruit trees brought in from the east dried up in the sun, what wasn't eaten by roaming cattle." He shook his head, "Tell you, the man ain't nothing more than talk with you doing all the work, but I gotta get along with him for now."

"Don't know when, Black, but something bad's going to happen back there. Only hope the women folk ain't made to suffer for Meeker's mistakes." Black Wilson agreed and with that the two men parted.

Nathan Meeker was fit to be tied when Black Wilson rode up to the agency office an hour later. He met the mail courier on the porch with several letters in his hands.

"How soon can you get these back?" Meeker asked Wilson. No greeting, no nothing.

"Dang, I just rode up, Nathan," Black Wilson said, dismounting. "I got to at least rest my horse some."

"Take one of the agency's horses. I've got letters both to Commissioner Hayt and Secretary Schurz that need immediate attention."

"That'll be fine, but I still got to rest some, grab a bite to eat."

"Do you have any mail from Fort Steele?" Meeker asked, ignoring Wilson's reply.

"No, don't think so." Meeker grew even hotter at Wilson's reply.

"I've written Major Thornburgh several times and I've yet to hear one single peep from him," Meeker fumed while Wilson stood there with the mail pouch in his hand.

"What's going on, Nathan?" Wilson asked, following the agitated agent inside.

"Plenty," Meeker responded. "First, I've been trying to get the army to check into this fire business and keep these Indians on the reservation. They roam over creation, buying whiskey and rifles from Perkin's and Peck's stores. They've been setting fires all over the place. Got half the population of settlers scared clean out of their wits."

"How do you know the Indians are settin' them?"

Meeker looked at the mail courier with cold eyes. "Because, Mr. Wilson, no settler in his right mind would start fires. And the army is ignoring the problem. And there's more. Just today, Douglas and Jack pulled their men off digging the canal we need to water the crops. Furthermore, they don't want us plowing up the land to plant more crops."

"Utes don't like work," Wilson commented, dumping the contents of his pouch on Meeker's desk.

"You can't get them to do *anything* closely resembling work," Meeker screeched. "All they want to do is ride their ponies, hunt and play cards. And since I've heard nothing from Thornburgh, I am leaving tomorrow for Denver to meet with General Pope whom I understand is visiting that city. Maybe through him, I can get these mettlesome Utes to stop setting fires and stay put and work their crops."

Black Wilson doubted anything Meeker could do right now would keep the Utes at home. They had spent their lives roaming across the mountains whenever they felt like it and until forced, would continue to do so. But he never told Meeker this. He gathered up the mail, stepped across to the boardinghouse for something to eat and saddled a fresh horse for the return trip to Rawlings. Only when he was beyond Yellowjacket Pass did he breathe a sigh of relief. The tension back at White River was thick enough to cut with a knife. Joe Rankin was right, the place was a powder keg with a short fuse. Question was, what would it take to set it off?

Four days later, Nathan Meeker was in Denver where he sought out Davit Moffat, cashier of the First National Bank where the agency account was maintained, and made arrangements to pay for the threshing machine he had ordered.

Next, he found General John Pope at the Grand Central Hotel where he was having dinner. Pope inquired about the agency affairs and Meeker obligingly launched off into a two hour tirade about the fires, the fact he couldn't get the Utes to do any work or to stay on the reservation so they could look after crops planted for them by agency employees. And Major Thornburgh had completely ignored his pleas for assistance.

"I wouldn't be surprised if these Utes didn't have an uprising if things don't get better. And to speak frankly, General, I'm about ready to resign from the whole mess."

"Don't do that, Nathan. Let me assure you, I'm well aware of your predicament and have ordered Captain Dodge and Company D of Hatch's Ninth Cavalry to Middle Park and Gore Pass to investigate these fires. Francis Dodge and his men are camped, as we speak, on Grand River at the mouth of Troublesome Creek. They are closer than Thornburgh's men at Fort Steele, so don't worry. At the first sign of trouble, they have standing orders to rush to your rescue. As soon as these Utes learn there is a Cavalry Unit so close, they'll behave."

Somewhat mollified, Meeker accepted Pope's argument, and boarded the Denver Pacific two days later for Cheyenne where he caught the westbound Union Pacific for the ride back to Rawlings.

Still, he doubted that Dodge's forty-four Negro troopers could do much if the Utes decided to cause real trouble.

As Meeker entered the palace car and took his seat, a striking army officer entered behind him and took a seat nearby. After the train had gone a few miles, Meeker got out of his seat and went over to the officer and introduced himself.

Thornburgh rose to his feet to grasp the White River Agent's hand, recognizing his name.

"I'm Major Tip Thornburgh, Commander at Fort Steele. I've been wanting to meet you."

"And I," Meeker said. "What brings you this far east, Major?"

"I've just served a week on General Court Martial at Fort D. A. Russell. Right now, I'm headed back to my Post."

"Are the Utes still roaming off the reservation?"

"They are!" Meeker said sharply. "Furthermore, you should know I've met with General John Pope back in Denver, since I've gotten no response to the two letters I sent you concerning the fires the Utes have been setting across Colorado. I asked General Pope for assistance in this matter."

"I'm sorry. I did send your request for assistance to General Crook in Omaha who sent it on to General Sheridan in Chicago and who furthered it on to General Sherman in Washington."

"And what did Sherman say?" Meeker prodded.

"I've yet to receive a response for your request to remove the Utes from the Little River and the Bear, although General Sherman requested I investigate these fires for Governor Pitkin."

"And what did you determine?"

"The reports from Wyoming settlers indicated no Indians had started any fires, even though a member of Jack's band had been seen hunting on French, Spring and Beaver Creeks."

"I'm not interested in what's happening in Wyoming. The fires are being set two hundred miles south of the North Platte Country you are talking about!" Meeker's hazel eyes snapped with rising anger.

"I've been tied up with forming a hunting party for General Crook and President Hays' son, Webb, the last three weeks."

"That's just as I figured," Meeker nearly shouted at the tall officer. "All you West Pointers are trained to do nothing but judge a
good bottle of wine, history and sports. Most soldiers are nothing
more than drunkards, and immoral in their practices upon Indian
women." Tip Thornburgh seemed to grow even straighter under the
tongue lashing. Meeker should have let well enough alone, but his
anger continued to flow.

"You officers are supposed to be civilized, yet you prove the opposite by murdering innocent women and little children at such places
as Sand Creek and Washita. Barbaric massacres like these cannot be
forgiven for supposedly educated white men."

Thornburgh looked down on the ranting White River Agent
with cold fury as the conductor came by to check their passes.

Tip Thornburgh flashed his elegant Union Pacific gold-lettered
card for the conductor while keeping his black eyes on Meeker who
fumbled for some minutes in his wallet for the soiled pass that was
so shabby, the conductor had trouble reading it. The Department of
Interior pass authorized the Union Pacific to collect twenty-one dollars for the agent's round trip.

After the conductor passed on by, it was plain further talk
between the two men was impossible and Meeker returned to his
seat.

Meeker regretted his outburst, even though the things he said
were essentially true. Attacking the major that way added little to his
side of the ledger.

In Rawlings, Meeker was met by Harry Dresser and a new
employee, George Eaton, whom he had recently hired. Of troubled
spirit, it only got worse for Meeker when the agency wagon turned
over on his arm while they were coming down Williams Fork. The
wagon was wrecked and Meeker was in such pain, Harry hurried on
to the agency and brought back another wagon for Meeker to ride
in.

The wagon carrying Nathan Cook Meeker lumbered into the agency and deposited him with Arvilla who saw him to bed in much pain. Restless more from a troubled soul than the painful, wrenched arm, Meeker realized he hated the Utes. They would never do as he asked. They would never give up their horses and settle down. But even in the depth of his dejection and frustration he still had the desire to succeed.

He would give the Utes one more chance. After that, he would see how they would deal with the force of a soldier's bullet, the feel of chains around their necks and prison.

CHAPTER 22

Deer Moon had come and gone along the Smoking Earth River and still the rains stayed away. And now they were half way through Hot Moon, that time the *Mericatz* called July.

Quinkent spent his days watching thunderclouds gathered over the distant peaks each afternoon, bringing nothing more than hot winds and lightning. More fires sprang up in Middle and South Parks, burning many acres. Quinkent paid little attention to these fires for they had been part of the People for as long as there had been mountains.

The two things that worried him the most were—the *Mericatz* were beginning to blame the People for starting these fires and, just as important, the searing heat of a long summer drought had sent the game deeper into the plains, away from the mountains. The

People still needed to hunt and the greater distances took their toll on man and beast.

One particular hot day when even the breeze from Smoking Earth River carried with it the feel of a cook fire, Canávish stopped by Quinkent's *carniv* to smoke and talk of the troubling times. For a long time, neither man spoke as they smoked the tobacco they had gotten from the storehouse at the agency. That was the one good thing the People had benefited from when this agent came to live in winter valley. They had plenty of tobacco, flour and oats for their horses.

Canávish was the first to break the silence. "There is something bad moving up from the earth beneath us. It moves around and is trying to get out, maybe to warn the People."

Quinkent did not like this thing Canávish spoke of for he too had noticed the change in the People. How Singing Grass had scraped a deerskin until a hole appeared and how *pana* was left on the cook fire too long and burned. Even the little children had become restless and cried for no reason. Quinkent felt this thing in the earth Canávish spoke of and wished he knew what to do.

"Perhaps, it is this plowing the *Mericatz* is doing. It hurts the land and leaves nothing for the horses to eat," Quinkent ventured.

"There is more, although, turning the soil upside down causes the earth to become sick. And so will the People."

"Pauvitz' *piwán* became very angry when this agent told the other *Mericatz* to plow up their land."

Canávish nodded, "This is a very bad thing this agent does. And now he blames us for setting fires in the parks. This agent has become angry at the People when all we want is peace."

"Unh!" Quinkent said, thinking of the angry words Nicaagat and the agent had exchanged only three sleeps before. And now Nicaagat was gone to talk with the governor.

Both men thought Meeker would settle down and start acting

like an agent should, giving out the presents when it was time and leaving the People to play games, hunt and race their ponies. But this agent only made it worse by telling the People they must work, that the land did not belong to them and if they didn't do as he said, he would bring in the soldiers.

Always the threat of soldiers! Always this agent was sending his words to Washington. Telling lies about the People. About the fires in Bear River Valley and Middle and South Parks.

And now, Nicaagat and Sowówic had gone to Denver to see the *Mericatz* who was governor and make him take this agent away for the lies he was telling on the People about the fires and other things this agent was doing that were not right.

As they sat there, Pauvitz came over from his *carniv* and joined them. After a moment he spoke.

"This agent held a council while you were away hunting with Tatitz. It had to do with this business of turning over the earth. This agent said Quinkent was not such good friends anymore and he ordered your land to be plowed," meaning Canávish's.

"How can this be?" the shaman said. "I was part of no council."

Pauvitz shrugged his shoulders like a *Mericatz*. "That is what this agent said."

"Perhaps, I will go and talk with this agent later," Canávish said, getting up to walk back to his own *carniv* to consider the matter.

Quinkent sat there like a man sick from eating too much and after a while, Pauvitz left to see if his *piwán* had cooked anything to eat.

Quinkent became aware he was alone and he got up from the ground and walked down to the river, seeking solace. But the spirit birds had gone north before Deer Moon and Quinkent found the river empty and silent. Once more he could feel this thing beneath his moccasins, working its way closer to the surface of the earth. What could he do? Who could he talk to about this agent that would change things here?

The pointy tips of his mustache drooped down over his lower lip as Quinkent thought of Nicaagat. Why hadn't he thought to go and talk with this governor for the People. He was *tawacz viem*!

In the end, he had no answer and he turned away from Smoking Earth River and back to where Singing Grass was mending his beautiful shirt after he had torn it while riding through dense brush. Perhaps, Canávish could talk with Meeker and he would start treating the People right again as he had when he first came to winter valley.

Canávish only picked at his food and his *piwán*, Tsashin, tried to lift the spirits of her husband, but nothing she said or did seemed to make any difference. After a while, she left him to his thoughts and went off to gather more firewood for the center fire that night.

Canávish sat there in the late morning sun staring out across his patch of grassy land and his racetrack where he and his two sons had won many horse races. Something moved beyond the trees, towards where the *Mericatz* lived.

A *Mericatz* grew into a shape large enough for him to see the two mules and the shiny contraption being pulled along by the mules.

Canávish watched as the *Mericatz* lifted aside a part of the wire fence that circled Canávish's racetrack and drove the mules and the shiny thing across the wire. Next the Mericatz put pieces of leather on the mules and hooked it to this shiny thing.

Canávish called to Tsashin as she came up with a load of sticks, pointing at the *Mericatz*. The shaman by now was standing and growing angry at the *Mericatz* for being on his land.

Tsashin dropped the firewood and hurried over to her husband. Suddenly the mules began to move forward and the shiny knife began to cut the grass and turn it under.

"I will go see this agent and tell him to stop cutting my land this way." There was dark anger on Canávish's face as he hurried up to the agency office.

Nathan Meeker was standing on the porch looking out at Shadrach Price plowing the racetrack. He gave Canávish a pleasant smile as the angry shaman came up to him.

"Hello, Johnson," Meeker said.

"Man plow my ground," Canávish said, without preamble.

"Yes, Johnson, I know."

"Don't wan land spoiled like dat. Why he plow?"

"I ordered him to," Meeker said, simply.

"Make him stop. Don't wan land cut up."

"Listen, Johnson, if you are ever going to have anything, we must plant a winter wheat crop there."

"Why you tell man dat?" Canávish took a step towards the porch where Nathan Meeker stood.

Meeker kept looking down at the racetrack where Shadrach Price had made several passes, laying the dark earth open.

"Because it was decided at the council yesterday to plow your land, Johnson."

"I no say man can plow. Who say dat?"

"I told you, Johnson, it was agreed by those at the council meeting. Washington wants all this land plowed."

To Canávish this did not sound right. None of the People would ever talk for someone who was not present. The People would wait until he could speak for himself in council. This agent was lying.

"Don't wan my land plowed. You lie," Canávish said to Meeker. Canávish stepped up on the porch as Meeker backed towards the door.

Meeker's face flushed red. "Don't you accuse me of lying! Go ask the others," Meeker shouted. Canávish followed the agent into the agency office.

"You lie! Don't want land plowed." Meeker looked around him and found himself being pushed back through the opened doorway by the angry shaman.

"The trouble with you, Johnson, is you need to kill some of your horses. They require too much land to graze. But I'm through talking with you! I want you to gather up your lodge and family and leave the agency!" Meeker was now standing outside once more near the edge of the porch with Canávish still advancing, only now with eyes blazing with full anger. "I'm tired of troublesome Indians!"

"No kill horses! Dis is my land. Washington build me house. I stay dere."

"I told you once, Johnson, what would happen if you people didn't do as I say. Either you better leave or I will have you thrown in prison."

Meeker's words only inflamed Canávish even more and he grabbed Meeker hard by the shoulder, who had one foot off the porch.

"You are bad agent . . . you lie, very bad agent," Canávish shouted. It had been a very long time since he had been this angry at another man. Meeker slipped over the edge of the porch, still backing up.

The air was taut with anger and some of the People were coming to see what was happening. Two *Mericatz* who had been nailing a roof on one of the buildings stopped hammering, and were staring at the whooping Indians who had gathered to watch.

Meeker tried to say something above the singing of the other Indians but his head went back and his feet shot out from under him as he flipped backward over the hitching rail, striking his head on the hard ground. Meeker sprawled in the dust and dung, his eyes blinking wildly. He pointed a feeble finger at Canávish, but no words came out of his mouth.

Ed Clark and Frank Dresser rushed over and helped Meeker to his feet, brushing the dust from his dark suit with their hats.

"Let's get him over to his house," Clark said to Dresser and the two men hustled Meeker away while the People picked up the chant again and led Canávish away with the sounds of the People coming from inside and outside of him until his mind was consumed by the ancient chant.

Nicaagat and Sowówic made a point to ride by and see for themselves the *Mericatz* house that had supposedly burned on Bear River as Meeker claimed, near the Hayden Settlement. Burned by fires set by two Utes.

Nicaagat had asked the agent to come with him to see for himself that the house was still standing, but Meeker refused, saying it was none of his business.

"How come dis iss not your business?" Nicaagat had asked. "You Indian agent."

"Because," Meeker had said, "it is not my business to go and find bad men in trouble like the Indians who set these fires."

"Dis talk iss no good," Nicaagat had said. "Somebody make paper say Indian bad. Maybe, paper lie. You come see dat dis house iss not burned."

"I am through talking about this matter," Meeker had said, and went into his office and closed the door.

Now as they rode through beautiful Bear Valley, Nicaagat was still troubled by what Meeker had said to him. Even though he had lost a lot of the *Mericatz* language, piece by piece over the years and had not tried to bring it back, Meeker's response to the charges two Utes had set fires had not made much sense. He was willing to blame Utes for this trouble not knowing if these charges were true. And as agent, he wasn't willing to go see for himself.

"I think this agent is a troubled man . . . too old and unhappy," Nicaagat finally said to Acari and Sowówic as they stopped to water their horses at a trickle of water that fell through a rocky gulch with its headwaters in the Williams Fork Mountains. The midday heat was like a hot center fire, sucking the already dry air free of any further moisture. Below them they saw the green trees marking Bear River as it cut its way across the broad valley of dying sagebrush and scrub chokeberry. Several dust devils raced along in the distance, carrying with them the red dust of the countryside. Also in the distance, along the river was the store and a little cluster of buildings.

"Perhaps, this agent will send words to Washington after we see the Governor and tell him Utes are not setting fires," Sowówic said. Nicaagat had nothing to say about this. He had given up long ago where *Mericatz* were concerned.

The trio rode slowly across the valley to the settlement and stopped at the store where a long bench had been built. Usually several *Mericatz* were sitting there talking and whittling. Today the bench was empty. A young boy who had been standing in the doorway of the store as they rode up, ran back inside.

Nicaagat and the others dismounted, tied their horses to the rack and went inside. There were noises in the back and presently the storekeeper came out and greeted Nicaagat by his *Mericatz* name. They shook hands.

"What brings you out here, Jack, more ammunition?"

"Come see if house iss burned, like paper said," Nicaagat said. Acari and Sowówic wandered around the store while Nicaagat talked with the storekeeper, peering into barrels and feeling of harnesses, saddles and other drygoods.

"There's been no houses burned around here, Jack."

"Dis agent say dat."

"Damn Meeker's hide anyway," the storekeeper said, rummaging behind the counter for a minute. "He's been trying to prevent me and the others like me, from selling your people goods and such." He showed Nicaagat the paper. "Meeker don't want your people roaming off the reservation. I told him he was crazy and besides, when does an Indian agent have authority off a federal reservation?"

"Dis paper say bad things 'bout Indian?" Nicaagat wanted to know.

"It does, and furthermore, these letters were sent out all over. Even to the Governor in Denver."

Nicaagat's black eyes fairly burned at the thought of the agent doing this to the People. This agent was telling lies on the People. He thought he had better go and see for himself that the house was not burned. He thanked the storekeeper and they shook hands again.

Acari and Sowówic followed Nicaagat out into the hot sunshine. They mounted their ponies and started away with Nicaagat taking the trail north, directly up river. The trail climbed through oak-brush hills that became mountains covered with aspen and pine across a rugged string of peaks the *Mericatz* called Gore Range. They rode past the log house that was still standing while Nicaagat told Acari and Sowówic about his talk with this storekeeper.

"Unh!" they both said, glad that they were going to talk with this governor and get the truth told. Washington wanted peace same as the People.

Nicaagat had not been to this place called Denver for four winters where the *Mericatz* huddled close together. This place smelled bad and was too noisy to stay there for very long. Nicaagat rode slowly down streets that now were as hard as rocks. The face of this place had changed. There were many stores and funny-dressed people who rode around in little buggies with tops on them. It took several tries before Nicaagat could get a *Mericatz* to tell him where the Governor stayed.

Eventually they found the large building with its shiny floor and tall granite columns. The floor was like a frozen lake and at first, Acari and Sowówic refused to walk across it until Nicaagat had done so.

They went into a room and saw a *Mericatz* behind an oak desk who told Nicaagat that unless they had an important man help them, they could not see the Governor. The *Mericatz* said such a man was Pius, the one the *Mericatz* called Byers. They turned and left the building.

"I do not understand why we must find another *Mericatz* to help us see this Governor," Acari said. He was tired and his belly gnawed at him from hunger. He would rather go eat but Nicaagat said they would first go see Byers.

"This Pius is an important *Mericatz* who makes newspapers. Perhaps, he will know something about what is being said about the People and the fires." Acari and Sowówic thought this was good.

They found the square-faced William Byers in his office and he shook hands with each of the Indians. Nicaagat told the editor why they had come and the newspaper man picked up his hat and went back with them to the Governor's office.

Inside the office as before, Byers had them wait on a bench while he disappeared into another room. Presently, he returned and ushered them into this office, much larger than the first.

Nicaagat saw another *Mericatz* sitting in a huge chair behind a desk. The man stood, smiled at them, and they all shook hands. This man, Byers told them, was the Governor.

"Please sit down," Governor Pitkin said as he took his seat again. Nicaagat did not want to sit down and he ignored the chairs as did Acari and Sowówic. Byers and this Governor exchanged glances the way only *Mericatz* can.

"Tell me, Jack, how are things going at White River?" Pitkin asked.

Nicaagat did not answer right away for there was much to speak of and he needed to use the correct *Mericatz* words to describe these troubles. Before he could speak, Pitkin rushed on.

"I've been receiving numerous complaints against your people,

Jack. How come the White River Utes can't be as peaceful as Ouray's?"

Nicaagat noticed that Byers, the *Mericatz* that made the newspaper was writing down words the Governor was speaking. Nicaagat chose his words carefully so others who read this newspaper would know he spoke the truth.

"Dis agent tell lies," Nicaagat finally said, having found no suitable way to say this clearer in *Mericatz* words. "He iss no good."

"You having trouble with Agent Meeker, then?"

"Much trouble. He iss bad agent. We want new agent."

"Now the newspapers are saying a great deal about your people Jack," Pitkin probed.

"Somebody tell lies to paper," Nicaagat said, watching Pius writing furiously in his note pad. "I come here to tell truth."

"Well, that is what we are after here, Jack," Pitkin said blandly.

"Maybe you know why somebody mad at Utes?"

"I don't think anyone is mad with your people, Jack." Pitkin picked up a letter from his desk and showed it to Nicaagat. "This is a letter from your agent. He says he's been trying to teach your people good things but that some of you are making trouble, not staying on the reservation. Mr. Meeker wants the Utes to farm so they can make their own living. Be independent. Work and have money like all white men. Explain to me why you don't want to do this, Jack?"

"Ute no farm, tear up earth, spoil grass. Ute no work like dat. Ute iss hunter to get food, like always."

"Everybody must work, Jack."

"You no work. You have fine place. Other people to do work." Nicaagat pointed at Pius who was scribbling even faster in his note pad. "He no work." And then Nicaagat pointed to his chest. "I no work." Both Pitkin and Byers laughed.

"You made a joke. Now maybe, we will all be good friends and they will help us get a new agent," Sowówic said.

"Perhaps," Nicaagat replied in the old language.

"I suppose you would like to be governor, then?" Pitkin asked Nicaagat, still laughing.

"Yes."

The two white men laughed even harder.

"What does he say?" Acari asked. Nicaagat told them. Sowówic and Acari laughed too. "Maybe, you will be governor tomorrow and sit in that fine chair."

In the mist of the laugher, Pitkin pointed to the letter from Agent Meeker again. His face became straight once more and Nicaagat had to listen closely to understand what he was saying.

"Your agent also says that some of your Utes have been setting fires. Agent Meeker says here that two Utes set Major Thompson's house on fire at the Hayden Community down on Bear River. The sheriff has gone to your reservation to arrest the two Utes responsible."

"That iss why I came," Nicaagat said. "This house iss not burn. I go see diss house. Thompson house not burned. Iss lie."

"That's not all," Pitkin said smoothly, ignoring Nicaagat's comment. "Meeker says there have been numerous other fires set all over Middle Park."

"There iss many fires dere," Nicaagat admitted, "but iss not from Ute. Lighting start fires. No rain, very dry. These lies come from agent. Meeker iss bad man for Ute. He say one thing today, 'nodder tomorrow. We want you write Washington. Tell Washington to send 'nodder agent, take diss one back."

Pitkin was looking at Byers who had stopped writing. There was a trace of a smile on his face. Finally, Pitkin looked at Nicaagat.

"Yes, Jack, I will write Washington if that is what you wish."

"Good, dat iss all we have to say."

CHAPTER 23

The telegraph key clicked rapidly at the railroad station in Rawlings, sending the message flashing across the country to the Bureau of Indian Affairs in Washington, D.C.

> September 10, 1879
> I have been assaulted by a leading chief, Johnson. Forced out of my own house and injured badly, but was rescued by employees. It is now revealed that Johnson originated all the trouble stated in letter Sept. 8; his son shot at plowman, and opposition to plowing is wide; plowing stops; life of self, family, and employees not safe; want protection immediately; have asked Gov. Pitkin to confer with Gen. Pope.
>
> N.C. Meeker, Indian Agent

"All hell's gonna break loose now," Haywood Grant said to Black Wilson as he straighten up from the key.

"Been coming for a long time. Just glad I made it back in one piece. And damned if I'll make another mail run for any amount of money. Meeker had a lick of sense, he'd get himself and his women-folk outta there while there's still time," Grant said, closing the flap on his mail pouch.

"You think they'll fight if Pope orders in troops?" the Union Pacific dispatcher asked.

"Best ask Joe Rankin that question. He's had more direct dealings with them through the years, but if I don't miss my guess, them Utes will fight. Hell, Captain Jack and his young bucks are spoiling for a fight most times." Black Wilson turned towards the door. "Right now, I'm headed down to Foote's place and get happy drunk."

After the mail carrier had gone, Haywood Grant leaned across the table on his elbows, speculating what he would do if he were trapped by a hundred crazy Indians, two hundred miles from civilization. Just thinking of it sent shivers down his backbone. That's when he began thinking maybe Wyoming wasn't the place for someone like him.

Still acting in Commissioner Hayt's absence, Ed Brooks took one look at the wire from Nathan Meeker and quickly penned a note to it and sent it over to Secretary Carl Schurz.

"I respectfully request this matter be referred to the honorable Secretary of War for action."

The last thing Carl Schurz needed right now was another Indian uprising, having spent the entire summer working to clear himself and President Hays of blame for relocating the peaceful Nebraska Poncas to Indian Territory to placate the troublesome Sioux. Even though he worried even more when he sent the request over to

George McCary, Secretary of War, Schurz knew he had no choice. An Indian Agent had to be protected at all costs.

McCary immediately approved Meeker's request for troops and instructed General Sheridan in Chicago to order the nearest military commander to forward troops to White River.

A reply for troops was sent back to Meeker at White River by Commissioner Brooks five days later after grinding slowly through the Departments of Interior and War.

> September 15, 1879
> Your request for troops approved. War department
> requested commanding officer nearest you to forward
> troops for your protection immediately. On their arrival
> arrest those Utes causing disturbance and have them held
> until further orders from this office. Report full particu-
> lars as soon as possible.
>
> E.J. Brooks, Acting Com'r

The wire was delivered to White River by Joe Rankin only after being promised triple wages by John Steele, a forthright Kansan, who owned the Rawlings-White River mail contract. Steele was not a happy man. He complained to Joe that he had been losing money on the contract for the last few months because of the Indian troubles. Rankin smiled, collected his money and rode to White River.

Meeker looked worried and sick and possessed none of the self-confidence he had shown Rankin that day, nearly three months before. To Rankin, the agent looked old and carried himself with a stooped posture.

What bothered Rankin more was the fact that Nicaagat's followers were breaking camp and their squaws were moving over Roan Plateau into the higher mountains. He mentioned this to Meeker who seemed to become even more depressed.

"Douglas is staying. I feel he wants peace and there is still hope this matter can be resolved without troops coming here."

Rankin looked at the agent with disbelief. "Douglas is an old man, Meeker. He's more likely to go along with whatever Jack decides to do, you can bet on it. Didn't you hear the war dance last night?" Rankin asked. "I dang shore did and I'm here to tell you, this is my last trip."

"They beat their drums all the time," Meeker said in a monotone. "It means nothing."

"You ain't heard nothing yet, once they learn the Army is headed here. Ute Jack will be fit to be tied."

"I've got to try to calm them. Before troops arrive. Douglas has promised to help. He doesn't want war either."

Rankin could see it was no use talking to the agent. He glanced over at Arvilla who sat before a window, reading from her huge book, *Pilgrims Progress*. He thought of blue-eyed Josie and the big-breasted Flora Ellen.

"Then at least you can send your womenfolk out with me this morning," he whispered to Meeker.

"We will be fine, Mr. Rankin. Here are several letters I wish to have telegraphed as soon as you reach Rawlings." One of the letters was Meeker's final payment to the estate of Horace Greeley. His spirits had been lifted by that simple act of writing the check, yet Joe Rankin had gotten him in a blue funk once again with all his talk of Ute trouble.

Rankin shook his head, accepted the letters from Meeker and shoved them into the mail pouch. One thing about it, Meeker had more guts than he had sense. Taking one last look around at White River and at the aspens turning gold on the higher slopes to the east, Rankin caught up his horse and rode away with a sigh. It was September seventeenth.

A worried Carl Schurz stopped off in Denver on his way from

California to confer with Governor Pitkin over the current Ute troubles. With Pitkin to greet Schurz at Union Station was William Byers of the *Rocky Mountain News.*

"Gentlemen," Schurz said, shaking hands with the two men. They immediately departed in the governor's gleaming carriage to his office where the three men settled down with glasses of fine whiskey from Pitkin's private stock.

"Tell, me, Governor, what is the latest with the Utes? Do you really think it's as bad as rumored?"

"News from White River has been sparse at best, Carl, but tensions are running high, right here in Denver. William can probably add more than I can." Both Schurz and Pitkin looked over at the pudgy-faced editor for comment. Byers held a half-smoked stub of a cigar clammed between his teeth. He removed the stogie and took a healthy sip of the smooth whiskey.

"Fred, how is it you never serve me whiskey like this when it's just the two of us?" Byers asked, grinning. And then his face grew serious once more. "Frankly, Mr. Secretary, news has been rather pitiful from that corner of Colorado. From what we've gathered, the Utes are really worked up over Meeker plowing their land. I spoke with William Fullerton, who returned not more than a fortnight ago on leave from White River and he indicated the tension there was growing worse with each passing day. Most nights the Indians beat their war drums and dance until morning light."

Carl Schurz sipped slowly at his drink, his face a serious study. "I have asked, as you both already know, for troops to be dispatched to the agency. This Indian business is really coming at a bad time." A studied silence filled the room as Pitkin and Byers contemplated what Schurz meant by this last statement.

Bad time? For *whom?* Byers thought. Surely not for the Indians. He concluded, trouble with all Indians came sooner or later. Possibly it was Meeker he was referring to and the womenfolk?

"Getting troops to White River may take some time, Carl. What about Captain Dodge and his colored troops over in Middle Park? If a dispatch was sent to them, they could ride immediately."

Schurz snapped his fingers, "By golly, Fred, you are right. Forgot about that colored unit." He jumped to his feet, drained his glass and reached for his hat.

"Where are you going, Carl?"

"Want to send another telegram to Sheridan. If we can get Dodge's boys rolling, we could have them there in just a couple days."

"I'll have my secretary come in and he can take down what you want to send General Sheridan. No need to leave," Pitkin said, getting up to open the door to summon his personal clerk.

"I just hope we are not too late," Byers said, expressing concern for the women and employees of White River.

"Amen," Schurz said, while Fred Pitkin refilled his glass.

"Only several weeks ago, three Utes paid me a visit," Fred Pitkin said, pouring more of the expensive whiskey into Byers outstretched glass. "Bill knows all about it. He was here as well."

"Who were they? What did they want?" Schurz asked.

"He's called Captain Jack, Mr. Secretary," Byers broke in. "Pretty powerful Ute. He and this Chief, Douglas, don't get along very well. Jack is something of a legend himself. Scouted for Crook against the Sioux and got rather high marks for it."

"Yes, I believe I've heard of him. What else?"

"He came to tell us that his people weren't the ones starting the fires in Middle Park and Bear Valley."

"Didn't I hear something about a couple of Indians burning a house or two?"

"You did, and after asking around among the Indians who hang around Denver, it came out that two Utes, Bennett and Chapman—don't know their Indian names—were the culprits."

"What did this Jack say to all this?"

"When Jack was here, he claimed Major Thompson's house had not been burned, but other people say different," Byers said, lighting his cigar. Fine whiskey deserved a good cigar and Byers settled back in the well-cushioned chair and inhaled deeply.

Schurz instructed Governor Pitkin's clerk to include in the wire to Commissioner Hayt, the two Indians' names and for Meeker to affect their arrest when the military arrived at the agency.

The trouble with all these wires flying back and forth was the fact Meeker had yet to receive confirmation to his request for troops in the first place, and as this new wire was being sent to him, Meeker was busy penning his own stinging telegram to Commissioner Hayt.

> September 17, 1879
> Conditions at White River have changed little over the
> past few days. Nothing is getting done. There is no plow-
> ing, nor will it til it can be done in safety. It remains to be
> seen whether the business and industries of this agency
> are to be conducted under the Indians or yourself.
>   N.C. Meeker, Indian Agent

For all the excitement being displayed both in Denver and Rawlings, deep in the wilderness of White River, Nathan Meeker and agency employees were trying their best to maintain some semblance of normalcy.

Josie was down to teaching just two Ute children now. Only the love-sick, Persune, continued to come to the schoolhouse to watch her teach, without fail.

In the sad days of late September, fall hung heavy in the dry afternoon air and Meeker became much of a recluse. And in these final days of autumn, Meeker slowly became distrustful of even his own employees, giving orders that countermanded those given previously without reason. He even got mad at Josie for seeming to enjoy her time with the normally happy Utes. And when he learned that Jack and Sowówic had gone to see Governor Pitkin about the fires, upon their return, he told them both they deserved to be hanged! He even accused them of starting more fires along the Gore Range in Middle Park where Captain Dodge held his Negro soldiers.

Depressed, and preferring his own company, Nathan Meeker rarely left his house now, spending his time writing news articles to be published in the *Greeley Tribune* or firing off telegrams to Commissioner Hayt or to the military.

The days passed slowly at White River and quieter, now that Captain Jack, angry at Meeker as well, had packed up his band and departed for the fall hunts in Wyoming. Douglas and his thirty lodges remained where they had been since before last winter. The only thing that still seemed normal was the big-bellied biscuit-eater, Colorow, who stomped into Arvilla's kitchen, unannounced, with a dark scowl on his face, demanding food just as they were getting ready to eat each day.

Things seemed to be turning backward once again as the Indians played games during the day and raced their ponies on that portion of the land where the plowing had stopped abruptly, after Tatitz had shot his new Winchester at the shiny object that was cutting the earth. Shadrach Price quit plowing after that and refused Meeker's orders to start up again.

This outward calm by everybody at White River Agency was nothing like the frenzied excitement going on at Fort Fred Steele when new orders came in for Major Thornburgh.

Private O'Malley took one look at the wire and called for his horse. Of all the times for Thornburgh to be away from the post. He hurried off to deliver the wire to Thornburgh's sub-commander, Captain Payne, but knowing already what the orders would be.

"What's up?" someone called to him as he double-timed it across the parade grounds. O'Malley simply waved his hand and kept moving.

Captain Payne looked up from the wire at O'Malley who stood waiting for further orders. Payne folded the wire and handed it to the private.

"Mr. O'Malley, you are instructed to take this wire to Major Thornburgh at once. Tell the Major I will be preparing the troops for field duty and await his return."

"Yes sir," O'Malley said, stuffing the wire in his tunic and giving the Captain a smart salute.

In a few minutes, O'Malley was dusting the trail at a fast cantor on the back of his big-chested horse who had plenty of bottom for such a fast trip.

O'Malley hurried up the North Platte River, passed out of the Red Desert and crossed the old Overland Trail and spent the night at the tiny, three-cabin settlement of Warm Springs. By the time the sun cleared the Medicine Bows the following morning, O'Malley had covered the twenty miles distance down the North Platte Valley to Grand Encampment. There he shared breakfast with the Culleton family, the first homesteaders to the valley.

While O'Malley sopped his plate with a fluffy biscuit, he listened as the homesteader recounted how the whole valley was once sacred ground of the Arapahos and how William Ashley's mountain men had held Rendezvous on this very spot some fifty years ago, bartering pelts for supplies, whiskey and squaws. Culleton spoke further of how fortutious he had been in securing land here for only a buck two bits an acre. O'Malley pushed back his empty plate, stood up, and allowed how much he had enjoyed the meal and the history lesson, but he was on an important mission and had best get to it.

With a full belly and a wave of his hat to the Culletons, O'Malley rode hard into the Sierra Madres and crossed the Continental

Divide as the sun reached the half-way mark in a sky the color of Robin's eggs.

Stopping to give his big horse a breather, O'Malley scanned the talus slopes below him and the pine-rimmed blue waters of Battle Lake. It was here one year ago, O'Malley recalled, Thomas Edison, as a member of the Henry Draper Eclipse Expedition, first conceived the idea of a non-conducting filament by the way the frayed end of his fishing rod behaved during a thunderstorm. And then his thoughts soured for it was Joe Rankin who had been Edison's guide to Battle Lake while other Expedition members were busy constructing a lookout in Rawlings to observe the total eclipse of the sun. Rankin was the last person O'Malley wanted crowding his thoughts just now. The private turned to his big horse and remounted and rode a little piece to get a better view of the lake. Finally, he spotted Thornburg's wagons and mules, but no signs of movement.

O'Malley rode nearly a mile along the sharp ridge towards the elk grounds located beneath Bridger Peak and found Thornburgh and his party enjoying lunch in the scenic beauty. O'Malley rode up to the party, dismounted and saluted the major who sat with his brother.

"O'Malley, what on earth are you doing here?" Thornburgh asked, fearing that something had happened to Lida or one of the children. He couldn't bear to lose another child.

"Afternoon, Major," O'Malley said, handing the wire from General Crook to Thornburgh. "Wire came for you late yesterday. I got here as fast as I could."

Thornburgh read the wire, looked up at O'Malley and handed it to his brother to read.

> Sept. 15, 1879, Omaha Headquarters
> Major Thornburgh, you will proceed with sufficient
> number of troops to White River Agency under Special
> Instructions.
>
> Gen. George Crook

"Captain Payne?"

"The Captain says to tell you he's busy preparing the men for field duty and ten days rations," O'Malley returned.

"What the hell, Tip," Jacob Thornburgh exploded. "We didn't come all the way out here just to play cards at the post. The United States Army isn't about to bust up our elk hunt! Dammit, Tip, send someone else!" An imposing figure, a Civil War Colonel and on a first name basis with two Presidents, Jacob Montgomery Thornburgh was also a ladies' man and charmer who had proved his skills by marrying the prettiest girl in Washington D.C.

Tip Thornburgh had always been in awe of his older brother and he valued his opinion highly, yet he knew there was nothing he could do. He had to go himself, thinking of the embarrassing Northern Cheyenne venture. He vowed to himself that this time he would not let Crook down.

"I've got to go, Jake, you can see that," Tip implored his brother.

"Well, then you go, but we are staying with the elk. Just leave us a wagon and Taylor to do the guiding."

"Jake, I need Taylor; he knows the country around White River."

"We need him here, Tip, you can plainly see that. Without him, we may as well head back ourselves. And the hunt's just started."

Tip Thornburgh fumed with himself for a moment and finally gave in. Never in his life had he crossed his older brother and he couldn't bring himself to do it now.

With O'Malley and a detail of soldiers, Major Tip Thornburgh started back to Fort Steele with a casual wave to his brother and the two banker friends from Tennessee.

CHAPTER 24

Thornburgh spent the next two days furiously organizing the trip to White River while Lida worried in silence at her husband's lack of rest. Since returning from Battle Lake, Thornburgh had gotten little sleep, going to bed long past midnight and up again two hours before reveille.

The "Special Instructions" referred to in General Crook's message gave Tip Thornburgh command of two Fort Steele companies. In addition, two companies of cavalry from Fort D. A. Russell in Cheyenne were to meet Thornburgh in Rawlings on the twenty-first of September.

The delay in having received Meeker's request for military assistance and the action now being taken by troops from Fort Steele, some eleven days later, was due, for the most part, to confusion at

Army Headquarters. At first, Headquarters wasn't sure just where White River Agency was and which Army district the reservation belonged under. And second, they were equally confused over which military commander was nearest White River. It took a couple of days of ludicrous back-and-forth communication before the orders finally arrived at Fort Steele.

The confusion in the delay resulted from the fact the guts of the Army's three Divisions under General Sheridan lay in the Division of the Missouri, commanded by General Sherman, and further divided into four Departments of which General George Crook commanded the Platte. The problem stemmed from the realization that Crook's department did not take in Colorado, in which White River was located, but was actually in General Pope's Department. Yet the nearest fort under Pope's command was five hundred very rough miles from White River at Pagosa Springs, home base for Dodge's Negro company currently guarding Middle Park.

To complicate matters further, not a man stationed at Fort Steele had ever been to White River Agency. O'Malley had gotten as far as the Little Snake on the ill-fated trip with Joe Rankin the winter before, but they had turned back considerably short of the reservation. And without Taylor Pennock to guide the expedition, Major Thornburgh faced up to the realization that only one other man could do the job: Joe Rankin.

Touching a match to his cigar, Tip Thornburgh leaned against the solid post supporting his office porch and watched the troops in action while recalling the only meeting he had had with Rankin. The experience had not been pleasant and he wondered if the man would even agree to become lead scout for the expedition, since Rankin felt the army had reneged on their promise to pay him premium wages. Thornburgh sighed deeply, inhaling a lung-full of blue smoke before expelling it. There was only one way to find out—ask him straight out—tomorrow when he led his troops through

Rawlings. Either way, he was determined to push on to White River, without a scout if necessary.

Sunday morning broke clear and inviting, as only a Wyoming autumn could. It was the twenty-first and while Tip Thornburgh stood, holding Lida by the hand at the Fort's postern while Olivia held to one of his long lanky legs, he cast a critical eye at his men as they filed past.

At the head of the column was Captain Payne, Thornburgh's sub-commander, followed by the Major's mule-drawn ambulance, driven by the red-faced Irishman, Private O'Malley. Riding with O'Malley was Dr. R.B. Grimes, Captain Payne's surgeon. The ambulance contained Thornburgh's rifle, trout rod, photos of Lida in her wedding dress, witch hazel for mosquitoes, a little Holland gin for ague, a box of Reina Victoria cigars and a small bible given to him by his sister upon graduation from West Point. The flyleaf inscription read, "To Brother Tip from Livvie. Please read one chapter every day."

Payne's company, F, Fifth Cavalry, followed the ambulance and consisted of forty-three well-groomed soldiers, some who were experienced Indian fighters. Next came the twenty-nine members of Fort Steele's Company E, Fourth Infantry, led by Lieutenant Butler Price, who spent his spare time collecting rare specimens for the Smithsonian. The supply train of thirty-three mule-drawn wagons, followed Price and was commanded by a young lad, Lieutenant Silas Wolf, just a year out of West Point. Charlie Davis's sutler wagon was part of this group as well.

The rear guard was led by none other than Fort Steele's Company E, Third Cavalry with a shriveled up old timer, Captain Joe Lawson, leading the group. At sixty, Lawson's crabapple cheeks seemed on fire as he passed by Thornburgh, giving him a snappy salute. The major smiled at the officer who seemed already to be well fortified with bourbon at this early hour and returned his salute. Lawson commanded a loose group of tough veterans, numbering forty-nine, who carried their whiskey openly and cussed a blue streak on general purposes. Nobody outside of Lawson's group, including General Crook, had fought more Indians. For all their roughness, Thornburgh was well satisfied with all of his men and his heart thumped heavily against his ribs, trying to conceal his pride.

Lida squeezed Thornburgh's hand and the tall officer turned his gaze from his departing troops to his lovely wife whose eyes were filled with worry.

"Now what's this I see," he said, chucking her beneath her chin playfully. "I should be gone only a month, tops. Jake and his banker friends should be back long before then, so please keep them company for me, okay?" He gave his pretty wife a smile and hugged her close.

"You know I will, darling," Lida whispered in his ear. He pulled back, looked at her briefly and planted a tender kiss on her upturned mouth.

Olivia, now aged four, pulled at her father's pant leg for attention while Bobby stood somber by his side, trying to act more like a man than a small boy of seven.

"What is it, Liv?" Tip asked, laughing as he swept his young daughter into his powerful arms, showering her with kisses. Olivia squealed with delight, yet fighting for her father to put her down again.

"Kisses yuk," Olivia said with mock seriousness. Both Tip and Lida burst out laughing, easing the tension of the moment somewhat. Thornburgh turned to his son and laid a hand on the boy's narrow shoulder.

"Take good care of Liv for me, will you Bobby?" Bobby looked up at his tall father adoringly, with gray-blue eyes.

"I will," Bobby promised.

"Good boy," Tip said, rustling his hair. He wanted to kiss his son, but thought better of it. He untied the reins of his horse and mounted the nervous animal.

"I love you all very much," he said, just loud enough for them to hear. With one last look at Lida, he turned the prancing horse away from the porch and cantered after his troops, sitting proudly in his saddle. What he couldn't see were the tears sliding down Lida's face nor the ones that filled little Olivia's eyes once she saw her mother weeping. A hard lump came into Bobby's throat and he turned away before his mother could see the growing mist in his own eyes.

For two miles Thornburgh's troops were stretched out along the road leading to Rawlings. And as he passed them on the way to the head of the column, his men called out gaily to him. He acknowledged their calls with a wave of his hand and a smile on his face.

Thornburgh and his force arrived in Rawlings that afternoon amid cheers and well-wishers. He found the two companies from Fort D.A. Russell waiting for him just south of town. Many of the troopers knew Thornburgh's men, having served at Fort Steele in the past and a few minutes were spent greeting one another. There was plenty of good-natured ribbing to go around at being thrown together like they were. Many wanted to know what it was all about anyway, since they were not part of Pope's Department.

Thornburgh ordered his men into camp beside the two companies and set off to find Rawlings first citizen, James France, for a conference.

He found the little man at his store, looking very worried. And in his usual directness, he launched into Thornburgh about his troubles.

"Had I been privy to Army's communication with you, Major, I would not have put two, four-mule wagons on the road to White River on the fourteenth, carrying four thousand pounds of flour. Three days later, I put John Gordon on the road with ten wagons loaded with ten thousand pounds of flour, pans, washtubs, red flannel shirts from Wanamaker's, meat cleavers and a wheelbarrow for Johnson not to mention saddles for Josie Meeker and Flora Ellen Price." France caught his breath and rushed on, describing in loving detail how his entire investment was now in jeopardy by this Ute uprising.

"That's why I've been asked to come to White River," Thornburgh edged in between the little man's pauses.

"Ain't through yet, Major. On the eighteenth, I sent Al McCarger and his son out with a wagon loaded with coal oil, thirteen thousand feet of barbed wire, spades and pick axes." And then France managed to grin ruefully. "Even shipped a sack of durn play-hatchets Josie ordered for them heathens."

"You done?" Thornburgh, knowing it would do no good until the little man had had his say.

"Almost. The day before McCarger went out, I sent George Gordon and two drivers out on three wagons loaded with pieces of Meeker's thrashing machine he ordered. One of the wagons carried the steam engine."

"Should be a lot of traffic on the road then," Thornburgh replied, wondering now if he should even bother with Rankin.

"Wished now I had waited after Secretary Schurz came rolling through here earlier. Should have figured then something was up at White River. Course, now that Black Wilson told me of Meeker's troubles, I'm really concerned now about all the annuities I got strung out on the road. And the men," France added as an afterthought.

"I'll be on the lookout for them, Mr. France and give them all the assistance I can." James France seemed somewhat relieved at this.

"Keep an eye on Carl Goldstein and a boy by the name of Julius Moore, Major. They are both inexperienced, but they were all the help I could get."

"I'll do that," Thornburgh promised. "Now tell me, is there anyone besides Joe Rankin knows that country? I'm in need of a scout."

"What happened to Taylor Pennock? Thought he was scouting for the Army now?"

A faint smile tinged Thornburgh's lips as he thought of Jake talking him out of his lead scout. "He busy guiding a hunt up at Battle Lake."

"France studied the Major's face for a moment. "I see. Well then, that leaves you with only one other choice, Major. Joe Rankin."

"I was afraid of that." Thornburgh told France of his only meeting with Rankin.

"You want me to speak to Joe for you?" France offered.

"Guess I better do it since this is Army business. Don't want anymore misunderstandings over money." Thornburgh turned to leave.

"Major, you be careful. I'm afraid what Meeker's been doing has stirred them Utes up to the boiling point."

"I'll do that, Mr. France. And I promise to keep your supply wagons safe as we possibly can."

Thornburgh found Joe Rankin working the kinks out of a stubborn mule that refused to stand for hitching. Even in the cool Wyoming air, Rankin was sweating. Thornburgh watched for a time before saying anything.

"Must be an Army mule."

Surprised, Rankin looked over at the lean Army officer in field dress uniform.

"Agency mule, but durn near the same," Rankin replied, attaching the single-tree to the wagon. "Took this'n on trade and it looks like I got the worse end of the deal."

"Maybe," Thornburgh commented, looking the mule over closely. "Appears to have good qualities to me."

"Ain't denying he's got a strong back and legs for pulling, but it's his head that's needin' adjustment."

Joe came over to the corral fence, dusting his clothes as he came. He looked at Thornburgh with steady eyes.

"Heard about the Ute troubles. Last time I was there, I told Meeker he better think twice how he was handling things. Utes don't understand plowing and digging irrigation ditches."

Thornburgh nodded his head in agreement. "You are probably right, Mr. Rankin but trouble is, I've been ordered there to size up the situation and secure the safety of the agency employees."

"Uh-huh. Know that too, Major."

"Then you probably already know too, that Taylor Pennock is not scouting for me this trip."

Rankin nodded, looking back at the mule now standing patiently in harness. He shook his head. There was just no understanding hard-headed mules. Rankin had spent the last two hours working with him to no avail. Now he was as docile as a worn out plug mare.

Thornburgh cleared his throat, "I know you don't have much love for the Army right now in view of the fact the wages you requested are in contention."

Rankin looked hard at Thornburgh. "Contention! Pretty damn plain what O'Malley told me. Course you officers don't hafta accept the word of an enlisted man, I know." Rankin's voice was edged with bitterness.

"Mr. Rankin, I'll come right to the point. You act as guide this trip to White River and I'll pay you premium wages plus double the wages for the trip you took with O'Malley."

Rankin studied on this for a minute. "There and back?" he quizzed Thornburgh.

"There and back," Thornburgh repeated.

"When do we leave?"

"First thing tomorrow morning. Guess you can find the camp," Thornburgh said, smiling.

"I reckon."

Grayson Toliver came out of the livery leading another mule the color of red clay. His pale-white complexion had been replaced by a youthful ruddiness of the out-of-doors living and his body had muscled up since leaving the Union Pacific job. He waved at the Army officer, turning the mule in the corral where the other one obediently stood.

"You want I should hitch up this one, too?" Toliver asked Rankin.

"That'll be fine, son. Then you can take them over to France's and load it up for him."

"He sending more stuff to White River?" Thornburgh asked, incredulous.

"Nah, this stuff is fer George Baggs. But I told France not to send any annuities 'til this thing came to a head. Now he's got fifty thousand worth of supplies on the road to an agency that's liable to be blown all to hell before they get there."

"I must return to my troops, Mr. Rankin," Thornburgh said, stepping away from the corral. "I shall see you at first light, then?"

"Expect so," Rankin said, eying Toliver as he moved the mule into position in front of the wagon. He fully expected the other mule to kick up a fuss but it didn't happen and Toliver completed the job in a few minutes. Rankin shook his head. There just wasn't anyway to predict cussed mule behavior. No way at all.

CHAPTER 25

The golden afternoon of a late autumn day bathed the *carniva* along the Smoking Earth River with warm sunshine. Upriver, the aspens were turning and myrtle warblers congregated among the trees before beginning their migration south. The feel of change was in the air and usually it was during this time, the People of the *Nüpartka* spend lazy days playing games, drying their meat for winter and caring for their horses.

But things were seriously different this fall. The People had not managed to save enough meat from the fall hunts to carry them through the Snow Moons. The drought of summer was still with the People. And there was this unpleasant business with the agent, who was holding back on the gifts from Washington once again. The long knife that the *Mericatz* used to cut the earth still lay on its side with wooden handles sticking straight out like the feelers on a grasshopper. None of the *Mericatz* had come to take it away since Tatitz had shot his new rifle at it. Now it lay gathering dew each morning and dust during the long day.

None of the People had seen the agent since Canávish had talked roughly to him. It was during this time, Nicaagat and the People who made their *carniva* near him, gathered their things together and departed north from Smoking Earth River. As was his custom, Nicaagat would spend the last Fall Moon hunting in Wyoming, preparing for winter.

The People who stayed behind with Quinkent tried to enjoy the quiet, pleasant days, but they could hear a stirring deep within the earth. They could feel it moving, like a sickness deep inside, trying to push its way to the surface. Even the sky seemed pulled tight, like a skin over a drum and men gathered in silent, watchful groups to smoke and think about this thing between Canávish and this agent that now affected the People.

Quinkent made many trips down to the agency to see this agent, but always, he returned without having seen him. This sickness seemed to grow inside Quinkent and the People. Even the spirit birds' haunting cries across the riverbottoms failed to soothe Quinkent's soul. There was anger across the land and Quinkent could do nothing about it.

It was during one of these sad days, when the sun was sinking towards the yellow benchlands to the west, that a pony carrying Tatitz, came thundering up to where Quinkent and Canávish sat smoking. Tatitz, who was fast growing into manhood, slid off his pony with his prized rifle in one hand. His face held the expression that he was carrying grim news.

"Nicaagat's camp is returning," Tatitz said, excitedly, not bothering to sit down with his father and Quinkent.

"Why is that?" Canávish asked his son.

"Father, there is talk the *swerch* is coming to Smoking Earth to put us in irons or hang us for what happened to this agent!"

"*Swerch!*" Quinkent blurted out, getting to his feet with the shaman. "This is the sickness I have felt for many sleeps now."

"We have done nothing. The soldiers cannot enter our reservation according to the treaty with Washington," Canávish said, pondering this sudden turn of events. When he looked at Quinkent, pure terror was etched across his broad face.

"I must go talk with this agent. He must stop the *swerch* from coming here," Quinkent said.

"Yes and I will tell the others," Canávish said, knocking the ashes from the bowl of his pipe. With his son by his side, Canávish hurried away, leaving Quinkent standing by his *carniv*.

Singing Grass appeared from the river with a load of firewood for the evening and Quinkent quickly told his *piwán* the news. Singing Grass became excited and began to cry loudly with fear, for like all the women of the People, she had heard all the bad things these soldiers had done to the people of the plains.

"I must go talk with this agent. He must stop these soldiers," Quinkent repeated. His heart was heavy with grief and the sickness was gnawing deep inside him now.

"I am afraid for you. This agent may hold you prisoner if you go down there now," Singing Grass said, her voice quivering with fear.

Quinkent managed a smile for his *piwán* and for a brief moment he held her close. He looked out across the river, but drew no comfort from the sight.

"Make ready to leave as quickly as you can. Tell the others to pack as well." With that, Quinkent released Singing Grass and started for the agency, his whole body feeling the sadness, the sickness that welled up from the earth.

The *Mericatz*, Post, was locking the door to the storehouse when Quinkent came up. The *Mericatz* looked as sad as Quinkent felt.

"Want to see agent," Quinkent stated.

"Mr. Meeker isn't seeing anyone now. He's at home and doesn't want to be bothered."

"Must see agent," Quinkent repeated, unwilling to leave with soldiers heading for the reservation.

"Douglas, there's nothing I can do. Fact is, Meeker hasn't been feeling well lately."

"He sick?"

"Yes, I believe he is," Post absently, looking around as if having misplaced something. "Every time something is laid down . . ."

"What is it?" Quinkent asked, thinking the *Mericatz* was a little crazy.

"I'll tell you, Douglas, you Utes steal everything that's not nailed down."

"You see Ute steal?"

"No, don't have to. Anytime something goes missing, an Indian took it."

Quinkent felt the anger rise in him and mix with the sickness. None of his people had ever stolen a thing from the agency.

"Maybe I go talk with agent about this stealing."

"I've already told you, Douglas," Post said, clearly exasperated, "you can't bother the agent now."

Quinkent looked at the *Mericatz* for a long moment and silently turned away. There was only one thing to do and that was to go see for himself if the soldiers were really coming to the reservation. But as it turned out, Quinkent did not have to leave Smoking Earth River to learn this fact.

Some of Nicaagat's people came into camp just before the last light left the skies. Quinkent quickly called a meeting to help him understand what was really going on with the *swerch*.

Canávish, Colorow, Pauvitz and several others listened carefully as two of Nicaagat's people told them what they knew. Nicaagat and his men were going to watch these soldiers carefully and if they crossed Little River, called Milk River by the *Mericatz*, they were going to attack these soldiers. Colorow said that he would ride north and talk with these soldiers and make them go back. Everyone knew that Colorow wanted to be with Nicaagat and in the thick of things should fighting start.

Listening to this talk made Quinkent even sicker and after a while, he simply left the hastily called council and walked down to the river to think.

Even in the cooling evening, dust still clung to the air, reminding Quinkent that it had been many moons since there had been any rain. His heart was heavy and everything seemed mixed up deep inside of him. Whatever the price, the People must not go to war with the *Mericatz*. He only wanted peace with Washington. So did the People.

Before the sun appeared above Sleepy Cat Peak, Quinkent, with troubled spirit, sat before his center fire, smoking his pipe and trying to decide what he must do as *tawacz viem*. His was a responsibility that tugged at his soul. So many of the young men who had come into camp last night, had danced and sung war songs until early light. Even now the camp was a flurry of activity, when most people should still be fast asleep.

Singing Grass threw back the elk flap on the *carniv* and brought Quinkent a cup of coffee. Without speaking, she returned to her cook pots. Near the far end of camp, Quinkent heard the sudden sounds of drums. Nicaagat's men were once again performing their war dances. Quinkent thought of his young days when he too had danced all night, singing and beating drums before a battle with the plains people. That had been a very long time ago. Never had the People gone to war with the *Mericatz*. These thoughts made the sickness in Quinkent rise up in his throat. He must get the agent to send his words to stop the *swerch*. That was the only way to prevent what he knew would happen if he didn't do otherwise.

This time when Quinkent walked up to the agency office, he found the agent at his desk, reading. The agent looked very sad and tired like he too had gotten little sleep last night with all the drums and dancing.

"Douglas, what brings you here so early in the morning?"

"There is much talk of soldiers coming to the reservation," Quinkent started in, concern crowding his voice.

Meeker leaned back in his chair and studied the old Indian for a moment as if searching for a place to begin.

"I told you and the others on plenty occasions what would happen if you displeased Washington," Meeker warned, running a bony hand through his thin gray hair. "I warned you," he repeated.

"Ute no want soldiers to come here," Quinkent responded.

"Makes no difference now, Douglas, soldiers from Fort Steele have been ordered here by Washington."

"Washington is friend," Quinkent said staunchly.

"Washington has always been friends of your people, Douglas. Trouble is, your people won't listen to Washington. I'm tired of trying anymore." The agent's voice was filled with hopelessness.

"You can make soldiers stop," Quinkent said, his face lined with worry. "You can send your words to this general and make him go home. You agent. Ute wants peace, not fight."

"Yes, Douglas, so do we all, but this time things are different. It is out of my hands. The Army is in control."

Quinkent returned to his *carniv* where Singing Grass was gathering their things for travel. The agent's words made him feel all twisted up inside. The agent would not help the People and the sickness grew within him.

Beyond, Quinkent watched as other *piwáns* were busy knocking down lodge poles and packing their bundles of food and supplies for the flight over Roan Plateau if conditions warranted it.

Quinkent decided to wait for the next courier from Nicaagat to tell him if the soldiers were still advancing before sending the women and children south.

The center fires offered nothing more than a faint, red glow when a horse approached Quinkent's *carniv* and stopped. The air was frosty and a cold mist clung to the river banks and blotted out the reeds and cottonwoods. The river had been aptly named by the *Nüpartka.*

Quinkent stirred beneath his warm robes and came fully awake as he listened to the approaching sound of footsteps. In an instant, Quinkent was out of the robes with his rifle in his hands, straining to hear more.

Someone made a scratching sound at the elk-skin flap and Quinkent knew immediately it was one of the People and he let out pent up air from his chest.

"Unh!" he grunted, turning to throw a few pieces of wood on the center fire.

Nicaagat came in looking like some wild animal, dark and threatening. Slung over one shoulder, Nicaagat carried a cartridge belt. In one hand, he carried his rifle. His face was grim and his black eyes hard like winter berries.

"*Maiquas,*" Nicaagat said softly as not to awaken Singing Grass, who was buried deep beneath the robes with her back to the fire. Quinkent returned the greeting, low and serious. For Nicaagat to seek Quinkent out at this late hour could only mean trouble. Quinkent offered his rival tobacco from his beautiful beaded pouch and for a short few minutes, both men smoked and offered up their prayers to the winds and sky.

Suddenly, Nicaagat started to speak in a conciliatory tone that surprised Quinkent. There had always been an undercurrent of tension in their talks but this time, Quinkent detected nothing more than worry and a need for cooperation.

"The *swerch* are camped as I speak on the Little Snake. We must put aside our differences for the good of the People and face this new challenge, should the soldiers continue south to Smoking Earth country."

Quinkent knew the threat had to be real for Nicaagat to come here and make such overtures for peace between them. It took a great man with wisdom to do this thing.

Quinkent looked into Nicaagat's hard eyes across the small center fire and saw only concern and worry in their depths. Of all the People, Nicaagat knew the *swerch* best and understood their ways.

"We should be more like the spirit birds that call back and forth across the river each night, seeking only friendship. We must be as one to face the *swerch* if they decide to come here to winter valley," Quinkent replied softly.

Nicaagat nodded, rolled another cigarette which he smoked like a *Mericatz*. "By treaty, these *swerch* should not come to our country, but they will not stop unless we get this agent to talk to them."

Quinkent grew sad at these words and he told Nicaagat of having gone to see Meeker just this day, demanding he stop the *swerch*.

"You must try again tomorrow. Tell this agent if the *swerch* cross Little River, we will fight." These words of war caused Quinkent to feel sick all over again and all he could do was nod his head that he understood.

"I will go see this agent and see if he will do this thing," Quinkent said.

"The People must go south in case there is war," Nicaagat said. "The women and children must be safe from the *swerch* if we do not stop them from coming here," Nicaagat ordered.

Quinkent nodded his understanding, hoping beyond all hope he would be able to get this agent to understand how serious things had become since their talk this afternoon.

"I must go back and keep watch on these *swerch* with Sowówic.

The young men will be encamped at Yellowjacket Pass if the *swerch* do not listen to reason."

"You will go to their camp, then?"

"There is no other choice. I will talk with their general and try to get them to stop at Little River." Nicaagat did not need to add more for the implied threat hung heavily in the cold air between them.

Both men stood, keeping the center fire between them. Quinkent made the sign of friendship. Nicaagat acknowledged the sign with his own before slipping out between the flap.

Quinkent took his seat before the center fire again and finished his cigarette. He sat there, unmoving, long past the time it took for the dying coals to come again to the center fire. The weight of the People's safety rested heavily on his shoulders, yet he was glad Nicaagat would share in the decision to fight the *swerch* if they crossed into the reservation. Quinkent prayed earnestly to Sunáwiv to protect the People and to send the *swerch* away from their peaceful valley here by Smoking Earth River.

When he sought his robes once again, Quinkent's troubled soul was eased somewhat by the sound of the calling spirit birds from the river. With their mysterious calls back and forth across the river, Quinkent drifted into a strange and troubled sleep filled with charging soldiers, blood and screaming children.

From a dense hillside, Nicaagat and Sowówic watched the *swerch* light their cook fires as morning came to the pretty valley surrounding Fortication Creek. Nicaagat counted the fires and grew deeply troubled. There were so many *swerch* present that to repel them would take the combined *carniva* of both bands of *Nüpartka* and he was glad he had gone to speak with Quinkent. For now, he would watch the *swerch* and sleep a little since he had gotten back from Quinkent's *carniv* only as light cast about among the deep shadows, swallowing up the darkness.

305

CHAPTER 26

After two days on the trail, Thornburgh's command reached the Little Snake, marked now by burnished oak and gold aspen. Serviceberries, crabapple red, clung to thick bushes where the river's life-giving waters had saved the fruit from the four-month-old drought.

Leading the expedition in his finest set of cream-colored leathers, Joe Rankin led Thornburgh and Sam Cherry down river to Bibleback Brown's where the major was able to hire the twinkling-eyed harmonica player, Charlie Lowry as mail courier.

Thornburgh kept everyone in camp that night to prevent some of the troopers wandering down to visit the half-breed Snake girls at Charlie Perkin's store and hotel. Rankin and Lowry proceeded to empty a bottle between them, once Rankin learned the orders applied to him as well. He had figured on another tryst with Maggie Baggs that evening. Instead, he was half-drunk by eight o'clock and sound asleep by nine.

The following morning, Private O'Malley couldn't help commenting on Rankin's condition and his lack of success with the rancher's wife.

"O'Malley, if your weren't in uniform, I'd gut shoot you were you stand," Rankin said grimly, not liking the personal digs being directed at him.

O'Malley threw back his head and let out a thunderous laugh. "You're a touchy one, now ain't ye! Expect ye'll just have to get by on short rations where women are concerned this trip, Rankin. Not a consenting female within seventy-five miles for ye to diddle."

Rankin settled his hat on his head, giving O'Malley a cold stare. His eyeballs felt like hot metal had been poured down the back of them.

"Oh, I don't know, O'Malley," Rankin replied calmly, packing up his bedroll. "There's still White River Agency. Visited there a few times in the past. Got a couple of young women there just might be more than willin' to give it a whirl."

The big Irishman's face sobered. "I swear, Rankin," O'Malley said, shaking his head before walking away.

Charlie Lowry stumbled up from the river where he had gone for a drink of water. He appeared wobbly-legged and looked flushed.

"What was that about?" Charlie asked, having caught only the last part of their exchange.

Rankin smiled, in spite of how he felt inside. "Just makin' conversation, is all."

The four companies of troops climbed over the divide and took their time moving down the other side. By mid-afternoon, Thornburgh called a halt at Fortification Creek at its juncture with Little Bear Creek. They had barely covered sixteen miles yet

Thornburgh seemed not to be in any hurry as he and the other officers lazed away the golden afternoon of an autumn day. Besides, the knee-high grass here was good and the water excellent, Thornburgh figured, and stopping over would allow him time to set up a supply depot with Lt. Price commanding the operation.

While the sun was beginning to set, Thornburgh called for Sam Cherry to take a letter for him.

> Headquarters, White River Expedition
> Camp on Fortification Creek Sept. 25

Mr. Meeker
U. S. Indian Agent
White River Agency:

> Sir:
>
> In obedience to instructions from General of the Army, I am en route to your agency, and expect to arrive there on the 29th instant, for the purpose of rendering you any assistance in my power, and to make arrests at your suggestion, and to hold as prisoners such of your Indians as you desire until investigations are made by your department. I have heard nothing definite from your agency for ten days, and don't know what state of affairs exists; whether the Indians will leave at my approach or show resistance. I send this letter by Mr. Lowry, one of my guides, and desire you to communicate with me as soon as possible, giving me all the information in your power, in order that I may know what course to pursue. If practicable meet me on the road at the earliest moment.
>
> > Very respectfully, your obedient servant,
> > T. T. Thornburgh
> > Major, 4th Infantry, Commanding Expedition

As Sam Cherry was copying out the letter, Charlie Lowry entered the big Sibley where the officers were seated. He looked rather agitated.

"Major, we got company. I spied a Ute in the brush, nearby."

Thornburgh jumped to his feet and rushed past Lowry to look for himself with Cherry on his heels. He looked in vain for sign of an Indian, but saw nothing.

"They were there, Major," Lowry said, standing firm.

"Fetch Joe Rankin will you please, Mr. Lowry?" Thornburgh asked. "And you can start for White River afterward," he said, handing Lowry the letter for Meeker.

"Yes sir, Major." Charlie Lowry hurried off to find the chief scout, leaving the two officers to enjoy what remained of a beautiful sunset.

Rankin was in the saddle by early morning, studying the moccasin tracks left by Nicaagat and Sowówic, near camp. He was more than a little chagrined that two Indians had come practically into camp without his knowing about it. O'Malley only grinned at the scout every chance he got. Rankin decided right then and there he would get back at the enlisted trooper, first chance he got.

At the mouth of Elkhead Creek on Bear River, Thornburgh called a halt for the day and went visiting at Tom Iles's ranch. While troopers lined the beautiful stream with fishing rods, Joe Rankin took the young Sam Cherry with him to visit Peck's store and to buy a few rounds of fixed ammunition.

Mrs. Peck, still carrying her baby around on an ample hip met them in the doorway.

"Afternoon, ma'am," Lt. Cherry said, tipping his hat to the woman.

"Who you got with you, Joe?"

"Lt. Sam Cherry of the Thornburgh expedition," Rankin said, trying to look past the woman. He saw shadowy figures moving around inside the cluttered store. "Who you got in there?"

Mrs. Peck stepped aside as Nicaagat and Sowówic came out of the store looking grim.

"Jack, how you doing?" Rankin asked, looking the two Utes over carefully. "Doin' a little trading?"

Nicaagat and Sowówic did not have to answer. Mrs. Peck answered for them.

"They cleared us out of fixed ammunition, ten thousand rounds."

"Oh," Rankin said, surprised.

"We go hunt diss time in Wyoming. Hunt bad here, no rain," Nicaagat explained. "Why iss soldier here?"

"There are many soldiers down by Bear River," Lt. Cherry broke in.

"Why are they dere?" Neither Rankin or Cherry answered. After a long silence the lieutenant finally spoke.

"My commanding officer is down at the river. I'm sure he would very much like to speak with you."

"Maybe, we come dere later," Nicaagat responded.

"Suit yourself," Rankin said. "Let's get back, Cherry."

Rankin and Cherry mounted up and rode upriver, leaving the storekeeper's wife and crying baby behind. Lt. Cherry looked worried.

"Relax, Cherry. Them Utes ain't lookin' to harm her. It's the soldiers got Nicaagat worried."

"Think he will come?"

Joe nodded, "He'll come all right, but in his own time."

Rankin was right. Before dusk, Nicaagat and Sowówic rode into camp and were stopped by a sentry on the road before letting them pass.

Major Thornburgh and the other officers, plus Joe Rankin, were seated before a fire, watching their approach.

As the Utes rode up and dropped from their horses, Major Thornburgh stood up and introduced himself, shaking each man's hand.

311

"Lt. Cherry and Mr. Rankin said they had seen you down at Peck's store earlier. I'm Major Thornburgh, this is my sub-commander Captain Payne. What are your names?"

Joe Rankin broke in, "Hell, Major, they ain't likely to tell their names. It's considered bad medicine for a Ute. That dark-faced one is Captain Jack or Nicaagat as he is called by his people. The other'n is Sowówic. He's the one I told you, Charlie Adams nursed back to health after he managed to go and shoot himself." Thornburgh nodded his head in understanding while Nicaagat's dark eyes remained on Rankin.

"So you are the one scouted for General Crook," Thornburgh said to Nicaagat.

"General Crook iss good friend."

"Well then, Jack, perhaps since you scouted for the Army you must understand something about why we are marching south."

"Best be careful, Major," Rankin warned. "This Ute is plenty smart and he understands good English. He'll tote it all back to the rest of 'em."

Thornburgh's face registered his slight displeasure at his chief scout.

"Mr. Rankin, I'm sure we have nothing to hide here from Jack or his people."

"Why iss soldiers come here?" Nicaagat asked.

"Army Headquarters has ordered I take my command to your agency," Thornburgh responded.

"This agent iss the one who wants soldiers dere?"

Thornburgh thought how to best put his next words carefully so the Ute would not misunderstand his response.

"There has been talk of trouble at your agency. That some of your people have set fires and even mistreated agent Meeker."

"Iss lies. Ute no set fire. I told diss to Governor Pitkin. Papers lie."

"There's still the matter of mistreatment," Thornburgh reminded the Ute.

"Diss agent say to Johnson he must kill hiss horses. Dat he hass too many. Ute get mad but agent iss not hurt. You go dere. See for yourself."

"That's what we intend to do, Jack. If there is no trouble, then of course we will go back to Fort Steele."

Nicaagat looked around at all the campfires now burning up and down the river. Many soldiers come with this general, Nicaagat concluded. Sowówic asked Nicaagat what was being said and Nicaagat took a minute to explain the situation.

Nicaagat addressed Thornburgh again. "I show you diss agent is not hurt. You come, maybe, bring four or five soldiers. Others day stay here. Lots of soldiers scare little children. Young men then get angry. You come. I show you diss iss all lies."

Thornburgh seemed to study on this for a moment before reaching into his coat pocket for cigars which he handed to the two Utes. He offered them matches and they lit their cigars. Thornburgh did the same.

While they smoked, Thornburgh said, "I'll talk it over with my staff. Meet me at Williams Fork tomorrow evening and I'll give you my answer."

Nicaagat nodded his head. "Long time ago I see dis man, President Johnson. He say we no fight. I say Ute no fight. Dis iss good. We like brothers." Joe Rankin stifled a small laugh, but Thornburgh ignored his scout.

"We are not looking for trouble, Jack. We are only looking for the truth and I sincerely hope there won't be any bloodshed."

"You come. Diss is all I want. We talk, then maybe no fight."

"I'm sorry Jack, but I have my orders and it does not include talk. I will give you my answer at Williams Fork."

Nicaagat nodded and turned away. Thornburgh called to him.

"Jack, I want you to know we are all brothers. I do hope there will be no need to fight. There will be deaths on both sides and nothing good can be accomplished that way. I have my orders which I must obey," Thornburgh said with sadness.

After the Utes had left, Captain Payne was the first to speak.

"Surely, Major, you don't intend to ride into the agency with five men?"

"Haven't decided," Thornburgh said, puffing on his cigar.

"Hell, Major, that's all Nicaagat wants. Get you separated from the rest of us and things'll go to hell quickly. You can't trust them far as you can spit," Rankin said, solidly.

"I think they only came here to spy," Lt. Cherry spoke up. Rankin laughed hard over this statement. Cherry gave him a hard look.

"What about the terrain up ahead, Joe?" Captain Payne asked. "Is there a favorable place the Utes can set up an ambush if they decide to do so?"

"Danged right there is, Captain," Rankin said eagerly. "Expect the best place will be Coal Creek Canyon. We get trapped inside those narrow walls, won't take half as many Utes to shoot us to pieces."

"I believe, Major, we ought to take Jack as hostage when he meets us at Williams Fork tomorrow. Since we'll be that much closer to the reservation, we can move forward quickly and once the Indians sees we are holding Jack, they'll be more cooperative," Sub-commander Payne added.

Major Thornburgh's brow furrowed as he thought about this new tactic. "I'll take it under advisement, Captain."

"Listen, Major, them Utes ain't got the guts to stand up to U.S. Cavalry. They won't fight," Rankin interjected.

"That remains to be seen, Mr. Rankin," Major Thornburgh said, yawning. "I'm about ready for bed, gentlemen. We'll have a long day of it tomorrow and I suggest you do the same."

With that the group broke up, with Payne and Cherry walking away together while Rankin went looking for a bottle.

Thornburgh opened his writing box and penned a note to his department commander. He would leave it with Peck to be taken out by mail carrier in the morning.

> Have met some Ute Chiefs here. They seem friendly and
> promise to go with me to the agency. Say Utes don't
> understand why we have come. Have tried to explain sat-
> isfactorily. Do not anticipate trouble.
>   T.T. Thornburgh, Maj. 4th Inf.

As he finished, a few drops of rain splattered the ground, stirring up little puffs of dust. In a few minutes it was over. The drought continued.

The continued march south overtook George Gordon's train bearing Meeker's threshing machine and Al McCarger's wagon. There was a two hour delay while Thornburgh's wagonmaster, William McKinstry, fixed one of Gordon's broken wheels.

Afterward, Thornburgh's command crossed the divide and went into camp at Williams Fork meadow where Deer Creek came in, the half-way point between Bear and White River. It was after supper when an agency employee, Wilmer Eskridge, rode into camp with two Utes, bearing a letter from Agent Meeker.

Thornburgh asked them to step down and help themselves to the last of the food and coffee. Both Eskridge and the smaller of the two Utes took him up on his offer. The big-bellied Ute, with a sullen face, refused.

Thornburgh read Meeker's letter.

September 27, 1879

Sir:

Understanding that your are on your way hither with United States Troops, I send a messenger, Mr. Eskridge, and two Indians, Henry Jim and Colorow to inform you that the Indians are greatly excited and wish you to stop at some convenient camping place and then that you and five soldiers of your command come into the Agency when a talk and better understanding can be had. This I agree to. But I do not propose to order your movements, but it seems for the best. The Indians seem to consider the advance of your troops as a declaration of real war. In this I am laboring to undeceive them, and at the same time to convince them that they cannot do whatever they please. The first objective now is to allay apprehension.

Respectfully.

N. C. Meeker

Thornburgh called a meeting of his officers, Payne, Cherry, Lawson, Wilmer Eskridge and the Ute interpreter, Henry Jim, to discuss Meeker's letter and asked Eskridge to brief him on the latest from White River.

"Things had been pretty quiet for the last few nights, Major," Eskridge began. "Mr. Meeker even thought for a while, there might not be a need for troops after all. He even asked Ed Mansfield—Ed works at the agency too—to stop by Middle Park and brief Captain Dodge of the latest lull on his way to Greeley for vacation. But that was after Jack came into the agency after meeting with you. They are pretty stirred up again and Mr. Meeker's doubled the guards on the storehouse after Goldstein showed up and began unloading supplies."

Colorow came over and eased his great bulk to the ground and picked up the talk, speaking through Henry Jim.

"I speak for Captain Jack. If you will come into the agency with only five of your soldiers, we will protect you. Your soldiers can camp on a nice spot where there is plenty grass, not fifty miles from White River."

"What do you think, men?" Thornburgh asked his officers. Old Captain Lawson and Sam Cherry thought it was a good plan and that given a chance, bloodshed could be avoided.

"I'm totally against the idea," Captain Payne said, emphatically. "We come here under military orders to settle things, not to be a mediator."

Thornburgh considered Payne's strong argument for a few minutes before replying, even though he already knew what he had planned to do all along. He was more interested in defusing the situation than starting another Sand Creek.

"I've decided to go along with the plan. The men will camp near the reservation boundary and I'll take five men with me and ride in and talk with Meeker and the Ute Chiefs." Thornburgh turned to Lt. Cherry. "Take a letter Lieutenant."

While the others listened, Thornburgh dictated the letter.

Camp on Williams Fork
September 27, 1879

N. C. Meeker
Sir:
Your letter of this date just received. I will move my command to Milk Creek or some good location for camp, or possibly may leave my entire command at this point, and I will come in as desired with five men. Mr. Eskridge will remain to guide me to the Agency. I will

reach your Agency some time on the 29th instant.
Very respectfully, your obedient servant,
T. T. Thornburgh
Major, 4th Infantry, Commanding Expedition

Thornburgh found the big Ute, Colorow, not half as friendly as Jack had been. When the major offered him tobacco for his pipe, Colorow refused and grew even more surly and distrustful when he peppered Thornburgh with questions similar to those asked by Jack. Nothing Thornburgh said pleased the big Indian and finally Thornburgh dismissed the entire group, after giving Henry Jim the letter to carry back to Meeker, but not before he told Colorow that the Army would fight if the Utes tried to stop his approach to White River.

Colorow left with Henry Jim, scowling back at the group of officers.

"Not a friendly fellow, is he?" Thornburgh said to no one in particular.

"That's the very reason I feel you could be in grave danger if you continue with this plan," Captain Payne spoke up.

Thornburgh gave his sub-commander a quiet smile, "Understand how you feel, Scotty, but I still believe it's the only way to keep this thing from coming to a head."

"Then at least let the command come as far as Coal Creek Canyon. I understand that's only a dozen miles from the Agency. If there is trouble, we can come on the double."

"We'll see," Thornburgh said, seeking his tent while leaving Payne standing there with a worried expression.

The following day, Thornburgh advised his officers that he would not leave his command so far from the agency, having thought about Captain Payne's comments of the night before. Payne looked instantly relieved.

"I will leave the command at Milk Creek and proceed from there with five men."

"What if, after dark, I take the cavalry column and slip down Coal Creek Canyon and place it near the agency?" Payne added, having thought of alternatives as well during the night.

"That's a good idea, Major," Old Capt. Lawson spoke up. "The Utes will see you leave and follow you in. They won't be keeping close tabs on us after that and we can make our move."

"I've got to admit, I like the idea of having the command closer, in the event of trouble," Thornburgh responded.

That evening they made camp on a grassy area at Deer Creek and the cook fires had barely been lit when Eugene Taylor came hurrying into camp with a worried tale. Taylor ran a sutler's tent for Charlie Perkins down on Milk River. Thornburgh and his officers with Joe Rankin listened as Taylor told the latest in the escalating tension.

"Not more than this morning, a dozen Utes rode in and confiscated all my fixed ammunition. They even stopped Black Wilson at Peck's and made him drop Saturday's agency mail there. Wilson high-tailed it back toward the Little Snake, but not before he swung by and helped Mike Sweet bury his guns and ammunition at the Good Springs Gulch." Sweet operated a sutler store there for Charlie Perkins.

"Don't sound good," Rankin interjected.

Major Thornburgh frowned at his chief scout. "Let Mr. Taylor finish, will you please."

Taylor gulped down his cup of coffee heavily laced with whiskey, courtesy of one of Capt. Lawson's men.

"Well sir, Old Black was making tracks when Jack and a few other Utes came up on him and they forced him back to Sweet's sutler where they tore the place up looking fer guns and ammunition. But Black said they never found where he and Sweet had buried them. Jack left hopping mad."

Suddenly a man thundered into camp on a big draft animal. It was Columbus Henry, one of John Gordon's bullwackers whose wagons were just ahead of the troops. His frightened eyes were wide and he talked in excited tones.

"Major, I just talked with that big-belled Ute, Colorow, and he told me if your men crossed Milk River, they was gonna fight. Just lookie here," Henry said, pulling a rumpled piece of paper from his pocket. He handed it over to Thornburgh who studied the penciled sketch of four army officers riddled with bullets. He passed it over to Capt. Payne.

"Told you them Utes couldn't be trusted," Rankin interjected for the second time.

Thornburgh looked worried enough. "Have you seen anything of Charlie Lowry?"

"Ain't laid a peep on Charlie for two weeks. Why, what's he up to?" Henry asked.

"I had him deliver a letter to Meeker and as yet he hasn't returned."

"Wouldn't worry none 'bout old Charlie. Them Utes might skin one of us alive, but they wouldn't hurt a hair on Charlie. They love his harmonica playing too much."

Rankin only shook his head over such foolishness. Harmonica or no, if it suited their purpose, Charlie Lowry would receive the same treatment reserved for any white man. This time he kept his thoughts to himself.

Late that night, Major Thornburgh was awakened to find Charlie Lowry standing there. Thornburgh rubbed the sleep from his eyes and sat on the side of his bed while he listened to Lowry give his report.

"Major, I'm mighty sorry it took so long gettin' back to you. I stopped off at Peck's for a little fixed ammunition, but he didn't have any."

"We have plenty, Mr. Lowry should the need arise," Thornburgh said, between two loud yawns.

Lowry nodded and launched into his story, seeing that the Army officer was still sleepy. What he had to say left Thornburgh wide-eyed and completely awake.

"All hell's broke loose at the agency, Major. Old Douglas and Jack's sent their squaws south over Roan Plateau toward Grand River. They war danced all night and here's the worst part, Ute Jack told me they were gonna stick a match to the agency and kill Meeker for having brought troops to the reservation. Tell you, Major, that's as close as I've ever felt to death. I played my harmonica danged near the whole night to try and calm Jack and Douglas down. When I left this morning, they promised they wouldn't do anything until you came in to talk."

Thornburgh was alarmed by this sudden turn of events and he immediately ordered his officers together for a staff meeting. After they had gathered, Thornburgh stood up and began to speak earnestly.

"I must admit, Capt. Payne was dead right. I should never have agreed to travel to the agency with only five troopers." And then he went on to explain the present status at the agency according to Lowry.

"With only seven white employees to guard the womenfolk from a hundred Utes, spoiling for a fight, we must bring a cavalry detachment as close to the agency as we can. I don't care if Ute Jack sees them or not. I have to know we can offer protection to those women."

"Only thing we can do, Major," Payne said with more than a little satisfaction in his voice.

Thornburgh turned to his chief scout who looked to be the worse for sleep, having spent the better part of the night sharing a bottle and conversation with Capt. Lawson. Both men had similar taste when it came to females.

"Mr. Rankin, you said earlier if we proceed through this Coal Creek Canyon the Utes may try to ambush us there, correct?"

"Correct you are, Major."

"What then, would you suggest we do to avoid this, yet not impede our progress to the agency?"

"We ought to take a few of your cavalry over the pack trail that runs just south of the canyon and check things out. If there's no Indians, then the rest of your command can move on through the canyon with no trouble."

Thornburgh studied on this for a moment and hastily wrote a letter to Meeker and handed it over to Wilmer Eskridge, who had stated earlier that he would be glad to take a message back to Meeker whenever Thornburgh asked.

"You don't have to do this you know," Thornburgh said to the agency employee.

"It's okay. I belong back there with Mr. Meeker. Just don't tarry on the road," was all Eskridge asked.

The latest letter to Meeker read:

> Headquarters, White River Expedition
> Deer Creek Camp
> September 28, 1879
>
> Mr. Meeker
> Sir:
> I have, after due deliberation, decided to modify my
> plans as outlined in my letter of the 27th in the following
> respects: I shall move with my entire command to some
> convenient camp near and within striking distance of the
> Agency, reaching such point during the 29th. I shall then
> halt and encamp my troops and proceed to the Agency

with my guide and five soldiers as communicated in your letter of the 27th. Then and there I will be ready to have a conference with you and the Indians so that an understanding may be arrived at and my course of action determined. I have carefully considered whether or not it would be advisable to have my command at a point as distant as that desired by the Indians who were in my camp last night and have reached the conclusion that under my orders, which require me to march my command to the Agency, I am not at liberty to leave it at a point where it would not be available in case of trouble. You are authorized to say for me to the Indians that my course of action is entirely dependent on them. Our desire is to avoid trouble and we have not come for war. I requested you in my letter of the 25th to meet me on the road before I reached the Agency. I renew my request that you do so and further desire that you bring such chiefs as may wish to accompany you.

T. T. Thornburgh
Major, 4th Infantry, Commanding

With no further discussion, Thornburgh ordered everyone back to their beds, while Eskridge saddled his horse and rode out of camp on the star-lit agency road.

CHAPTER 27

The People were frightened. Nothing like this had ever happened to the People before. No one really knew how to prepare for it or what to do now that the dreaded *swerch* were finally marching into their country. Young men strutted around openly at the agency in full war paint, yet Quinkent knew their boldness was due in part to Nicaagat's urging, now that both families of the band had left camp and gone south. He still saw the quiet fear in each of the young men's eyes.

Only a few scattered *carniva* remained along Smoking Earth River and these were occupied by men only. In the shortening days of autumn, Quinkent slept little and prayed to *Sunáwiv* that the *swerch* would not come into their lands. He spent a good portion of each day talking to the young men and enjoying the quiet company of Canávish who spoke of how his two sons were now men and favored war like the other young men of the *Nüpartka.*

Quinkent listened to the sadness in Canávish's voice, yet a voice also tinged with pride now that his two sons were old enough to be men.

Quinkent thought of how much things had changed so quickly when this new agent came to their country. First, things had been good for the People, but like all agents who were never satisfied, this agent began to change and demand things of the People that were not good. Quinkent decided that the insistent plowing of the land had been the single-most factor that sealed their fate with this agent, yet he knew too that with agents, if it had not been the plowing, it would have been something else. *Mericatz* were never satisfied with things as they are and almost never happy like the People of Smoking Earth River.

Now that the *swerch* were moving closer to winter valley, Nicaagat rarely came to the agency anymore, preferring to send runners, as many as five and six a day, to report the latest developments.

"Will you fight if the *swerch* comes into the reservation?" Quinkent asked his friend, Canávish. It was a question he had been considering himself now for more than seven sleeps. Yet he was no closer to the answer than the first sleep. And with Singing Grass gone, and the troubles facing the People, his sleeping became less each day.

"This is a serious thing these soldiers do by coming here. This agent had no right to ask them here," Canávish said, relighting his pipe.

"Unh!" Quinkent responded.

"The People have never made war with the *Mericatz,* even when Ouray gave away a great piece of our land. Not even later, when the *Mericatz* came deeper into our mountains, digging in the ground for stones, did we threaten war. We have tried to be friends with the

Mericatz even as pieces of our country grew smaller and smaller. But," and here Canávish pointed to the river now lined with golden cottonwood and red alder, "this is a far more serious thing the *Mericatz* do by bringing the *swerch* into our country."

"By treaty they cannot come into our lands," Quinkent interjected, knowing that the shaman already knew this, but being caught up in the moment, he felt like it was important to say it again. Quinkent felt the anger growing within him again.

"If the *swerch* crosses into our country, I will stand beside Nicaagat and do what I must do," Canávish said simply.

"I will not fight the *Mericatz* there. Only if they come to Smoking Earth River."

"What about this agent? Will you make war against him as some of the young men suggest?"

Quinkent thought of this for a long while. This caused the sickness deep within him to stir around again and he could feel this strange thing gnawing its way closer to the surface of the ground. All the People could feel it. And it grew stronger with each sleep.

"I have a responsibility to the People. Therefore, I must put aside such thoughts of war and try to do what is best for the People. That is what a *tawacz viem* should do."

"Yes, that is what a *tawacz viem* should do," Canávish repeated quietly.

Quinkent felt a little better for having someone as powerful as Canávish to agree with him. Part of the sickness left him.

"I will go down and talk with this agent and see what he knows."

"We need to know," Canávish agreed. Both men had seen the new agency employee, Wilmer Eskridge, ride up to this agent's house very early this morning. They knew the *Mericatz* brought words on paper from the *swerch* for this agent. Quinkent should learn what these words were so he could effectively perform his duties as *tawacz viem*.

Quinkent started for the agent's house and after he had walked a little ways, he looked back to see Canávish riding towards the north with his big rifle, one the *Mericatz* called a Sharps. Among the People, there was no better shot with a rifle than Canávish. Quinkent knew the shaman was going to join Nicaagat's men, who now watched the road below Yellowjacket Pass.

He turned back and kept walking, his heart heavy in his chest. Could he manage to keep peace with the *swerch* so close by?

When Quinkent entered Meeker's office, he found the agent putting words down on paper again. This agent was always doing that and anger flared suddenly in Quinkent. Was he sending more lies so the *swerch* would come and drag the People away with chains around their necks like the agent had repeatedly threatened?

"Hello, Douglas. I was just writing a note to Major Thornburgh, the commander of the soldiers now at Milk River."

This interested Quinkent very much and he fought the anger back down so he could learn more.

"You and I can meet the Major tomorrow on the road at Coal Creek Canyon and have a talk. Jack should be there as well."

Quinkent's tight face relaxed. It was good to talk, not make war.

"He leave men at Milk River?" Quinkent asked. It was one thing to talk with only a few *swerch* around, but with many, the People become scared and the young men eager to fight.

"That's the plan, Douglas," Meeker said smoothly, knowing otherwise, having just read Thornburgh's recent letter. "The soldiers do not wish to fight. Only your people can see to that."

"Ute no fight. We go meet, talk."

Wilmer Eskridge came into the office looking ready to ride. Quinkent did not look at this *Mericatz.*

"Your letter about ready, Mr. Meeker? I don't start back now, it will be midnight before I see the Major."

328

"Almost, Wilmer. Just a line or two more." Meeker signed his name and sat back to read the message through once more.

White River Agency
September 29, 1879 —1 P.M.

Major T. T. Thornburgh
White River Expedition, In the Field, Colorado
Dear Sir:
I expect to leave in the morning with Douglas and
Serrick to meet you. Things are peaceful and Douglas
flies the United States flag. If you have trouble getting
through the canyon let me know. We have been on guard
three nights and shall be tonight, not because we know
there is danger but because there might be. I like your
last programme. It is based on true military principles.
Most truly yours,
N. C. Meeker, Indian Agent

That last part Meeker referred to was in response to Thornburgh's bringing his troops closer to the agency rather than leaving them far behind.

Meeker looked up and handed the letter to Eskridge.

"Well, gentlemen, how about lunch?" Quinkent grinned broadly.

Together, the three men crossed to Josie's boardinghouse and sat down to lunch with the Greeley boys, Frank and Harry Dresser, Sowówic and Arvilla.

After lunch, Josie packed supper for Eskridge and two Utes, Ebenezer and Antelope, who were going to guide him safely through to the troops.

Quinkent left feeling the sickness in him completely gone now. He wandered down to the beautiful river in hopes of catching sight of the spirit birds. He had not seen them now for three sleeps. The spirit wind rustled the cottonwood leaves and Quinkent closed his eyes to the soothing sound. This time tomorrow, he would meet with this *swerch* and put an end to the troubles.

Thornburgh broke camp early, the frosty morning cut cleanly in a man's lungs. It was a beautiful day to be alive and Thornburgh reveled in the clear mountain air and the timbered slopes of Sleepy Cat Peak caressing the bright September sky. Among its folds of spruce and aspen Thornburgh knew were elk and deer slowly making their way down into the valley for the winter. If only there was time to go hunting and his brother Jacob were along. This area was much more beautiful than where his brother now hunted. Beyond Sleepy Cat, were the enfolding Flattops and Trapper's Lake Joe Rankin had told him about that was full of fish. He thought again of catching fifty-two red sides at Battle Lake in thirty minutes. That had been a day to remember.

Thornburgh dismounted near the headwaters of Milk Creek and drank deeply of its chalky-white waters. They continued across the valley floor and three hours later came to the Milk Creek Crossing where the drought had reduced the river to stagnant pools.

Milk Creek curved away to the northwest and disappeared behind a triple-knobbed mountain that rose some fifteen hundred feet above the bench. Scattered juniper and piñon dusted the top while large bands of yellow sandstone marked its two mile base. A series of five gray sand dunes lay at its foot from where the bench, covered with sage, ran gently down to Milk Creek.

Rankin came riding back from across the river and joined Thornburgh, who was busy studying his next move.

"Major, they ain't enough here to keep the animals watered if you order the men into camp," Rankin said.

"I was just thinking that very same thing, Mr. Rankin. Where is the nearest good supply of water?"

330

"Beaver Springs, Major." Rankin paused, a slight grin creasing his face, "Five miles inside the reservation."

"Captain Payne!" Thornburgh called back to his sub-commander. Payne came forward on the double.

"Yes sir, Major?" Payne said, coming alongside the officer.

"Mr. Rankin says the nearest source of water sufficient enough to support our needs lies five miles inside the reservation at Beaver Springs. I originally intended to leave the main body of the troops here at Milk River with you bringing a support unit of the cavalry in behind me as you suggested. With no water, I don't really see how we can hold to that agreement promised Chief Jack."

"Neither do I, Major," Payne said quickly. "We must have good water."

"But what do think the Utes will make of this after having promised we would bring troops no further?"

Payne rubbed his jaw, his eyes studying the distant ridge. The afternoon was a deep blue and across the river, golden cottonwood leaves rustled in the slight breeze. Although the morning had begun with frost, the temperature now was nearing eighty degrees.

"If Utes are watching, surely they can see we cannot stop where there is insufficient water for our animals. And if a good supply is only five miles from here, as Joe says, then I'm for pushing on. Five miles shouldn't make that much difference to the Utes."

Rankin smiled and shook his head. Payne had been too long back east as far as he was concerned. He knew even less about Utes than Thornburgh, yet the Major was willing to learn.

"I disagree with you Captain, but not about the need to push on for suitable water. It's the five miles that'll get us in trouble, I figger." Lt. Sam Cherry and three privates rode up and joined the group.

"You think they still set to attack at Coal Creek Canyon?" Major Thornburgh asked.

"My best guess," Rankin replied. "The road is tight against the walls in spots and the canyon lies about fifteen hundred feet from the top. A few sharpshooters up there and we could be in a pickle."

"Well, we can't stay here and I will not order a retreat just to find water. That would put the troops too far from White River Agency and of little help should the need arise."

"I agree with you, Major," Rankin said, "just wanted you to know how these Utes think. They ain't never had to deal with Army troops on their land before and they are more than a little frightened. They've heard how the plains Indians were rounded up and they want no part of that. Ain't helped none to have Meeker telling Jack and Douglas about how the soldiers would come and drag them away with chains around their necks to prison or to hang."

"Meeker said that?" Thornburgh asked, not wanting to believe his ears.

"I can speak a little Ute, Major. That's the rumor going around among the Indians."

"Damn!" Thornburgh said explosively. "No wonder they are more than a little edgy about us being here."

"Should I bring the troops up, sir?" Payne asked Thornburgh.

"Yes, Mr. Payne, you may do so," Thornburgh said, tiredly. "Only pray to God you are wrong about us moving forward, Mr. Rankin."

"Could be, Major, but I doubt it."

"Lt. Cherry, why don't you and the privates ride out with Mr. Rankin. Another four sets of eyes may be of some help to you, Mr. Rankin. And be careful. If you make contact with the Indians, you are not to fire on them," Thornburgh admonished.

"Yes sir, Major," Sam Cherry said, gathering up his reins.

"We get across, you men kinda spread out some and keep your eyes peeled. See anything don't seem right, you let me know," Rankin ordered, before lifting his own reins on his horse and moving forward.

Thornburgh watched the small group of men move across the shallow river and climb through the golden cottonwoods and red willows. He turned in his saddle and watched as Captain Payne got the whole expedition moving forward again. A good two miles back, Thornburgh could see the huge cloud of yellow dust being stirred up by John Gordon's bull train.

Joe Lawson's rough-and-ready company of veterans rode behind Thornburgh's ambulance, still driven by Private O'Malley. Thornburgh joined Lawson's group to discuss the situation with the old captain.

Behind them at an interval of several hundred yards, rode Captain Payne and his Company F, Fifth Cavalry. A good quarter-mile back of Payne was Quartermaster Wolf's supply wagons and Lt. Paddock's Company D, Fifth Cavalry. Now riding with Charlie Davis's sutler wagon, Surgeon Grimes brought up the rear along with John Gordon's ponderous ox train.

Thornburgh's troops were spread out over a two mile stretch of benchland yet Thornburgh did not really worry too much about this. They were still a good ten miles from Coal Creek Canyon where everyone had agreed an ambush might be staged by the Utes. Long before they ever reached the canyon, Thornburgh fully intended to tighten the line.

CHAPTER 28

Canávish arrived at the site selected by Nicaagat to watch the wagon road where Little River crossed the benchland. One time a *Mericatz* turned his wagon over in Little River and shiny little cans spilled out and floated away. There were women at the river that day and they brought these shiny cans filled with milk back to their *carniva*. For several days more women went to the river and brought back these milk cans to their *carniva*. After that, the *Mericatz* began to call it Milk River.

With Canávish was his two sons, Tatitz and Saponse, dressed in their war paint and looking eager to prove their manhood. Canávish wore the traditional war paint of three red, yellow and blue bands on each side of his cheeks with a bright yellow line that ran across the left eye and shot diagonally across the bridge of his nose. On his forehead were three crimson streaks.

The combination of yellow, red and blue bands were repeated again on both his upper arms. In his braided hair tied up with otter skin was a single eagle feather with the tip pointing downward. He carried the big rifle that shoots louder than the other People's weapons in the cradle of one arm.

He found Nicaagat before a small campfire where meat, skewered on green sticks, was being cooked, for no *piwáns* were there to cook for the hundred young men.

"*Maiquas*," Nicaagat said as the shaman and his two sons dismounted. Acari and his son, Sáponise, came over to the fire and joined in. They all greeted each other quietly for the thought of war with the *Mericatz* had now become a real possibility and such thoughts sobered even the most warlike of the People.

Acari spoke first saying, "If you will give the power and wisdom of Quigat to my son, and your sons as well, I will give you the best of my ponies," he said to Canávish.

Canávish indicated with a nod of his head that he was willing to do so, even though the time for war was growing close.

Nicaagat and Acari left the young men there beside the fire with Canávish and went off to check the road for soldiers.

Canávish settled next to the fire and brought out his stone pipe and smoked it to the powers and then he told the young men of the story of *Sunáwiv*, the God, who lived on the greatest mountain and wore the finest buckskin.

"*Sunáwiv* became lonely and he made a brother and together they sang and danced and went on fine hunts. This brother was *Sunáwigá*, whom the *Mericatz* call Holy Ghost. When *Sunáwiv* went away one day to hunt by himself, he warned his brother not to open the little buckskin bags he kept tied up, but as soon as Sunáwiv left, his brother began opening the little bags after he heard tiny voices calling for him to let them out. As he opened the bags, little men hopped out and ran away. In the last bag were men who were very noisy. They were the Sioux. *Sunáwigá* became frightened after they jumped out and he closed this last bag tightly when he heard his brother coming back. *Sunáwiv* knew what his brother had done and he told him that now all these people would make war, for they were not ready to be turned loose across the earth yet. *Sunáwiv* was very angry at his brother and changed him into Old Man Coyote because he had spoiled things.

"And then *Sunáwiv* opened this last bag and let out the people he had been saving for last. These were *Nüntz*, the People. Then he told them they were his People. He told them they needed to fear only four things: fire, flood, wind and war. And then he told them how to protect themselves. For fire, always carry a little piece of rabbit brush and crouch down and the fire will burn over you. For flood, take a few feathers which will grow into a boat and carry you over deep water. For wind, carry little stones to hold you near the earth. But for war, I have nothing that will protect you. You must look inside your heart for the truth. After that day, *Sunáwiv* went away to live in the sun and the People spread out across these mountains and it has been this way since before the old ones, who knew of these things."

None of the young men had said a word throughout Canávish's talk. They were honored at having the shaman bless each of them with *Quigat's* power at such an important time. Now they each thanked him and went away to watch the road with the others. Tatitz took his rifle and followed after his brother, Sáponise.

Canávish ate some of the meat hanging on the green sticks and walked over to where Nicaagat and Colorow watched the road.

Nicaagat was on his feet near the high ridge, with his hand shading his eyes when Canávish came up. For a long moment there was silence and then Nicaagat pointed so Colorow and the shaman could see what he was looking at.

Deep in the great bowl that was Milk Creek Valley, all three men watched as two soldiers moved slowly up to the drying river and stopped. And behind these *Mericatz* came a long line of soldiers, stirring up much dust.

Nicaagat finally spoke. "This is where the soldiers will make camp. I will go down later and talk with this general again and things will be all right." Colorow lay belly-down on the ground and pushed his rifle across the top of the ridge.

"What if they do not stop here?" Canávish asked, looking around at the young men who were gesturing excitedly at the soldiers with their rifles.

Nicaagat took his eyes momentarily from the scene below and looked at the shaman. "We will fight."

The words were barely out of his mouth before Colorow's deep voice spoke.

"They cross Little River!"

Both Nicaagat and Canávish looked quickly down into the hole and saw five *Mericatz*, four of them *swerch* riding with another *Mericatz* who wore a fine set of cream-colored buckskins, cross Little River and head directly alongside the grassy ridge where the People waited.

Now all the young men stood up and lined themselves along the ridge so they could see better. No one said a word and the stillness of the afternoon heat beat gently down on Indian and soldier alike.

Nicaagat watched as others behind the five *Mericatz* started across Little River and anger filled his chest so tightly he could barely breathe. The general had not kept his word, yet Nicaagat still felt compelled to avoid a war. He could still remember how badly the soldiers had whipped the Sioux.

"I will go down there a little ways and talk with these *swerch*. Get them to stop."

"Unh!" Colorow growled like a huge bear from the ground. He

gripped his rifle so tight that his knuckles were white. There was a lot of fear in the young men as well.

Canávish said he would go with Nicaagat if he wanted, but Nicaagat shook his head.

"These *Mericatz* know me. Things will be all right," he said as he eased over the grassy ridge and started slowly down the gentle slope.

"Where is Rankin taking them?" Thornburgh asked Charlie Lowry who had come alongside.

"It's a short cut, Major. It rejoins the agency road at the end of that long ridge," Lowry replied, pointing at the grassy ridge. "It'll spare the horses some."

Thornburgh nodded and looked back at his command only to see Captain Payne gesturing at something up ahead. Next he motioned for Thornburgh to retreat.

"What's that?" Thornburgh said, bringing his glasses to his eyes and focusing on the grass ridge. What he saw caused his heart to beat heavily against his ribs. There were at least fifty, possibly more, Indians standing along the edge of the ridge, looking down at them.

"Utes!" Charlie Lowry said forcefully.

Thornburgh looked back and saw that Payne was closing ranks behind Joe Lawson's veterans. Suddenly Joe Rankin saw them too and he trotted back towards Thornburgh leaving Cherry and his men in the field.

"Capt. Lawson, deploy your men over there!" Thornburgh shouted, pointing to the right side of the agency road. When Payne came rushing up with his men, Thornburgh had them placed onto the left of the road among the sage.

Rankin came riding up and reined in next to Thornburgh, his face telling it all.

"Never figgered they would try to hit us here! Them's Jack's men and if I were you I'd commence to shooting now!"

"I'll wait, Mr. Rankin. There's still the chance we can conclude this by peaceful means."

Rankin shook his head.

Thornburgh rode out alone a little distance from Rankin and stood up in his stirrups and waved his hat at the line of Indians. Just below the ridge, he saw a lone Indian moving down the slope. The Indian waved back at Thornburgh. He couldn't be sure from this distance, but Thornburgh thought the Indian was Ute Jack.

Thornburgh sat back down in the saddle and watched as Cherry, now dismounted waved his hat and began limping up the slope.

Suddenly, someone along the skirmish line mistook Cherry's hat as a signal to open fire and rifles pinged up an down the line of soldiers. Immediately, the Indians began returning their fire and little puffs of smoke rose up above the ridge were the Utes were stationed.

The battle of Milk River was on.

Thornburgh lifted his engraved Colt from its holster and brought his horse around just as he saw three Utes fall and two of Payne's men. He saw mounted Utes slipping north behind the sand dunes at the base of the lone mountain. Thornburgh thought of the supply wagons and knew they had to be protected and he wheeled his horse around and started back through the cottonwoods.

"Private O'Malley, bring up the ambulance," he called to his orderly without looking back.

O'Malley bawled to the mules at the top of his lungs as he brought the reins down on their backs. The bowl was thundering with guns of every size and description. O'Malley managed to get the ambulance turned when a Ute bullet caught the lead mule in the head and dropped him in his tracks.

"Jesus, be damned!" O'Malley cursed, jumping quickly from his seat to cut the harness from a mule. He mounted up and looked for Thornburgh but the Major had completely disappeared.

Riding alone through the tall grass above the Milk Creek

Crossing, wholly preoccupied with the beginning battle, Major Thomas Tipton Thornburgh never felt the big bullet from a Ute sharpshooter that caught him just above his ear and lifted him free of his saddle. He rolled over once and ended face up on the ground, still tightly clutching the Colt his men in Maryland had given him on his thirty-first birthday with his name engraved in silver on the butt. More than likely he had died before his lanky body hit the ground.

After O'Malley could not find Major Thornburgh, he rode the mule over to Captain Payne's company and found the sub-commander clutching his arm, in great pain. His mount lay dead nearby.

"Cap Payne," O'Malley said hoarsely. "The Major is alone in them cottonwoods."

"Rankin, you and Sergeant Dolan go have a look and see if you can find the Major," Payne shouted, his face twisted in pain. He finally sat down on the ground.

Rankin led the way with old Sergeant John Dolan bringing up his rear. Emerging from the cottonwoods, Rankin caught a riderless horse by the reins.

"Ain't this the Major's?" Rankin asked.

"It is."

"Here, take the reins, it looks like the Major may be dead," Rankin said, giving Dolan the reins. "You best get back and tell Captain Payne while I see if I can give Lieutenant Wolf a hand with the supply wagons."

Dolan nodded, grabbed the reins and galloped back through the cottonwoods.

Rankin found the young West Pointer completely disorganized and trying to ward off Ute sharpshooters from the sand dunes while forting the wagons. Rankin found Lieutenant Paddock with two bad bullet wounds.

With Rankin's help Paddock managed to corral the twenty-five wagons one hundred and fifty yards away from the meager waters of Milk River. Rankin had left a gap for John Gordon's ox train to fill in, but in a few minutes Gordon appeared on foot with his bullwackers looking scared out of their wits. The steady fire from Ute rifles had forced them to abandon the oxen. This left a large gap between Paddock's men and Payne's with nothing to fill in the hole with.

By sheer will, Payne got to his feet to deal with the predicament after Dolan returned with the sad news about Thornburgh.

"Sergeant Grimes, get back to the supply wagon and bring up ammunition for Lawson's men." Lawson still held the right side of the agency road. When Grimes returned, Payne withdrew his Company F from the left side of the road and back to the supply train. Once there, he directed a detail to dig a big central triangular pit for the wounded men of Company F. Payne still faced what to do about the hundred and twenty foot gap in the circled supply wagons. Even in his pain, the wounded acting commander knew there was but one thing to do.

"You men line those mules and horses up in this gap and start shooting them," Payne shouted, sick at having to give such orders. The troopers did as ordered and soon a breastworks of dead animals was formed to complete the circle formed by the rest of the wagons. Payne was beginning to think things were under some semblance of control once again when he heard Rankin call his name.

"They've fired the sage!" Rankin shouted hoarsely.

With a stiff breeze blowing up from the north, an eight foot wall of yellow-orange fire raced towards the corralled wagons.

Thinking quickly, Payne turned to Sergeant Poppe. "Crawl out there and set a back fire," he ordered. Everyone watched as Poppe crawled out and lit a fire. He scampered back to the corral with his own fire chasing him.

"Look out!" Rankin shouted, "It's gonna set the wagons on fire."

Sure enough, the fire entered the corral and soon the canvas wagon tops were ablaze. With every trooper beating at the flames, Utes bullets rained in on them. Five troopers were killed. Rankin watched as the fire passed beyond the corral and set John Gordon's bull train on fire.

"There goes Meeker's red flannel shirts," John Gordon said quietly as black smoke billowed up into the blue sky.

There was a sudden lull in the fighting as Ute warriors rode out to catch the oxen who had escaped the fire by crossing Milk River.

Dr. Grimes laid out ten bodies and ordered them covered with a thin layer of dirt. Rankin came over to see who had been killed.

"Ain't that old Charlie Lowry?"

"Him all right," Grimes said grimly. "Took a hit in the front of his head."

"Guess them Utes'll just hafta live without harmonica music from now on," Rankin said, trying his hand at black humor. None of the troopers assigned to dig the shallow graves were amused as they eased old Sergeant Dolan down beside Lowry and began covering them both up with a thin layer of soil.

The afternoon grew even warmer in the boardinghouse where Arvilla, Josie and Flora Ellen were busy cleaning away the dinner dishes. Through an opened window, they could see Arthur Thompson spreading a layer of dirt on the roof of one of the new buildings Meeker had ordered constructed. Frank Dresser and Shad Price were busy throwing dirt up to Thompson.

"Just look at that Ute ride," Josie exclaimed. The three women watched as a Ute rider tore down the wagon road from the north and yanked his lathered pony to a stop before Douglas's lodge.

"They've been doing that all week," Arvilla replied, handing Josie a slippery pot to dry. "Ever since Jack moved his band north to hunt."

"Do you know what day this is, Mother?" Josie asked taking the pot from her.

"I haven't the slightest idea, child," Arvilla replied, reaching for another dirty plate.

"Father says on this day in 1066, William the Conqueror landed in England!"

"That's so much like Mr. Meeker to remember such details," Arvilla replied, rinsing the plate she had just washed.

Flora Ellen wiped her hands dry on a corner of her apron.

"I better look after May," she said, referring to her three year old daughter. "I'm not careful, she'll be right amongst all that dirt her father is shoveling."

Flora Ellen stepped out on the porch and was alarmed to see Ebenezer tying his horse to the corner of the bunkhouse rack. What was he doing back, she wondered? He was suppose to be riding north with Wilmer Eskridge to deliver Meeker's letter to the Army troops.

In the distance she saw Douglas coming up the road with several Utes at his side. There was a strange look on his face. One Flora Ellen had never seen before and instinctively, she clutched the chubby-faced May close to her. Those walking with Douglas were Pauvitz, Antelope and Persune. She thought Jata, Johnson's brother was among them as well.

And then disaster struck without warning.

Several of the Utes simply lifted their rifles and began firing at the toiling men.

Flora Ellen screamed in horror as Art Thompson tumbled headlong from the roof, being the first to die.

Stricken-faced, Shad Price shouted to his wife, "For Godsakes, Flora, grab the babies and run!" A second later, Shadrach Price staggered sideways and collapsed, clutching his stomach.

By now, little May was screaming wildly. Flora Ellen turned to go back inside the boardinghouse just as young Frank Dresser bounded up at full speed, wide-eyed and shoeless.

"Get back inside, hurry now," Dresser commanded, pushing Flora Ellen towards the door. Behind them they could hear in a clear voice, William Post begging for his life.

Suddenly, Indians seemed to be everywhere at once and their rifles sounded like firecrackers at a Fourth of July picnic. Inside the boardinghouse, both Arvilla and Josie were too stunned to move. It was hard to think that less than two hours before, they had sat down to lunch with some of the Indians now killing their menfolks.

"Everybody, quick, into the bedroom," Frank Dresser shouted, trying to get the shocked women to cooperate. Normally shy, the curly-haired Dresser was barely out of knee pants, yet today he was acting more like a grown man. Dresser raced to the bureau and picked up Shad Price's loaded Winchester and shot Canávish's brother, Jata, through the opened dinning room window.

The women all crowded into Josie's bedroom and hid beneath the bed with Flora Ellen's two children, May and little Johnnie. They lay for quite sometime, listening to crackling guns.

"I smell smoke," Frank Dresser said, from his position near the door. He held the Winchester tightly in his small hands, his face ashen.

"Oh, God! They've fired the agency," Arvilla said, making whimpering sounds.

"Where is father?" Josie asked.

"At the office. God only knows . . ." Arvilla's voice trailed off, not being able to complete the unthinkable sentence.

"Listen, while they are busy breaking into the storehouse, we best go hide in the milk house," Dresser said, his thin voice shaking. "It'll only be a matter of time 'til they check here. Once it gets dark, we can make a run for it."

When the women came out from beneath the bed, Josie noticed young Frank's bloody leg.

"You've been shot."

Frank nodded grimly, shoving them through the bedroom door.

"Been too busy to even feel the pain."

They ran across the street to the adobe milk house. Once inside, Frank Dresser spent a few anxious moments piling can goods, jars of food and sacks against the door.

Arvilla Meeker spent her time sobbing into a corner of her long dress and wondering out loud about *poor, Mr. Meeker*. Flora Ellen had her hands full just tending to little Johnnie and May. Josie cleaned and dressed Frank Dresser's leg wound.

"You are very lucky, Frank. It's only a flesh wound. The bleeding's already stopped."

"Thank you, ma'am," Dresser said shyly after Josie had finished with the wound.

"You did a brave thing today, Frank, protecting us," Josie said, her voice betraying her sadness.

"Aw, I ain't done nothing," the lad replied, blushing deeply in spite of their dire situation.

"Oh, but you have." And then her face changed to disbelief. "I simply can't believe the Utes are doing this terrible thing. Douglas has been so sweet, the others as well. Jack must be behind this. He is the one always talking about fighting."

After that, silence filled the little milk house as they listened to sporadic gunfire, benumbed and too helpless to do anything more. And darkness was still hours away . . .

Attracted by the shots, Nathan Meeker came out of his office on a stumbling run only to catch sight of the carnage going on around him. There were Indians firing at his agency employees and he started toward them on a dead run, shouting for the Utes to stop. He heard the hoofs of a horse fast approaching him from behind and

Meeker turned to see a Ute riding his pony with the reins in his teeth and a rifle aimed at him.

"Oh, God, noooo!" Meeker whispered as he saw the puff of dark-yellow smoke come out of the barrel of the Ute's Winchester. Something slammed hard into him but he thought it funny that he felt no pain.

CHAPTER 29

Captain Payne rested briefly with Joe Rankin beside him, whose big Winchester barked whenever a Ute had the temerity to test Rankin's skill with the heavy weapon.

"Captain, you better have the sawbones check your wounds. As pale as you are, there can't be much blood left in you."

"Directly, Mr. Rankin," Payne said weakly.

"Uh oh," Rankin said, pointing with the barrel of his Winchester. "Looks like they fired the agency."

Payne rose up enough to see the black smoke billowing upward in the distance above the Danforth Hills.

"Then all hope is lost of saving Meeker and his family," Payne said bitterly.

"Most likely, Captain. But the Utes won't harm the womenfolk."

"That's hardly something positive, Mr. Rankin. I've heard the stories of what Indians do with captive women. I doubt they'll survive the ordeal."

"The women at White River are a lot tougher than you might think, Captain. Don't go selling them short just yet."

"Corporal Roach!" Payne shouted at the enlisted trooper, two wagons down. Roach zig-zagged his way to Payne, staying low to the ground.

"Yes sir?"

"Set up a water detail when it gets dark between the creek and the corral. We need to fill every bucket we got tonight. There's no telling how long we'll be pinned in this hole."

"Yes sir," Roach said, starting to turn away.

"One more thing, find Lieutenant Cherry and have him do a head count. I need to know how many men we got who are still in fighting condition." Roach scrambled away.

There was a long silence between officer and scout. Finally, Payne looked over at Rankin's tense form.

"What do you think of our present situation, Mr. Rankin? What I mean is, you know these Utes better than most. How long do you think they'll keep us pinned down here before they leave?"

"Hate to tell you, Captain, but Nicaagat, and I suspect now, old Quinkent himself, will do their dangest to keep us here 'til we are all killed or starved to death. Case you ain't noticed, they hold the cards right now. Like shooting down into a fish bowl from up there."

"Thought that was what you'd say," Payne responded softly.

Lt. Sam Cherry came skidding up, scattering dust and gravel. His young face was streaked with sweat-dried dust. He was breathing hard, yet still game.

"Report, Lieutenant."

"We got ninety-six men still on their feet, sir. That's out of a force of one hundred and forty-two."

Payne nodded, seeming to accept the grim news well. Rankin merely grunted his reply, keeping his eyes peeled. What he hadn't told Payne yet was, towards dark, the Utes would make another major charge. For now, he could hold off with this news.

"What about the animals?" Payne queried Cherry.

"We got fifty horses and mules left."

"We could sure use some of Gordon's oxen now for food. They will serve the Utes far longer than we can survive on our limited rations," Payne calculated.

As if reading his thoughts, Cherry added, "We got rations to last us through Thursday."

"And this is Monday," Payne said sadly.

"And all they got to do is sit tight up there and watch us starve to death while taking pot shots."

"Ain't but one thing to do and the sooner I get to it the better our chances of survivin' this," Rankin spoke up.

Both officers looked questioningly at the big scout.

"What are you suggesting, Mr. Rankin?" Payne asked.

"Simple. We got to get the word out. Get Merritt's men up here to lend a hand. And since I know this country better than anybody in your command, I propose slipping out under cover of darkness and high-tailin' it for Rawlings and the telegraph."

Payne only deliberated for a moment, seeing the logic in Rankin's proposal. It was the only way to get help.

"I agree, but take one other man with you in case one or the other of you don't make it," Payne said. All three men knew what would happen if a white man was caught out alone now. The Utes would put them through slow torture.

Rankin considered this for a moment. "Best man I know would be John Gordon. He knows the roads and such pretty good."

"Fine. I'll prepare the messages," Payne said, somewhat fired up.

Rankin figured he may as well go ahead and give Payne the bad news so his men could be better prepared.

"There is one other thing."

"What's that?"

"Expect a strong attack around twilight."

"While I get the messages, Mr. Rankin, would you and Lieutenant Cherry see to the men's positions. Place them where you think is best. And pass the word about the attack."

Both Cherry and Rankin nodded and slipped away.

Just as Rankin predicted, the Utes rose up out of the sage, and screeching at the top of their lungs, attacked the corralled wagons in force. But Rankin had placed the sharpshooters well and Utes fell like grains of wheat. The drive lasted less than five minutes and silence crept back across the darkened benchland.

Captain Payne, finding his shoulders carrying the weight of the command, hunkered down and began writing out messages, one to Lt. Price at the supply depot, one for Captain Dodge and his Negro troopers, and a telegram for General Crook which read:

> Milk River, Colo.,
> September 29, 1879
> 8:30 P.M.

> This command, composed of three companies of Cavalry, was met a mile south of Milk River by several hundred Ute Indians who attacked and drove us to the wagon train with great loss. It becomes my painful duty to announce the death of Major Thornburgh, who fell in harness: The painful but not serious wounding of Lt. Paddock and Dr. Grimes, and killing of ten enlisted men and a wagon master, with the wounding of about twenty men and teamsters. I am corraled near water, with about

three fourths of my animals killed. After a desperate fight since 12 N. We hold our position. I shall strengthen it during the night, and believe we can hold out until re-enforcements reach us, if they are hurried. Officers and men behaved with greatest gallantry. I am also slightly wounded in two places.

Payne, Commander

Two of Payne's Fifth Cavalry troopers volunteered to take the risk along with Rankin and Gordon, Corporals George Moquin of Company F and Ed Murphy of Company D.

Rankin laid out the plans to the men as other troopers got their horses ready.

"Listen good 'cause I ain't likely gonna get a second chance to say it. We go out with the water detail and slip north to the agency crossing. After that we make a flat out run for it. Any trouble, I expect you to cover me if the Utes finds us. That happens, I'll take to the brush and move cross-country."

"But what if they don't?" Corporal Moquin asked.

"Good question, Moquin. That be the case, we head for Peck's on the Bear. Gordon will ride like the devil from there to Middle Park where Captain Dodge is encamped. I want you two men to take the Fortification Creek trail and find Lt. Price's supply depot and get him started south. As for myself, I'll push on north to Rawlings and telegraph General Crook." Rankin paused for a moment. "Any questions?" No one said anything. "Good. We ride in ten minutes, then."

Captain Payne stood by listening to Rankin and he found no fault with the scout's plan of action and told him so.

Rankin looked at the commander in the flickering light of a near-by campfire. "Captain Payne, you look about done in. Soon's we on the road, you get medical attention."

Payne managed a weak smile. "That an order, Mr. Rankin?"

Rankin gave him a tight smile. "If that's the way you want it."

Payne stuck out a pale hand which Rankin gripped. "Be careful out there. Sorry about the full moon, Joe. Good luck."

"Count on it."

It was nearly ten thirty when Rankin and his small group crept out of the corral with the water detail.

Payne and the others held their breaths, waiting for shots that would indicate the group had been discovered. Thirty minutes passed and the water detail came back into camp with their buckets brimming.

Scott Payne felt the tension recede from his wounded body and he knew he wouldn't last much longer. He turned to old Captain Joe Lawson, who was busy working a huge chew around in a mouth and whiskers stained golden by tobacco.

"Mr. Lawson," Payne said weakly.

"What?" the old veteran asked, not one given to military protocol most times, and especially now.

"Captain Lawson, the command is yours." Whereupon, Scott Payne, having worked tirelessly with three wounds since noon that day, promptly fainted.

Lawson spit a big glob on the ground and grunted his amazement. "He cutt'er close," Lawson said to Quartermaster Wolf who was kneeling beside the fallen commander. "Best get the Captain over to Doc Grimes and have him look after his wounds. The man's earned my respect."

"Yes sir," Wolf said, beckoning to nearby troopers for assistance.

Lawson turned back to the moon-lit ridge and wondered how Rankin and the others were making out.

Silently, Joe Rankin cursed the silvery brilliance of the valley as he led the small group back up Deer Creek Divide without encountering a single Ute. Once they reached Deal Gulch above Williams

Fork, Rankin was breathing a little easier and he pushed the horses at a faster clip now.

Away from the besieged troops, the moon now became a major asset, and Rankin pushed the horses even faster now that the silvery trail was plainly visible.

At three in the morning the small group thundered up to Peck's store on the Bear and dismounted stiffly. Rankin was already off his horse and banging on Peck's door. His banging awakened the baby and Rankin could hear the youngster squalling. The darkened window suddenly framed yellow light. A minute more, and the storekeeper called out from behind the solid wooden door, asking their intent.

"It's me, Peck, Joe Rankin!" the scout said.

The door flew open and Peck stood there with a lantern in his hand, gaping at Rankin and the others.

"What in tarnation!" Peck peered closer at the others behind Rankin. "You got soldiers with you, Joe? What the hell's going on?"

"Best gather up your kin and whatever you think is most valuable and get out of here," Rankin said after giving Peck the bad news about Major Thornburgh and his trapped command.

Mrs. Peck was sitting on a sack of grain in the corner of the cluttered store, innocently nursing her baby from an engorged breast to keep him quiet. It reminded Rankin of Maggie Baggs and it was a second or two before he was able to get his mind back on track.

"Lordy, Lordy," Peck said, pacing back and forth, wringing his hands. "We got so much here. I don't know how I can leave it behind."

Rankin looked around at the mess. "Ain't nothing you got here can't be replaced, except that woman and child over yonder."

The storekeeper stopped his pacing and looked at Rankin in a new light. "By golly, Joe, you are right." He went over to his wife and helped her to her feet with the child still attached to his mother, sucking furiously. "We'll be gone by morning."

Rankin and the others turned to the door. "We got to git. Lot of riding still to do."

"I want to thank you men for stopping by and warning us," Peck said, profusely. "Say, why don't you fellars help yourself to whatever you want. Danged Utes will probably burn what they don't haul off."

"Thanks, but we ain't got the time nor the way to carry anything. Luck." Rankin turned to John Gordon, the bullwacker. "Expect you know your way east from here to Middle Park. Just stay on the Gore Pass road. You should run into Captain Dodge's boys before long."

"I'll find them, Joe," Gordon said grimly. "Remember, I got a brother that was hauling freight ahead of us on the road to White River. Got to see he has a chance."

Rankin nodded, mutely. Most likely, Gordon's brother was already dead, but he said nothing.

With that, they mounted up and were gone.

Fearing the two corporals would get themselves lost, Rankin rode the full distance to Lieutenant Price's supply depot on Fortification Creek. They splashed across the beautiful little creek at seven that morning.

Lieutenant Butler Price was shocked by the news of Major Thornburgh's death and while Rankin ate a hasty breakfast, a fresh mount was brought up for him to ride.

By noon, Rankin was at George Baggs' ranch, having pushed the army gelding for all he was worth.

"Lord, Joe, but that animal is winded," Baggs said as Rankin came into the yard at full gallop and skidded to a halt. White foam flecked both the horse's neck and Rankin's clothes.

Rankin quickly filled him in while Maggie Baggs set him down to a quick lunch. While George hurried off to select one of his best animals for Rankin, Maggie planted a wet kiss on Rankin's lips. She wrinkled her nose.

"You could do with a bath, Joe."

"No time, darling," Rankin grinned, shoving down the last piece of steak on his plate. He reached up and squeezed one of her big breasts. "Got to take a rain check this time, Mag."

"Have you heard anything of Mike Sweet?" the woman asked, pouting a little. "George made him take over the sutler's tent at Good Spring Gulch and I'm worried about him with these Utes on the warpath."

"Old George finally caught on to you two, huh?" Rankin said, standing up to put his hat back on. "Well, I wouldn't worry, we ran into Black Wilson a few days back and he helped Mike bury his guns and fixed ammunition to keep the Utes from getting them. Expect Mike'll show up around here before long." Rankin turned and hugged the buxom woman to him for a second. "Know I would."

"Joe Rankin, you are the devil reincarnate." She kissed him hard and pushed him towards the door. George Baggs was coming up from the corral leading a deep-chested chestnut mare.

"She's the fastest thing I got around here on four legs," the rancher said, giving his wife a knowing look. Maggie lifted her head, pretending she hadn't heard the intended remark aimed at her.

"Thanks, George. I'll see she gets good care." Rankin mounted up, taking the reins from the rancher.

"Good luck, Joe," Maggie called from the porch.

Rankin lifted his hand and was gone in a cloud of dust. George Baggs was right, the big mare's long legs seemed to eat ground with every step.

By early Tuesday night, Rankin was at Sulphur Springs where he was fed supper and given a fresh mount, a wiry little pinto. Joe took the flatter trail through Alamosa Gulch and arrived in Rawlings at 2 A.M. Wednesday morning, October first.

The little horse trotted along the Front Street railroad tracks carrying Rankin to Foote's Saloon where he dismounted and went inside. Sweat-stained and grimy, Rankin's buckskins looked the worse for wear. And he slumped at the bar while an excited bartender poured him a glass of whiskey.

Surprised by Rankin's sudden return, a few drunken patrons and bar girls crowded around the scout while he downed a couple stiff drinks and told them the news from Milk River. Rankin had spent twenty-seven and a half hours in the saddle, covering one hundred and sixty miles since leaving Thornburgh's Command on Milk River.

Rankin set his glass back on the bar and a bottle appeared, ready to pour him another.

"No more, I got to get over and wake up Adams," Rankin said, waving the bottle away. J.B. Adams manned the Western Union Telegraph and once Rankin had him on his feet and over at the office, Adams was more than a little shocked by the message Rankin handed him from Captain Payne to send to General Crook, Army of the Platte. Without a word, Adams stroked the telegraph key and fired the message off. When it was done, he leaned back and stared at Rankin, slumped over in a chair.

"My God, Joe, but you look a sight. Go get some rest, you deserve it."

The door burst open and both Bobby and James Rankin stood there, looking sleepy-eyed and excited.

"Lord, Joe, you okay?" Sheriff James Rankin asked his brother, laying a hand on the scout's drooping shoulder. Rankin straightened and looked up at his brothers.

"Dammnest ride I ever made," he whispered. "Bobby, take that little pinto over to the livery and treat him to a rub-down and a couple buckets of oats. He deserves a good meal and rest too."

"Be glad to, Joe," Jailer Bobby Rankin said, feeling somewhat proud for his brother.

Inside of an hour, the whole town was awake and buzzing with the news about Thornburgh's death and his besieged troops. Whiskey flowed like water at such places as Little Van's and Foote's. Even the chippies down on Lower Row found themselves facing eager and excited customers.

Adams sent Payne's message to Laramie City where the next nearest army post was located, at Sheriff Rankin's urging. Immediately, the post telegraph clicked and the message was sent south to Denver and Governor Pitkin.

Joe Rankin stirred himself and made Adams send a third wire to Commissioner Hayt expressing his belief that Meeker and his employees were all murdered as well by the rampaging Utes.

"Good God! I had completely forgotten about the agency," James Rankin whispered. "Are you sure?" he asked his brother.

The begrimed scout gained his feet and stood their swaying for a minute. "That's what I believe. Black smoke was rising above Danforth Hills where the agency should be. To me that means the worst."

"What about the women?" Bobby Rankin inserted.

Joe Rankin shook his shaggy head. "You know Utes." With that, Chief Scout for Major Thornburgh's Expedition left Western Union, crossed the street and went to bed.

Back in the Western Union office, the three men, with perplexed expressions, looked from one to the other for answers.

"What did Joe mean by that last statement, James?" Adams asked the sheriff.

Sheriff James Rankin took a deep breath and turned to the door with Bobby right behind him.

"Your guess is as good as mine, Jim," Rankin said, leaving the telegrapher still without an answer.

CHAPTER 30

Quinkent looked like a man dying from a sickness and in a way he was. The shooting of the *Mericatz* who worked at the agency was mere destiny fulfilling its course across time. Even though Quinkent had wanted nothing to do with Nicaagat's plan to attack the soldiers if they crossed Milk River, all that was lost forever in the cloud of dust of Nicaagat's runner, Cojoe, who brought him the urgent news that twenty of their young men had fallen to the guns of Thornburgh's soldiers. Nicaagat's message was simple . . . kill all the *Mericatz* at the agency and burn the buildings.

For thirty minutes, Quinkent had argued against such a policy, but with the hot-headed Jata, screaming for their blood, the others fell in line behind him. Hopeless to stop them now. Quinkent had gone up to the agency with the young men, thinking he might be able to change their minds once confronted with the real situation of having to kill unarmed *Mericatz*.

Even Quinkent was stunned by the sudden killings of the agency *Mericatz* who were shoveling dirt onto the roof as the bullets from the young men's rifles cut them down.

Jata fired his rifle first and the others joined in the killing spree. There was nothing Quinkent could do but stand there and watch the carnage.

And now, darkness had crept across winter valley, filling it with the sickness of what they had done. Quinkent stood motionless before the burning agency office, the yellow flames captured by the reflection in his sad eyes.

All around him, he could hear the noise of the young men looting the storehouse and shooting their guns into the air in a victory dance. Quinkent knew the victory would be short and hollow, for the People had never fought the *swerch* before. He also realized this would probably be their last night here in the valley of the Smoking Earth River that he loved.

Some of the young men found a supply of whiskey and a bottle was thrust into Quinkent's hand by a passing brave. Without thinking, Quinkent drank long and deep, trying to shut out the smell of gun powder and the crackling sounds of buildings lost in wood smoke.

"Aheeee! Aheeee!" one of the young men shouted as he galloped across the hard-packed ground, dragging a dark object behind his ponies. As he swept past Quinkent, the stark white form of Nathan Meeker slithered by on the end of a logging chain. Quinkent tipped the bottle to his lips once more, unnerved by the sight of the dead agent.

Suddenly, through the din of warhoops, gunshots and thundering horses, Quinkent heard perfectly the cry of a spirit bird from the river, yet its voice seemed different now, more haunting and with a deeper sadness as if knowing what had taken place here today. He turned his face from the burning building, towards the river, listening intently. But the dark river was silent once more, accusing.

A shout from one of the men refocused Quinkent's thoughts and he turned back to see the agency women and one of the young *Mericatz* scampering across the flame-lit darkness through the gate where Meeker had fenced a field.

Several shots rang out and Quinkent saw Meeker's woman stumble and fall as several men ran after the fleeing women. The young *Mericatz* crossed the opening like a fleeing antelope and was gone into the night.

Quinkent, filled with anger, ordered the women not to be harmed. Again he drank deeply from the bottle but the contents seemed to have no effect.

He watched as a big Ute the *Mericatz* called Thompson rushed over to help Meeker's woman.

Quinkent turned and wandered down to the storehouse, hoping to obtain one of the *Mericatz* rifles kept there. He saw the sprawled body of the *Mericatz*, Post, in the entrance, oddly holding sacks of flour under both arms. There was blood coming from a bullet wound in his head. The area around the storehouse was littered with annuity goods and emptied flour sacks, causing the ground to look like snow in deep winter. Quinkent stepped over the body and started plundering the storehouse.

"I am sorry, heap sorry," the young Ute said to Arvilla Meeker as he helped her to her feet. "Can you walk?"

"Yes sir," Arvilla said weakly. The Ute guided Arvilla back across the fenced field and as they passed her house the Indian asked if she had any money inside.

"Very little."

"You get money. Hurry. We ride a great ways tonight," the Ute instructed her.

Arvilla went quietly into the house which was burning at one corner calling, "Nathan, Nathan," softly, more to herself than in hopes of hearing a reply from her husband. She managed to find twenty-six dollars in bills and four dollars in silver.

The young Ute escorted her over to Douglas's *carniv* and Arvilla gave the money to the old chief who had returned from the storehouse after finding no rifles. It was then she saw Josie holding the chubby-faced May on her lap while seated on a pile of blankets. Beside her, stood Persune, who had been in love with Josie ever since she first came to White River. Josie saw her mother and gave a sad smile to let her know she was holding up under the circumstances.

Further away, the little Ute, Ahutupuwit, stood next to Flora Ellen, who loomed over her captor. Arvilla looked around at the Utes and she asked each one as they passed by her if they had seen her husband. The Utes merely shrugged and said nothing.

As the night deepened, the air grew colder and Arvilla asked Quinkent if she could go and get a few clothes and blankets.

Quinkent sent her with the Ute, Thompson, back to the burning house for clothes. Arvilla loaded the young Ute down with blankets, coats and a small box of medicines. While she was there, Arvilla found her hat and shawl and put these on. A needle packet went into her coat pocket as she picked up the huge illuminated volume of *Pilgrim's Progress* and walked out of the house. A little ways beyond, she came suddenly upon the stark white body of a man, clad only in a shirt and lying perfectly straight with arms by his side.

Arvilla nearly dropped the huge book when she realized it was Nathan Meeker she was looking at. He had been shot in the side of his head. She dropped to her knees sobbing quietly and calling his name. Arvilla leaned forward to kiss her dear husband, but thought the young Ute would not understand such a morbid act. The Ute helped her to her feet and she wiped away the tears and continued on to where the others were being held captive.

A little while later, the Utes loaded their captives aboard horses and left winter valley by way of the Grand River trail and south toward Old Squaw Camp on Piceance Creek.

Flora Ellen rode by Arvilla with little Johnnie in her arms. Around her neck Ahutupuwit had hung William Post's gold watch as a mark of possession.

Quinkent, still tippling from the bottle, lifted the wounded Arvilla to the back of his raw-boned pony and mounted in front of her.

"You hold on, Mother," Quinkent told the woman as they started up the trail, now lit by the full moon rising above Sleepy Cat Peak to the east. Arvilla glanced behind her and saw Josie getting on a fine horse by stepping on Persune's back while the young Ute bent over. She turned back around and looked out across the old chief's shoulder as he continued to drink.

Their only hope lay in Frank Dresser who had escaped up Strawberry Creek. If he reached Thornburgh's troops in the morning, they could be freed within a few days. For comfort, she clutched the big book, *Pilgrim's Progress* to her as the old chief slowly got drunker each mile they traveled.

It had been a long four days for the trapped men of Major Thornburgh's expedition since Joe Rankin had slipped out of the besieged camp to spread the news of the massacre. Amid the warm weather, the breastworks of dead animals were swelling and beginning to putrefy. Swarms of green-bottle flies covered the strutted carcasses, laying eggs by the millions. Troopers who were assigned to guard that area of the corral became ill under the awful stench of death.

Captain Payne and the other wounded soldiers were in painful shape. Even those not wounded suffered from the effects of exposure to the relentless sun, poor rations and lack of sleep.

From his sickbed, Payne still commanded the expedition with what few orders were necessary. Mostly, his orders were routine and already put in place by Sam Cherry or Joe Lawson. Together, they kept the men in fighting condition, day after interminable day of waiting for relief troops to arrive and deliver them from this hell hole of death.

Everyday, Captain Payne, without fail, asked Cherry if Dodge's men were near, and if not, where were they? It was the exact same question all the Milk Creek soldiers were asking one another. John Gordon had gone out four days ago with Rankin. Surely, that was sufficient time for Gordon to ride to Middle Park where Dodge was encamped. Had Gordon been caught and killed by the Utes? Many hours were devoted to such discussions by both officers and men of Thornburgh's command.

Each new day brought an emptiness to the valley and left their questions unanswered. The troops continued to suffer under the warm sun and rising stench. Even the Utes seemed to have settled into a routine of their own with only occasional shooting during the day or whenever a trooper became careless. After the first day's charge, the Utes preferred to hang near the top of the grassy ridge, shooting into the hole from time to time. By the fifth day, the Utes seemed more or less a nuisance to the troops entrenched at Milk River, much like the blowflies that gathered like a green carpet over dead and alive alike.

Soon, very soon now, Dodge and his Negroes would come thundering into the valley and ease their misery, every soldier said to himself and aloud to anyone who cared to listen.

The trouble with Captain Dodge and his fighting Negroes of Company D, Ninth Cavalry, was the plain fact they didn't know whether they were coming or going. For almost three months now,

Dodge had been trying to keep an eye on the Utes, under standing orders from General Pope and to offer assistance to Nathan Meeker at White River if required. He had even gone so far as to take his colored troops all the way to Peck's store on Bear River when there had been rumors of trouble at White River, only to learn from the mail carrier, Black Wilson, that everything was just fine at the agency. That had been in mid-September.

As the battle raged at Milk Creek, Dodge and his forty-three colored troops were encamped on a pretty spot in Twenty Mile Park, along the trail that wound over Gore Pass and down to Hayden and Peck's store. It was during this time a courier from General Sheridan galloped up, ordering Dodge and his troops to White River on September twenty-ninth.

Dodge started out for White River immediately, only to have a second courier catch up with him with another order countermanding the first. The message stated that Dodge wasn't needed after all and that Major Thornburgh was proceeding to White River from Rawlings to settle the trouble.

"By heaven, I wish General Sheridan would make up his mind," the confused Dodge said to the courier as he studied this latest message. He turned to his troops who looked ready and willing to ride straight into hell if Dodge was to so order.

Captain Francis Safford Dodge was especially proud of his colored regiment, not that Dodge could be considered a conventional army officer. Raised a gentleman New Englander, Dodge had found himself in command of the Second U.S. Colored Cavalry through the Civil War siege of Petersburg and greatly admired the Negro troops for their courage and fighting ability. Following the war, Dodge asked to be given command of Company D, Ninth Cavalry and for a dozen years, Dodge and his colored troops toured the Southwest, giving aid to travelers, fighting Indians and scouting along the border.

"Turn them around, Sergeant," Dodge said to the waiting men, "guess sooner or later, things'll settle down." With that, Company D, Ninth Cavalry faced about for the third time and rode back up the trail and camped at Gore Pass in Egeria Park. As they were saddling up the next morning, they were met by flocks of terrified settlers from Bear River, rushing east. Dodge was just putting away his own personal gear when the first wagon rumbled into camp driven by a gaunt-faced man, a wife and two kids. Their wagon was piled high with various clothing, furniture and boxes on which the two children perched.

"What's going on?" Dodge asked, with his hand on one of the man's sweating animals.

"Man, ain't you heard?" the driver asked, bug-eyed.

"Heard what?"

"Major Thornburgh's been ambushed on Milk River! There's talk even Meeker and his men have all been killed down on White River. I'm gettin' my family over to Denver til this thing's over." As if to emphasize his point the man slapped the reins across the backs of his horses and left the befuddled Dodge wondering what in hell was going on. Thornburgh ambushed? Nathan Meeker dead?

"Okay, boys, it's back to Peck's store," Dodge ordered, mounting his own animal and setting a fast pace back through Twenty Mile Park the following morning. A note tied to a bush caught the attention of one of his sharp-eyed troopers. Dodge frowned, studying the wrinkled note.

Hurry up. The troops have been defeated!

E. E. C.

"This time, boys, we are not stopping until we get to Milk Creek and see for ourselves just what the hell is going on," Dodge told his waiting men.

They rode hard and fast and when they arrived at Hayden on Bear River, they found John Gordon, fresh from the besieged troops who set Dodge straight about the facts. The news was grim. He hated to hear of Thornburgh's death, having known and liked the officer before his transfer to Fort Steele. With Gordon, was Ed Clark, agency employee, who had left the note on the trail.

"We got to get back as quick as we can, Captain," John Gordon said. "Otherwise, them Utes will starve 'em to death."

"Yes, I'm aware of that, Mr. Gordon," Dodge said, thinking quickly. He turned again to his waiting troops.

"Men, you've heard what's been said by Mr. Gordon and Mr. Clark, here. It will be dangerous, no doubt. We are a small group and may face odds many times greater by the Utes, but we have to try and rescue those trapped men. What do you say?" There was an immediate roar from the group of Negro soldiers and Dodge broke into a grin, in spite of the circumstances.

When they arrived at Tom Iles' ranch at the mouth of Elkhead Creek, Dodge ordered his men to strip down to three days' rations and one hundred and twenty-five rounds of ammunition for the forty mile ride to Milk River. Next, he sent Ed Clark with eight of his soldiers with Company D's supply wagons to Lt. Price's depot on Fortification Creek to bring needed food and blankets to the besieged troops. With the rest of his command and John Gordon acting as guide, Dodge hurried off to Milk River.

The first signs of the Utes' fury came in the form of Al McCarger's wagon of destroyed goods, except for Josie's order of play hatchets, left lying beside the trail. Further along the trail, after ascending Morapos Creek past Monument Butte, they came upon the carnage of George Gordon's three supply wagons. Near the steam engine, toppled over into a ravine, lay the bullet-riddled, stark-white bodies of George Gordon and his two helpers.

"Oh, Lord! No!" John Gordon said, filled with horror as he slid from his horse and skidded down the ravine to where his brother lay.

Dodge and his men watched as Gordon's shoulders shook from grief as he knelt beside his brother. The Negro troops appeared stunned by the violence the Utes had displayed here. Meeker's threshing machine was smashed to pieces and littered the trail.

In a few minutes, Gordon crawled out of the ravine after covering his brother's body with his own coat. His eyes were wet with pain.

"I'm terribly sorry, Mr. Gordon," Captain Dodge said quietly, as John Gordon mounted his horse.

Gordon nodded his head, pulling his hat lower over his red eyes. "Let's go get the bastards that did this!"

As dawn broke over Milk River Valley, Gordon led Dodge's men over Williams Fork and down along the sage bench in front of the lone hill that would soon be known as Thornburgh Mountain.

"Keep the troops here, Captain, while I work my way close to the corral. Don't want anybody to get killed now."

"Where are the Indians?" Dodge whispered. Everything seemed strangely quiet for a siege to be taking place.

"On that ridge, last time I was here," Gordon said, snaking off through the sage and up to the corral. When he felt he could go no further, he hallooed the camp.

"That you, Gordon?" came a whispered reply from a sentry.

"It is," Gordon said. "I got Dodge's men with me."

"Thank, God! Bring 'em in, man!"

As Gordon led the Negro soldiers into the stench-filled corral, cries from atop the ridge followed by rifle shots from the surprised Utes did no harm and Dodge and his men arrived in camp with no casualties while the besieged troopers returned fire. But the captain was appalled by what he found. The gaunt troopers of Thornburgh's command cheered the arriving troops and old Captain Lawson summed it up best.

"You men of the Ninth Calvary are the whitest black men I have ever seen!" Proud of his Negro troops, Dodge beamed.

The young men had long ago lost interest in the *Mericatz* trapped in the hole below the ridge. At first, there had been much fun and cries of *aheeeee, aheeeee!* could be heard all along the line of Ute men who shot their rifles at the funny *swerch* who scrambled around trying to hide from their bullets.

Beside a small fire, Colorow sat with his son, Acari and Nicaagat, talking and smoking in low tones. Colorow was telling them how a nice, fat, prairie dog puppy roasted over their fire would be good to eat right now. As if to emphasize his point, his stomach growled loudly.

Nicaagat passed him a buckskin bag containing old *pana* and pieces of dried meat. Glumly, Colorow took a few pieces and began eating, wishing his *piwán* was there to cook him a hot meal.

Canávish came up out of the weeds with a strange look on his face, carrying a shiny rifle. He looked old and very tired.

"I have seen my son," Canávish said simply.

Puzzled, Acari looked at the shaman. "But you have two sons."

"Now I have one," Canávish replied, laying Tatitz's new rifle on the ground. Afterward, he turned and walked away. He would need to be alone now and cut his hair off. Only after it grew back would things be right again.

Acari looked at the new rifle and knew it was meant for his own son. It was the right thing to do with a possession of someone who had died.

Suddenly, a few of the young men standing guard cried, "Aheeeee! Aheeeee!" all at once. "*To-Mericatz!*"

Nicaagat moved swiftly to the edge of the ridge and scanned the distance. Colorow lumbered up next to him seconds later, breathing hard. In the dim light of dawn they could see specks moving into the hole down below. Several of the young men began shooting at the black-whitemen, filling the air with little puffs of stinking gunpowder.

Soon, all the *To-Mericatz* were safe in that hole and the shooting stopped. As the sun grew larger in the sky, it chased away the broken pieces of clouds and the day became blue again.

As Nicaagat and the others watched, a line of *To-Mericatz* marched out from the hole with what looked to be rifles on their shoulders and the men shouted again, lifting their rifles for another fight.

Nicaagat watched as the soldiers stopped before a dead horse, bloated by the sun, with its legs sticking upward into the blue sky. They began digging in the ground with shovels that the young men had thought were rifles. Nicaagat continued to watch as the soldiers buried the animal and moved over to another and continued the process. The young men dropped their rifles to their side, disappointed by the *To-Mericatz*, some moving off to repaint their bodies, others to their own cook fires.

A shout went up and Nicaagat saw four ponies coming fast along the trail. In the lead was Quinkent and Sowówic with Pauvitz and Piah bring up the rear. When Quinkent drew near, Nicaagat saw the old chief was bare chested with stripes of yellow across his chest while his forehead and face carried the colors of the People at war. Quinkent's beady little eyes looked at Nicaagat as he dismounted.

"*Maiquas!*" Quinkent said, with a tight smile on his face. Nicaagat returned his greeting while Colorow only muttered to himself and went over to the fire and sat down heavily.

"The *To-Mericatz* has come," Nicaagat said simply, going over to his fire where Colorow sat sipping loudly at a coffee cup. Quinkent and the others followed.

"How is the fight going?"

"Well," Nicaagat said, rolling himself a cigarette. "The young men want to fight on, but we have killed about as many as we have lost. I think it is about time to leave."

"Tomorrow, I will go down into that hole and shake the soldiers hands and tell them we had a good fight and then they can go home," Colorow rumbled loudly.

A rising wind, coming down from the tall mountains already covered with snow, sent Quinkent scrambling for a blanket and Nicaagat and the others after wood for their fires. Soon, the snow would creep down from the flanks of those mountains like Old Man Coyote and cover the ground where they were now.

As night approached, sleet rattled the hardened leaves but by the following morning, the sun was bright once more as the men drew near their fires for warmth. Others wandered down to the ridge to check on the *Mericatz* who were holed up there. From across the wide valley a strange sound floated up to the young men, like some lost animal calling to its mate.

Nicaagat sprang up from the ground at the first sounds for he knew immediately what had made the noise. He walked quickly over to the ridge with Quinkent at his side. The strange sound continued.

"What makes that noise?" Quinkent asked.

"It is a soldierhorn," Nicaagat said simply. He had heard the horn many times while scouting for General Crook against the Sioux. Nicaagat pointed out across the valley to a blue line of moving objects.

"*Swerch!*" Quinkent said. "A great many soldiers come."

"It is time we leave," Nicaagat said. "These soldiers have come to free those we hold down there in that hole."

"Will they follow?"

Nicaagat turned to face Quinkent, and the metal hanging around his neck and given him by President Johnson shone like a new piece of silver in the early morning sun.

"This general will march to the agency. He will find this agent that you killed and he will follow us into the mountains to get the women back."

Quinkent looked as if he were going to be sick. "I tried to keep the men from shooting all those *Mericatz* and this agent." He shook his head slowly. "Now I do not know what will happen."

As they stood there these new soldiers rode up and only one dismounted and went into the hole. Soon he came out and suddenly many soldiers started up the hill at a dead run with their weapons firing.

The young men grew excited by their charge and began firing at the soldiers until they were all driven back, leaving some of their men on the open field.

They heard horses behind them and Nicaagat and Quinkent turned to see two men on horses, one a *Mericatz*, but not a soldier. Both men began walking towards them.

When they came close enough, Nicaagat recognized the *Mericatz*, an agency employee from south of the tall mountains where Ouray made his home at Los Pinos. The other was Sapovanero, second in command to Ouray and his brother-in-law as well. The two men rode up and stepped down from their horses.

"I come with this *Mericatz*, Brady, to stop this fighting. It is bad for all our People," Savopanero explained as soon as his feet touched the ground. The *Mericatz* stepped forward and handed Nicaagat a note which read:

> Los Pinos Indian Agency
> October 2, 1879
> To the chief captains, headmen, and Utes at the White
> River Agency:
> You are hereby requested and commanded to cease
> hostilities against the whites, injuring no innocent
> persons or any others farther than to protect your own
> lives and property from unlawful and unauthorized

combinations of horse thieves and desperadoes, as anything farther will ultimately end in disaster to all parties.

Ouray

The *Mericatz* handed another piece of paper to Nicaagat, and this one read:

Los Pinos Indian Agency
October 2, 1879
To the officers in command and the soldiers at the White River Agency:
Gentlemen:
At the request of the chief of the Utes at this agency, I send by Jos. W. Brady, an employee, the enclosed order from Chief Ouray to the Utes at the White River Agency. The head chiefs deplore the trouble existing at White River, and are anxious that no further fighting or bloodshed should take place, and have commanded the Utes there to stop. I hope that you will second their efforts so far as you can, consistent with your duties, under existing commands.
This much for humanity.
Very respectfully, your obedient servant,
W. M. Stanley,
United States Indian Agent

Quinkent asked Nicaagat to translate what this *Mericatz* was doing here and what words the pieces of paper held. Quinkent hated doing this thing but he had no choice for only Nicaagat could read the words. Nicaagat spoke the old language and soon a relieved look crossed Quinkent's painted face. Now the *Mericatz* and the People could be friends once again, he told Nicaagat.

Nicaagat said nothing, cutting a piece of white tent cloth away which he tied to a long stick. Next, he carried it to the top of the hill and stuck it into a little pile of stones where it fluttered in the breeze.

Like magic, the soldiers stopped their firing. The young men, who had been shooting back, laid down their rifles and a strange stillness came over the place. It was then Quinkent and the young men knew the fight was finally over. In a little while most of the young men caught up their ponies while talking of their *piwáns* and of seeing their children again. As they gathered up their things to ride south to Grand Mesa, slowly the desire to fight was washed from their minds.

Quinkent rode away with these young men, leaving Nicaagat and Colorow to deal with the soldiers. As they were leaving, the *Mericatz,* Brady, rode slowly down the hill and entered the hole.

Nicaagat stood there a long time waiting for him to return.

CHAPTER 31

With the arrival of Colonel Merritt's men, the besieged soldiers of Thornburgh's command as well as Dodge's Company D were jubilant. Colonel Wesley Merritt commanded the Fifth United States Cavalry. With him were four companies of calvary, one hundred and fifty foot soldiers in wagons and a cart full of newsmen, including John Dyer of the *New York World.* Leading the expedition was old Jim Baker, whom Merritt had hired at the Little Snake.

It didn't take long to put the camp in order, even while his own troops engaged the enemy on the hillside. The attack ended suddenly and soon Merritt and the other officers saw the reason why. A large while flag flapped in the early morning breeze from atop the high ridge.

"Guess they see they are outnumbered," Dodge said to Merritt.

"Wouldn't be too sure, Captain," Merritt returned. "I fully believe the possibility exists that Ouray has ordered his own Uncompahgres to join the fight and are waiting for us on the other side of Coal Creek Canyon."

"I've always heard Ouray is too smart to be drawn into a fight with us. He knows our strength. He's been to Washington."

Merritt smiled faintly, crawling beneath a wagon to nap. "Mr. Dodge, I have it on good authority that this Captain Jack is leading the fight from that very ridge and he, sir, has been to Washington with Ouray on several occasions." With that, Merritt leaned back and closed his eyes.

Dodge walked off from the Colonel to study the white flag more. He spied Captain Payne with Cherry and Lawson talking with Jim Baker and he joined them.

"Look, someone's riding in," Lawson said, pointed a gnarled finger up the hill. "And damned if it ain't a white man," Payne said, still not feeling well. The astonished officers watched as Joseph Brady rode up and dismounted.

"Can you gentlemen tell me who's in charge? I'm Joe Brady from Los Pinos Agency."

"He's over yonder, taking a nap beneath that wagon," Lt. Cherry answered.

"I've got messages for him from Chief Ouray and from William Stanley, Los Pinos Indian Agency."

"Right this way," Cherry said, walking over with the agency employee.

"Excuse me Colonel," Cherry said. "There's messages here for you from Chief Ouray and William Stanley of the Los Pinos Agency."

Merritt opened his red eyes and stared for a moment at Brady as if deciding whether the man was merely a spy sent by the Utes. He read the two messages with his head supported by his forearm.

"You Brady?" Merritt asked.

"I am. Chief Jack told me to tell you the Utes want peace. Also, they want Uriah Curtis as their agent."

"I see," Merritt said, not moving from his place. "What about Nathan Meeker?"

"Well, old Jack didn't come right out and say it, but he hinted Meeker and all the agency employees are dead. The women they took with them."

Colonel Merritt came out from under the wagon with anger riding his shoulders. He took Cherry one side.

"This is the damnest thing I have run across. What are kidnappers and murderers doing sending an employee of the Indian Bureau to make their demands? I got a notion to arrest everybody I can, including this Brady for conspiracy or something."

"Think I ought to tell this Brady fellow to let Jack know that it's the Army in charge here and no deals will be cut with any Ute. Further, Jack ought to immediately surrender."

Merritt nodded, "Good idea, Sam." With that, Merritt lay back down beneath the wagon and closed his eyes without having looked again at Brady. Cherry proceeded to tell Brady the facts and in a few minutes, Brady mounted his horse and rode up the hill.

Cherry grabbed his glasses and watched as Brady stopped amongst the milling Indians. In a few minutes Brady rode away with the Utes, heading in the direction of Yellowjacket Pass.

With the Utes gone, Dodge sent two of his men out looking for Major Thornburgh while the forty-three wounded were moved upstream to a new camp, away from the stench. The two Negroes found Thornburgh's long body face up in the cottonwoods, still clutching his engraved Colt. Nothing was disturbed about his body other than finding Thornburgh's gilt Union Pacific Railroad Pass and other papers scattered about him. Pinned to his tunic was a drugstore photo of old Colorow.

The one big excitement of the day came when old Charlie Lowry rose up out of his shallow dirt grave after six days. Several troopers who were busy removing the bodies to a new location nearly came undone at sight of the apparition.

"What's the matter, boys?" Lowry asked.

"Good God almighty, Charlie," a trooper answered. "We gave you up for dead days ago."

"Best get the Doc over here quick," another trooper said and one of their number left on a dead run.

"Lordy, but I'm thirsty," Lowry said, looking around him.

Someone fetched the harmonica player a cup of coffee as Dr. Kimmell, Merritt's surgeon came puffing up with his bag.

"I don't believe this," he said as he looked at the bullet hole in Lowry's head. "I'm going to have to probe for the bullet," he said, fumbling in his bag for a steel instrument.

Charlie Lowry took a sip of coffee and held still while Kimmell brushed the dirt away from the wound and inserted the needle-like probe. Suddenly Lowry slumped over.

"Ease him down, men," Kimmell ordered who felt for a pulse on the side of his neck.

"Old Charlie gone this time?" a trooper asked.

Kimmell nodded, sighed deeply and put the probe back in his bag. "May as well lay him with the others." With that Kimmell went off to embalm Major Thornburgh for the trip back to Fort Steele, leaving the troopers gaping down at the body of Charlie Lowry.

"Damnest thing I ever seen," one of them whispered as they gently placed Lowry's body with the others.

Four days later Merritt's force was strengthened to nine hundred by the arrival of Colonel Gilbert's six companies of the Seventh Infantry from Fort Snelling, Dakota Territory. Merritt sent Thornburgh's men back to Fort Fred Steele with the body of their commander under Dodge's Company D escort. Some of the wounded were transported on to Fort D. A. Russell to be cared for there.

On Saturday, October 11, Merritt's huge force started for White River Agency, led by the grizzled-faced, red-haired Jim Baker. About mid-way through Coal Creek Canyon, near the old Danforth coal mine, Jim Baker, still as sharp-eyed as ever spotted a trail of blood near the stream bank. Taking two soldiers with him, Baker followed the bloody trail upward to the old mine where they found Frank Dresser.

"Would you look at that," one of the soldiers whispered. Young Dresser was lying supine with his coat neatly folded beneath his head. In his hands, he still clutched Shadrach Price's cocked Winchester.

"Boy had a tough time of it, no doubt," Baker said, observing the chest and leg wound. Both his feet were bound with pieces of buckskin. One of the soldiers checked the boy's coat pocket and found a letter addressed to Thornburgh from Meeker telling the major to leave his troops fifty miles away and come in for talks.

"Guess the boy never had a chance to deliver that message," Baker said dryly.

"Look at this," a soldier said, pointing to a message scribbled on a mine timber.

"What's it say?" the old mountain man asked. The soldier peered close at the scrawlings.

"Have been here twenty-one hours. All killed at the Agency. Send my money to my mother at Greeley. Frank Dresser."

"Damn!" old Jim Baker said in the ensuing silence. He turned to go. "At least now we know they ain't nobody to save at White River."

Colonel Merritt's skin grew tight around his eyes as Baker related what they had found in the cave and handed him the message from Meeker.

More grim bodies turned up the closer they got to White River Agency. They passed the burned wagon and the bodies of old Carl Goldstein and his teen-aged companion, Julius Moore. Later, as they entered the Narrows, they found the body of Wilmer Eskridge, still carrying the last dispatch from Meeker for Thornburgh when he was killed by the two Utes, Ebenezer and Thompson.

Merritt's force entered the charred ruins of White River Agency with the American flag still flapping in the breeze atop the flagpole. Below, the ground was utter ruin and bodies were scattered across what was once the neat yard of the agency and outbuildings. The only building still standing was the storehouse where they found William Post's body, shot through the head and partially blocking the entrance. Nearby were the bullet-riddled bodies of young Fred Sheppard, the fiddle player, George Eaton, his face nearly chewed off by wild animals, and Frank Dresser's brother, Harry.

Colonel Merritt looked around him in total disgust. "Spread out and look for Nathan Meeker's body," Merritt ordered. He dismounted with visible anger clouding his face.

"Mr. Baker, I intend to fully pursue these Utes. Would you be available to guide this expedition in that endeavor?"

"Be my pleasure, Colonel," Baker said, his hard blue eyes looking Wesley Merritt dead in the face. Someone shouted and Merritt and Baker walked the distance in silence, their eyes roving across the yard, littered with broken plows, spilled flour sacks, washtubs and an assortment of hardware.

"We found him, Colonel," a grim-faced private said, pointing at the half-nude body of Nathan Meeker.

"My God!" Merritt said, taking in the sight. "They've dragged him around by a logging chain."

"Ain't all, Colonel," the private said, kneeling beside the body. "They shoved a barrel stave down the poor man's throat."

General Charles Adams had been keeping up with the latest news from the battle front and was dismayed to learn that Meeker and his men had been massacred by such good friends as he considered both Sowówic and Quinkent. It was hard to believe anything could have driven them to do such deeds. He recalled his days as White River Agent in the early seventies and how he had nursed Sowówic to full health. And now the headlines read that the agency women had been carted off into the wilderness to face God knows what.

The more the burly German read of Vickers' article, the more Adams became convinced he must act to prevent an all out war with the other bands of Utes, not part of the tragedy, as Vickers indicated. He caught the first train out leaving Leadville for Denver and conferred with Governor Pitkin at his Welton Street home. Adams convinced the governor to rein in Vickers concerning the expulsion of all Utes from Colorado at least until the women had been rescued. Pitkin promised, and as Adams made ready to catch a train south to Colorado Springs for his home in Manitou, a telegram intercepted him from Secretary Carl Schurz, asking him to become a special agent and penetrate the Ute wilderness of mountains and passes and rescue the captive agency women.

Adams sent a wire back to Schurz accepting the position and one to Ouray that he would be arriving at Los Pinos as quickly as he could to confer with the chief on how to get the captives released.

Both Ouray and his *piwán*, Chipeta were relieved to see Adams. Ouray was dressed out in full Ute regalia, looking deeply depressed and thinner than usual. Chipeta, normally very happy, was distressed and looked harassed. Both men talked in Spanish as they shared a fine bottle of Ouray's Spanish wine.

"There was a time I thought of committing suicide," Ouray freely admitted to his friend. "Even worse, there was that moment I considered joining the *Nüpartka* with my Uncompahgre warriors and with Ignacio's men as well and fight Merritt until we were all killed."

"I am thankful you did not, my friend," Adams replied, sipping his wine. "I have spoken with Governor Pitkin and he has promised not to talk further of removing the Utes from their homeland."

Ouray's sick black eyes looked at the burly German. "Not until the women are freed," he added.

"Yes, Ouray, I should have added that," Adams said sadly.

"What Nicaagat and Quinkent have done at Smoking Earth River will be the end of our life here as we know it," Ouray predict-ed.

"Not if I am able to get the captive women released without being harmed, my friend. There is still the good chance, the people of Colorado will not hold you and the southern Ute bands guilty of anything more than trying to help ease the tension."

"I hope your are right," Ouray said. "What you are able to do in the next few days could easily seal our fate along with Nicaagat's and Quinkent's if things are not resolved peacefully."

"I can only do my best, but as you know, the rest will be up to Nicaagat and Quinkent."

"I have been thinking on this while I waited for you to arrive and Sapovanero will ride with you and twelve of my men who will show you the way to Quinkent's camp. Stanley has promised two agency employees and a wagon to bring the women back from Grand Mesa once you talk with Quinkent and the others."

"If we can just delay Merritt's advance, give the nation a little time to cool off, there's a chance no further bloodshed will occur once the snows close the high passes."

But both men were thrown into a dark mood when a runner came in from Quinkent's camp informing Ouray that the war drums were beating along Grand River and there was talk of killing the women captives and Charlie Adams as well if he showed up.

Adams left the following morning with Sapovanero and twelve other Utes as guides and escorts along with two agency employees,

George Sherman and W.F. Saunders who drove the supply wagon. Adams' old friend, Captain M.W. Cline, drove a buckboard in which the captive women would ride.

Wasting no time, the small group came to the Gunnison that evening, forded the river and made camp near the site of Antoine Robidoux's trading post, below the vast purple mantle of Grand Mesa.

Nicaagat's runners, Cojoe and Henry Jim appeared by their fires that night with terrifying news. The soldiers were advancing toward Roan Plateau and Nicaagat and the others were working themselves up into a fevered pitch to do battle.

"There is much talk the white women will be killed if Merritt continues south," Cojoe remarked, looking over at bearded Charlie Adams.

"We must push on then, tonight," Adams said to Sapovanero. "There is no time to waste."

"We are still sixty-five miles from Quinkent's camp," Sapovanero replied. "We must cross the north rim of Grand Mesa and that takes us out of the way by fifteen miles."

An old Ute rose from his place by the fire, pulling his blanket around his shoulders to ward off the growing chill.

"There is another way," Old Shavano said, quietly. "A deer trail that could save at least twenty miles."

"Then I'm for it," Adams shot back.

"It is too steep for the wagons," Shavano replied. "They must be left at Whitewater."

"Tell me more of this trail, old man," Sapovanero probed. "I know of no such trail."

Shavano smiled at his secret. "It is very old and not used since I was a young man."

"Can you find it?"

"I can see it now," the old man smiled, gazing off at the thin slice of quarter moon rising in the distance.

"I say it's worth a try, considering how dangerous the situation has come for the women. Nicaagat just might carry through with his threat if Merritt continues south," Adams said, picking up his bedroll which he tied behind his horse. "And God forbid if that happens."

"This trail will be very hard on the horses and men as well," Shavano warned.

"I don't care," Adams responded. "We are wasting precious time."

Under scant moonlight, the group climbed twisted defiles and towering cliffs, choked with sand and loose rock. Finally they topped out on Grand Mesa at nearly eleven thousand feet. The place was flat and eerily quiet. It was home of departed Ute souls, Thigunawat. As dawn approached, the tiny group of tired riders reached a crystal-clear pond formed by the stream's downward plunge. They stopped and cooked breakfast.

"Quinkent's camp is at the head of this water, twelve miles that way," Sapovanero pointed. It was all Adams could do to sit still and eat his breakfast, with visions of seeing the Meeker women mutilated by Nicaagat's angry young men.

Near noon, they topped a rise and Adams found himself looking down at the sweeping vista of a wide valley with thirty-odd lodges strung along the course of the waterway. Beyond, were the red and gray Book Cliffs and Roan Plateau. Adams could see Ute women slowly plodding back to camp with loads of wood on their back. Not a man was in sight.

"I go find Quinkent," Yanko said and broke away from the group. Yanko was Ouray's personal runner and Quinkent would know that Adams was near.

For now, there was nothing more to do than wait for Yanko to return. Meanwhile, Adams' head ached with excitement to be so close to the women. He prayed they were still safe.

CHAPTER 32

For Arvilla and the other captive women, it seemed time stood still. They had ridden away from the agency across rushing streams and up steep slopes, past leaping waterfalls for what seemed like days instead of hours. It was nearly morning before Quinkent had called a halt and helped her down from the bony nag. For a minute, Arvilla had to lean against the horse for support, so tired were her numbed back and legs. Quinkent mumbled something under his drunken breath and stumbled off into the night to relieve himself.

Others around her were preparing to camp for the remainder of the night and soon Quinkent came back, pointed his rifle at Arvilla's head and let out a drunken laugh. And then he took the gun away. Josie called to her across the darkness.

"Do not worry, Mother, I am fine."

"Thank God, Child. Do nothing to cause them to mistreat you," Arvilla called back.

But that was not to be the case for Josie. As soon as Persune's *piwáns* had made the lodge, Josie was brought inside and told to undress on the robes. They laughed and made obscene gestures which frightened Josie terribly.

Soon, Persune came into the lodge and spoke to the laughing women who scampered through the opening, leaving the love-sick Ute alone with Josie. Even in his drunken state, the Ute was gentle with Josie, telling her he would protect her now with his life. Josie cried herself to sleep, thinking what her mother must be enduring as well. And what of Flora Ellen and the children?

Persune came to her every night while they continued to climb higher and higher into the mountains. Soon they reached a stream that meandered across a lovely little valley and a permanent camp was made. Tried from the ride and heart-broken at Persune's continuous outrages, Josie refused the Ute that night.

"Do you want to kill me?" Josie said in a tired voice.

"Yes," Persune replied.

"Then get up and shoot me and let me alone." A silence filled the lodge and after a few minutes, Persune turned over and went to sleep.

Now that they were in camp, Josie was given more freedom and she spent the time making warm clothes for herself and Flora Ellen's children. She saw to her mother's needs as well. Arvilla spent most of her days reading from *Pilgrim's Progress* and praying for their safe return.

During this time, both Quinkent and Nicaagat spent their time riding back and forth to Roan Plateau, watching the soldiers advancing deeper into their country.

Angry councils were held and Canávish and his *piwán* favored killing the women captives if Merritt's men advanced much further.

Many of the people became frightened by such talk and it took hot words from Quinkent to calm them down again.

It was during one of the mild days with bright sunshine coming down when Yanko raced across the swift stream with the news that Charlie Adams and Sapovanero were waiting up the hill to ride in for a talk. Yanko was told that Sowówic and Quinkent would be back soon and he recrossed the stream and rode to where Adams stood waiting and gave him the message.

Adams said nothing, mounted his horse, and spurred the animal down the hill and across Plateau Creek. Behind him he could hear the others following. He rode down the length of lodges until he came to a tent where two Ute women were holding a blanket across the entrance.

As he rode up, the flap was pushed aside and the anxious face of Josie Meeker looked up at Charlie Adams.

"Are you all right?" Adams asked, studying Josie's tanned face and bobbed hair.

"I'm glad to see you, Mr. Adams!"

"Lord, are the others all right?" Adams asked, barely trusting his voice.

"Quite well, considering."

"Forgive me, Miss Meeker. Do you know who killed your father and the others?"

"I do not, sir. I can only guess."

"Did they treat you well, the men I mean?"

"Better than expected."

"What I mean is, did the Ute men commit any indignity to your person?"

"Oh, no, Mr. Adams. Nothing of that occurred."

"Thank God. That will make things easier to get you and the others on the way home."

Horses thundered across the valley and Adams looked around to

see Nicaagat and Quinkent with a number of other sub-chiefs crossing Plateau Creek.

"Excuse me, Miss Meeker while I have a talk with these chiefs,"
Adams said, tipping his hat.

"Certainly, sir," Josie said and ducked back inside the lodge.

Quinkent and Nicaagat were anything but cooperative and their
mood was ugly when they learned Adams had come for the women
without offering any concessions to the Utes. The council was
stormy.

"The women will be released when you stop this general from
coming any further into our country," Quinkent said, harshly.

"I will do so only if the women are released first," Adams said
firmly. Over and over the demands were repeated, followed by
Adams' refusal to budge from his position. The council continued
for five weary hours and Adams was beginning to think he would
fail his mission when Sapovanero rose suddenly from his seat and
looked around at the tired faces.

"I have heard enough. I come from Ouray and speak for him."
Sapovanero pointed at the eagle feather Canávish carried and said
the oath out loud for those to hear.

"There is but one spirit above the sky and the earth and he looks
down on me now and sees what is on the earth as well as in the sky.
Therefore, I cannot speak anything but the truth."

Adams had never heard such an oath before and he thought it
beautiful. The others remained silent, waiting for Sapovanero to
talk.

"If the women do not arrive safely at Ouray's farm in three sleeps,
then Ouray will lead the Uncompahgres north and seize the captives
and drive the *Nüpartka* into the guns of the soldiers. That is all I
have to say." Sapovanero took his seat. For a long moment there was
a strained silence around the council. Adams had known what
Sapovanero was going to say for he had discussed it with Ouray

before leaving Los Pinos. "Can you stop the soldiers?" Quinkent asked.

"I am on this mission by the authority of President Hays. I think Colonel Merritt will listen to me."

"Iss not right. You stop these soldiers first, den we give up women," Nicaagat said, still trying to hold to the only thing they had for negotiating.

"It's like I said earlier, Jack. I will do nothing for you as long as you hold the women captive."

Quinkent stood up and looked out across the strained faces. He was still *tawacz viem.*

"The women are free to go," he said, simply.

Adams let out a long sigh. "That is good, Douglas. Sapovanero and I will start for the soldiers' camp first thing tomorrow."

"Sowówic must go with you dere," Nicaagat said, not fully trusting Adams to do the right thing.

"Fair enough," Adams said, getting up from the floor. The council was over and he went out to find the women and tell them the good news.

Arvilla was walking towards Adams from the creek willows where she had been hidden. The old woman wore a calico dress, shawl and a sunbonnet with Josie and Flora Ellen walking beside her. May Price skipped along behind the women.

Adams studied the women, noting Mrs. Meeker's pale face and gaunt frame. She was also limping from an old wound.

"Dear Mrs. Meeker," Adams said, taking the woman's frail hand in his big fist. "I have good news. Right after supper, you will all be escorted back to Los Pinos and from there, back to Greeley."

"Thank you so, Mr. Adams," Arvilla Meeker said, weeping openly. "I have prayed fervently for this moment, for Josie's sake. As for myself, I don't care. Mr. Meeker is gone. I have nothing more to live for. You see, Mr. Adams, I am sixty-four years old. An old lady, you might say."

"You have many good years left, I assure you, Mrs. Meeker." Then he turned to the plump Flora Ellen, noting her withdrawn eyes and sunburned face.

"Have you been treated well?" he asked her.

"Yes sir," came the reply.

"How did the men treat you? Did they do anything outrageous?"

"No sir. Other than the normal abuse." Arvilla was watching her closely.

"I see," Adams said, more than a little disturbed by her response which seemed almost rehearsed, like Josie's had been. Adams felt vaguely uneasy, but decided not to question the woman further. There would be time for that later when the official commission was established to inquire into such matters. He wrote out a wire and gave it to Yanko to take to Western Union at Del Norte via Elk Mountain trail and Cochetopa Pass which read:

> Camp on Plateau Creek
> October 21, 1879
>
> C. Schurz
> Secretary, Washington, D. C.
> Arrived here this morning and have succeeded in
> persuading Indians to release Mrs. Meeker, Miss Meeker,
> Mrs. Price and two children without condition who will
> leave here tomorrow with sufficient escort. I go to White
> River to communicate with General Merritt. The Indians
> are anxious for peace and desire a full investigation of the
> trouble.
>
> > Charles Adams
> > Special Agent

Before dark, he saw the women off with the agency employees and the Ute escort provided by Ouray. Only when they were clearly out of camp and beyond Plateau Creek, did Adams begin to breathe easier. Now, if he could only convince Colonel Merritt to withdraw his troops. Since it was so late, Adams decided it would be best if they started for Merritt's troops the next morning.

They were riding up Grand River the following morning when a Ute runner arrived to report another crises. Two Utes had been killed by two of Merritt's men who were subsequently killed.

The runner glowered at Adams while he spoke. Then he implied that Adams had planned it all along to make things worse for the Utes.

"Sowówic, you know I am a man of my word," Adams said to his friend. "This is as much news to me as it is to you."

Adams was met with stony silence and in the end, Adams simply spurred his horse forward. They rode into Merritt's encampment late the following evening only to be told that Colonel Merritt had retired for the evening.

The soldiers were in a stew over the recent killings of the two civilians Merritt had brought along. And now with the enemy in their camp with a white man they didn't know, more than a few enlisted men suggested that maybe Adams was nothing more than a Ute spy and should be hung.

Adams was incredulous by such comments and he didn't feel fully safe again until Wesley Merritt greeted him the next morning, having known Adams for a number of years. Adams told Merritt about getting the women released.

"Thank, God, General," Merritt said.

"There's more, Colonel," Adams continued.

"Please continue."

"I promised the Utes I would try and get you to stop your advancement against them now that the women have been released."

Merritt smile ruefully. "On that score you have my word," Merritt said. "Actually, I received a wire from General Sherman, ordering me to stop my advancement until Secretary Schurz had a try at getting the women safely out of the Utes hands." He smiled again at Adams. "Looks like it worked."

Adams spoke to Sapovanero and Sowówic and told them what the army officer had said and watched as the strain of the last few weeks vanished from their faces. Sowówic pounded the burly German on his back and said good-bye. He left camp riding like the wind, at full gallop, to take the message back to Nicaagat and Quinkent who was now camped on Grand River.

Adams turned to Sapovanero. "Looks like that's the end of it for now," Adams said, touching the Ute's shoulder. "Without your invaluable help and Ouray's, a peaceful solution would have been impossible."

The big Ute smiled at Adams and wandered off to the nearest cook fire for breakfast, leaving Adams alone with his thoughts. Finding a rock, Adams wrote out a message to be wired to Secretary Schurz from Rawlings by one of Merritt's couriers.

When Charles Adams finally returned to Los Pinos and reported to Ouray, there was a telegram waiting for him from Secretary Schurz.

> Department of the Interior
> Washington, D. C.
> October 26, 1879
>
> General Charles Adams, Special Agent
> Los Pinos Agency, via Del Norte, Colo.
> Dispatch of the 24th from White River received. Your
> dispatch from Plateau Creek also received. President
> Hays desires me to express his very high appreciation of
> the courage and good judgement displayed in the

performance of your task. You will now insist upon the
following terms: The White River Utes are to move their
camp temporarily to the neighborhood of Los Pinos
Agency. A commission consisting of General Hatch,
yourself and Ouray to meet at Los Pinos as soon as
possible to take testimony to ascertain the guilty parties:
The guilty parties so ascertained to be dealt with as white
men would be under like circumstances. The White
River Utes or at least the mischievous elements among
them, to be disarmed. These terms, approved by the
President and General Sherman, are fair, and the most
favorable that can be offered. State this to Ouray.

C. Schurz, Secretary

Adams slowly folded the wire. There it was, a commission to
investigate the crimes of those Utes responsible for the deaths of
Major Thornburgh as well as Nathan Meeker and the agency
employees. Furthermore, it carried with it the highest authority in
the land, both the President and General Sherman for the military.

There was a sadness about him, Adams could not explain. He
thought of the Meeker women and Flora Ellen. He hated to be the
one given the task of officially interviewing them for the commission. To reopen, so soon, the hurt they must be carrying inside.

And then the reason for his sadness surfaced in his mind like a
water ousel from a mountain stream. If the women were only trying
to protect themselves when asked about possible outrages by the Ute
men, and in reality it had occurred, Adams felt sure that would be
the final straw needed to break the back of all the Utes and force
their removal from their wonderful blue-sky country forever.

He left the stoop of the Los Pinos Agency and took the short
walk down to where Ouray's house was located. He was going to
have dinner with his old friend, suffering badly now with Bright's

Disease. Afterward they would sit down over a glass of fine wine and cigars and discuss what plans they needed to make concerning the Ute Hearings.

EPILOGUE

The Ute Peace Commission, consisting of General Hatch, Charles Adams and the Ute Chief, Ouray, met some forty-two times between November 12, 1879 and January 7, 1880, producing some 182 pages of testimony from twelve white witnesses consisting of Captain Scott Payne, Lieutenant Sam Cherry and Josie Meeker. Ouray, Quinkent, Nicaagat, Sowówic, Chipeta, and Henry Jim had their say, requiring 221 pages more. For the most part, the meetings were confusing, boring and accomplished little. A second commission met, at Ouray's urging, in Washington between January 15, and March 22, 1880, but added nothing new to the Los Pinos Peace Commission as to who killed whom. What did come out of it was a proposal to move the White River Utes out of Colorado to the southern part of the Uintah Reservation in Utah. The pivotal, and most damaging testimony came in the form of sworn depositions, given by the women, held for twenty-three days and raped repeatedly by several of the Utes, including Quinkent, Canávish and Persune. The hue and cry following news of these rapes by the citizens of Colorado was as much responsible for banning the Utes from Colorado as were the carnage left behind at White River Agency and Milk River.

The Ute delegation, led by the very ill Ouray, finally approved the plan as well as payment of annuities to relatives of the ten white men killed at White River Agency. But Congress balked, demanding that some of the accused Utes surrender for trial, before the plan be ratified. Only Quinkent agreed to stand trial and was thrown in prison at Fort Leavenworth, Kansas in February, 1880.

With failing health, Ouray accepted the awful task of trying to explain to his people why they would have to give up their beautiful mountains and their way of life after some eight hundred years. Sadly, Ouray clung to life through the summer of 1880 until the Ute Bill had been ratified by the majority of all Ute bands. He died on August 24, 1880.

For the Utes as a whole, 1880 was the turning point in their lives and as they sadly departed their homeland on the 350 mile trek to the burning desert of Utah, the Army opened the flood gates, allowing settlers, miners, and anybody else who wanted a piece of this beautiful high country to madly rush in. Marching under the orders of General R.S. Mackenzie, the Utes moved north with 8,000 ponies, 10,000 sheep, and goats and 1458 Ute men, women and children. Only the big-bellied Colorow and fifty followers, in full war paint, made a final desperate attack, but were turned back by Mackenzie's rifles and booming cannon.

Joe Rankin spent the better part of the 1880's basking in the glory of fame for his famous ride that terrible night. Rankin was named U.S. Marshal of Wyoming by President Benjamin Harrison when he took office. Sheriff Jim Rankin gained fame by arresting the train robber, Big Nose George Parrott, while jailer Bob Rankin became famous for having been knocked cold by Big Nose George Parrott with his leg irons before the outlaw was finally hung and his hide tanned to make purses for the tourist trade.

Major Thomas Tipton Thornburgh was buried with full military honors in Omaha on October 22, 1879. Into the single grave with Thornburgh went the small coffin of Lida's Centennial baby, George Washington Thornburgh, exhumed from the cemetery at Fort Steele. Thornburgh's pretty widow, Lida, never remarried and contented herself by spending time with the progeny of her daughter, Olivia, and her husband Dan Casement. Lida died in 1930 at her son-in-law's famous Juanita Farm in Manhattan, Kansas.

Of the men who served with Major Thornburgh during the Battle of Milk River, twenty received Medals of Honor or Certificates of Merit. Captain Payne, Captain Dodge and Major Thornburgh were not cited by Congress for gallantry until the mid-1890's. Scott Payne's wound at Milk River caused his health to decline even more and he retired from service in 1886 and died in 1895.

Lt. Sam Cherry was the victim of sad mischance. On the trail of robbers, one of his own men, Thomas Locke, drunk for two weeks, developed delirium tremens and began shooting wildly, killing Cherry, May, 1881.

After Milk River, old Captain Joe Lawson's health failed rapidly and he died in 1881, while Lt. Silas Wolf rose to Lt. Colonel before retiring in 1910. Captain Francis Dodge became an Army Paymaster and by 1904 was Paymaster General. Lt. James Paddock carried the two bullets he received at Milk River for the rest of his life.

The burly German, General Charles Adams, was rewarded for his heroism at Plateau Creek in freeing the captive women when

President Hays sent him to Bolivia as U.S. Minister for two years. He returned to Colorado as Chief Inspector for the Post Office and died in Denver on August 19, 1895 when the Gumry Hotel's steam boiler blew up. He was fifty years old.

As for the Meeker children: Mary married in 1881 and had a daughter whom she named Josie. Two years later, Mary died in childbirth. Josie Meeker went to work in Washington as assistant secretary to the new Secretary of Interior, Henry Teller. Josie died, holding to her brother Ralph's hand, on December 30, 1882, of pneumonia. She had never married.

Arvilla Meeker finished out her days with her son, Ralph, in White Plains, New York and died of senility in 1905.

Lusty, Maggie Baggs, finally ran off with Mike Sweet to California after she sued George Baggs for half the value of the ranch. She couldn't sue for divorce since they were not legally married. When the money ran out, Maggie wound up in Galveston, Texas, running an apartment house, minus Mike Sweet.

The only one ever incarcerated for his part in the Meeker Massacre, Quinkent was held at Fort Leavenworth for 348 days without ever being charged for any crimes. He was released under secrecy in February, 1881, to protect the War Department and other government officials from embarrassment. Following his release, Quinkent began to drink heavily and was finally killed by a member of his own band one night in 1885 after a drinking spree in Meeker Town.

Nicaagat refused to go to Uintah Reservation and became a teamster on the Rawlings-Fort Washakie road. Nicaagat was finally killed by the army in 1882 after being accused of horse stealing. Rather than give up, Nicaagat shot to death Sergeant Casey after which a mountain howitzer shell was fired into the tepee in which Nicaagat had run, killing him instantly.

The old biscuit-beggar, Colorow, had a few more clashes with the

Mericatz before he finally died in his sleep at his camp near the mouth of Smoking Earth River, December 11, 1888.

Piah committed suicide in 1888, while Ouray's old rival, Kaneache, was struck by lightning near Ignacio not long after Ouray's death.

The relatives of those slain at White River Agency received the following compensation: Arvilla Meeker, $500; Josie Meeker, $500; Flora Ellen Price, $500; George Gordon's wife, Maggie, $500; George Dresser, father of Harry and Frank Dresser, $200; William Post's widow, Sarah, $500; Wilmer Eskridge's parents, $200; Arthur Thompson's parents, $200; and Mrs. Eaton, George Eaton's mother, $200.

Arvilla Meeker's five pound volume of *Pilgrim's Progress* resides at the Meeker Memorial Museum, Greeley, Colorado. An inscription by Ralph Meeker is pasted opposite the flyleaf and ends with these words: The Indians took much interest in the book and they improved every opportunity to look at the pictures. As a "Spirit Book" they attached a mysterious value to it and preserved it for you, good friend, to read and admire. R.M.

ABOUT THE AUTHOR

Jess McCreede is the pen name for Jerry O'Neal who has written several historical western novels. He is the Regional Ecologist for the U.S. Fish and Wildlife Service in Atlanta, Georgia. Jerry lives in Marietta with his wife and one child.